The Divine Pymander and the Emerald Tablets of Thoth Hermes Trismegistus

Including the Glory of the World, the Table of Paradise. the Science of the Philosophers Stone and the Alchemical Catechism

By Hermes Trismegistus, Translated by John Everard, Compiled by Marilynn Hughes

The Divine Pymander and the Emerald Tablets of Thoth Hermes Trismegistus

Including the Glory of the World, the Table of Paradise. the Science of the Philosophers Stone and the Alchemical Catechism

By Hermes Trismegistus, Translated by John Everard, Compiled by Marilynn Hughes

The Divine Pymander and the Emerald Tablets of Thoth Hermes Trismegistus

Including the Glory of the World, the Table of Paradise. the Science of the Philosophers Stone and the Alchemical Catechism

By Hermes Trismegistus, Translated by John Everard, Compiled by Marilynn Hughes

CONTENTS

The Divine Pymander and the Emerald Tablets of Thoth Hermes Trismegistus

Including the Glory of the World, the Table of Paradise. the Science of the Philosophers Stone and the Alchemical Catechism

By Hermes Trismegistus, Translated by John Everard, Compiled by Marilynn Hughes

INTRODUCTION

A Letter from the Rosicrucian Brotherhood

(Bolded items are Additional Comments or Commentaries Added by Marilynn Hughes)

From a Letter from the Brothers of the R.C. Concerning the Invisible, Magical Mountain, And the Treasure therein Contained

"There is a mountain situated in the midst of the earth, or center of the world, which is both small and great. It is soft, also above measure hard and stony. It is far off, and near at hand, but by the providence of God, invisible. In it are hidden most ample treasures, which the world is not able to value. This mountain by envy of the devil, who always opposeth the glory of God and the happiness of man, is compassed about with very cruel beasts and other [sic] ravenous birds, which make the way thither both difficult and dangerous; and therefore hitherto, because the time is not yet come, the way thither could not be sought after nor found out. But now at last the way is to be found by those that are worthy, but notwithstanding by every man's self-labor and endeavors.

"To this mountain you shall go in a certain night (when it: comes) most long and most dark, and see that you prepare yourselves by prayer. Insist upon the way that: leads to the mountain, but ask not of any man where the way lies: only follow your Guide, who will offer himself to you, and will meet you in the way but you shall not know him. This Guide will bring you to the mountain at midnight, when all things are silent and dark. It is necessary that you arm yourselves with a resolute heroic courage, lest you fear those things that will happen, and so fall back. You need no sword, nor any other bodily weapons, only call upon God sincerely and heartily.

"When you have discovered the mountain, the first miracle that will appear is this. A most vehement and very great wind, that will shake the mountain and shatter the rocks to pieces. You shall be encountered also by lions and dragons and other terrible beasts, but fear not any of these things. Be resolute and rake heed that you return not, for your Guide who brought you thither will not suffer any evil to befall you. As for the treasure, it is not yet discovered but it is very near. After this wind will come an earthquake, that will overthrow those things which the wind hath left and make all flat. But be sure that you fall not off.

"The earthquake being past, there shall follow afire, that will consume the earthly rubbish, and discover the treasure, but as yet you cannot see it. After all these things and near the daybreak there shall be a great calm, and you shall see the Day-Star arise and the dawning will appear, and you shall perceive a great treasure. The chiefest thing in it, and the most perfect, is a certain exalted tincture, with which the world (if it served God and were worthy of such gifts) might be tinged and turned into most pure gold.

"This tincture being used, as your Guide shall reach you, will make you young when you are old, and you shall perceive no disease in any part of your bodies. By means of this tincture also you shall find pearls of that excellency which cannot be imagined. But do not you arrogate anything to yourselves because of your present power, but be contented with that which your Guide shall communicate to you. Praise God perpetually for this His gift, and have a special care that you use it not for worldly pride, but employ it in such works which are contrary to the world. Use it rightly and enjoy it so, as if you had it not. Live a temperate life, and beware of all sin, otherwise your Guide will forsake you, and you shall be deprived of this happiness. For know this of a truth, whosoever abuseth this tincture and lives not exemplary, purely, and devoutly before men he shall lose this benefit, and scarce any hope will there be left ever to recover it afterwards."

A Letter from the Brothers of R. C. Concerning the Invisible, Magical Mountain, And the Treasure therein Contained

From Hermes Trismegistus

"For there can be no Religion more true or just, than to know the things that are; and to acknowledge thanks for all things, to Him that made them, which thing I shall not cease continually to do."

The Divine Pymander of Hermes, Hermes Trismegistus, Translated by John Everard, 1650

CHAPTER ONE
The Divine Poemander Interpreted by Manly P. Hall

From the Secret Teachings of all Ages

"POIMANDRES, THE VISION OF HERMES

The *Divine Pymander of Hermes Mercurius Trismegistus* is one of the earliest of the Hermetic writings now extant. While probably not in its original form, having been remodeled during the first centuries of the Christian Era and incorrectly translated since, this work undoubtedly contains many of the original concepts of the Hermetic cultus. *The Divine Pymander* consists of seventeen fragmentary writings gathered together and put forth as one work. The second book of *The Divine Pymander*, called *Poimandres*, or *The Vision*, is believed to describe the method by which the divine wisdom was first revealed to Hermes. It was after Hermes had received this revelation that he began his ministry, teaching to all who would listen the secrets of the invisible universe as they had been unfolded to him.

The Vision is the most: famous of all the Hermetic fragments, and contains an exposition of Hermetic cosmogony and the secret sciences of the Egyptians regarding the culture and unfoldment of the human soul. For some time it was erroneously called "The Genesis of Enoch," but that mistake has now been rectified. At hand while preparing the following interpretation of the symbolic philosophy concealed within *The Vision of Hermes* the present author has had these reference works: *The Divine Pymander of Hermes Mercurius Trismegistus* (London, 1650), translated out of the Arabic and Greek by Dr. Everard; *Hermetica* (Oxford, 1924), edited by Walter Scott; *Hermes, The Mysteries of Egypt* (Philadelphia, 1925), by Edouard Schure; and the *Thrice-Greatest Hermes* (London, 1906), by G. R. S. Mead. To the material contained in the above volumes he has added commentaries based upon the esoteric philosophy of the ancient Egyptians, together with amplifications derived partly from other Hermetic fragments and partly from the secret arcanum of the Hermetic sciences. For the sake of clarity, the narrative form has been chosen in preference to the original dialogic style, and obsolete words have given place to those in current use.

Hermes, while wandering in a rocky and desolate place, gave himself over to meditation and prayer. Following the secret instructions of the Temple, he gradually freed his higher consciousness from the bondage of his bodily senses; and, thus released, his divine nature revealed to him the mysteries of the transcendental spheres. He beheld a figure, terrible and awe-inspiring. It was the Great Dragon, with wings stretching across the sky and light streaming in all directions from its body. (The Mysteries taught that the Universal Life was personified as a dragon.) The Great Dragon called Hermes by name, and asked him why he thus meditated upon the World Mystery.

Terrified by the spectacle, Hermes prostrated himself before the Dragon, beseeching it to reveal its identity. The great creature answered that it was*Poimandres*, the *Mind of the Universe*, the Creative Intelligence, and the Absolute Emperor of all. (Schure identifies Poimandres as the god Osiris.) Hermes then besought Poimandres to disclose the nature of the universe and the constitution of the gods. The Dragon acquiesced, bidding Trismegistus hold its image in his mind.

Immediately the form of Poimandres changed. Where it had stood there was a glorious and pulsating Radiance. This Light was the spiritual nature of the Great Dragon itself. Hermes was "raised" into the midst of this Divine Effulgence and the universe of material things faded from his consciousness. Presently a great darkness descended and, expanding, swallowed up the Light. Everything was troubled. About Hermes swirled a mysterious watery substance which gave forth a smokelike vapor. The air was filled with inarticulate moanings and sighings which seemed to come from the Light swallowed up in the darkness. His mind told Hermes that the Light was the form of the spiritual universe and that the swirling darkness which had engulfed it represented material substance.

THOTH, THE IBIS-HEADED.

From Wilkinson's Manners & Customs of the Ancient Egyptians.

It is doubtful that the deity called *Thoth* by the Egyptians was originally Hermes, but the two personalities were blended together and it is now impossible to separate them. Thoth was called "The Lord of the Divine Books" and "Scribe of the Company of the Gods." He is generally depicted with the body of a man and the head of an ibis. The exact symbolic meaning of this latter bird has never been discovered. A careful analysis of the peculiar shape of the ibis--especially its head and beak-- should prove illuminating.

Then out of the imprisoned Light a mysterious and Holy Word came forth and took its stand upon the smoking waters. This Word--the Voice of the Light-- rose out of the darkness as a great pillar, and the fire and the air followed after it, but the earth and the water remained unmoved below. Thus the waters of Light were divided from the waters of darkness, and from the waters of Light were formed the worlds above and from the waters of darkness were formed the worlds below. The earth and the water next mingled, becoming inseparable, and the Spiritual

Word which is called *Reason* moved upon their surface, causing endless turmoil.

Then again was heard the voice of Poimandres, but His form was not revealed: "I Thy God am the Light and the Mind which were before substance was divided from spirit and darkness from Light. And the Word which appeared as a pillar of flame out of the darkness is the Son of God, born of the mystery of the Mind. The name of that Word is *Reason*. Reason is the offspring of Thought and Reason shall divide the Light from the darkness and establish Truth in the midst of the waters. Understand, O Hermes, and meditate deeply upon the mystery. That which in you sees and hears is not of the earth, but is the Word of God incarnate. So it is said that Divine Light dwells in the midst of mortal darkness, and ignorance cannot divide them. The union of the Word and the Mind produces that mystery which is called *Life*. As the darkness without you is divided against itself, so the darkness within you is likewise divided. The Light and the fire which rise are the divine man, ascending in the path of the Word, and that which fails to ascend is the mortal man, which may not partake of immortality. Learn deeply of the Mind and its mystery, for therein lies the secret of immortality."

The Dragon again revealed its form to Hermes, and for a long time the two looked steadfastly one upon the other, eye to eye, so that Hermes trembled before the gaze of Poimandres. At the Word of the Dragon the heavens opened and the innumerable Light Powers were revealed, soaring through Cosmos on pinions of streaming fire. Hermes beheld the spirits of the stars, the celestials controlling the universe, and all those Powers which shine with the radiance of the One Fire--the glory of the Sovereign Mind. Hermes realized that the sight which he beheld was revealed to him only because Poimandres had spoken a Word. The Word was Reason, and by the Reason of the Word invisible things were made manifest. Divine Mind--the Dragon--continued its discourse:

"Before the visible universe was formed its mold was cast. This mold was called the *Archetype*, and this Archetype was in the Supreme Mind long before the process of creation began. Beholding the Archetypes, the Supreme Mind became enamored with Its own thought; so, taking the Word as a mighty hammer, It gouged out caverns in primordial space and cast the form of the spheres in the Archetypal mold, at the same time sowing in the newly fashioned bodies the seeds of living things. The darkness below, receiving the hammer of the Word, was fashioned into an orderly universe. The elements separated into strata and each brought forth living creatures. The Supreme Being--the Mind--male and female, brought forth the Word; and the Word, suspended between Light and darkness, was delivered of another Mind called the *Workman*, the *Master-Builder*, or the *Maker of Things*.

"In this manner it was accomplished, O Hermes: The Word moving like a breath through space called forth the *Fire* by the friction of its motion. Therefore, the Fire is called the *Son of Striving*. The Workman passed as a whirlwind through the universe, causing the substances to vibrate and glow with its friction, The Son of Striving thus formed *Seven Governors*, the Spirits of the Planets, whose orbits bounded the world; and the Seven Governors controlled the world by the mysterious power called *Destiny* given them by the Fiery Workman. When the *Second Mind* (The Workman) had organized Chaos, the Word of God rose straightway our of its prison of substance, leaving the elements without Reason, and joined Itself to the nature of the Fiery Workman. Then the Second Mind, together with the risen Word, established Itself in the midst of the universe and whirled the wheels of the Celestial Powers. This shall continue from an infinite beginning to an infinite end, for the beginning and the ending are in the same place and state.

"Then the downward-turned and unreasoning elements brought forth creatures without Reason. Substance could not bestow Reason, for Reason had ascended out of it. The air produced flying things and the waters such as swim. The earth conceived strange four-footed and creeping beasts, dragons, composite demons, and grotesque monsters. Then the Father-- the Supreme Mind--being Light and Life, fashioned a glorious Universal Man in Its own image, not an earthy man but a heavenly Man dwelling in the Light of God. The *Supreme Mind* loved the Man It had fashioned and delivered to Him the control of the creations and workmanships.

"The Man, desiring to labor, took up His abode in the sphere of generation and observed the works of His brother--the Second Mind--which sat upon the Ring of the Fire. And having beheld the achievements of the Fiery Workman, He willed also to make things, and His Father gave permission. The Seven Governors, of whose powers He partook, rejoiced and each gave the Man a share of Its own nature.

"The Man longed to pierce the circumference of the circles and understand the mystery of Him who sat upon the Eternal Fire. Having already all power, He stooped down and peeped through the seven Harmonies and, breaking through the strength of the circles, made Himself manifest to Nature stretched out below. The Man, looking into the depths, smiled, for He beheld a shadow upon the earth and a likeness mirrored in the waters, which shadow and likeness were a reflection of Himself. The Man fell in love with His own shadow and desired to descend into it. Coincident with the desire, the Intelligent Thing united Itself with the unreasoning image or shape.

"Nature, beholding the descent, wrapped herself about the Man whom she loved, and the two were mingled. For this reason, earthy man is composite. Within him is the Sky Man, immortal and beautiful; without is Nature, mortal and destructible. Thus, suffering is the result of the Immortal Man's falling in love with His shadow and giving up Reality to dwell in the darkness of illusion; for, being immortal, man has the power of the Seven Governors--also the Life, the Light, and the Word-but being mortal, he is controlled by the Rings of the Governors--Fate or Destiny.

"Of the Immortal Man it should be said that He is hermaphrodite, or male and female, and eternally watchful. He neither slumbers nor sleeps, and is governed by a Father also both male and female, and ever watchful. Such is the mystery kept hidden to this day, for Nature, being mingled in marriage with the Sky Man, brought forth a wonder most wonderful-- seven men, all bisexual, male and female, and upright of stature, each one exemplifying the natures of the Seven Governors. These O Hermes, are the seven races, species, and wheels.

"After this manner were the seven men generated. Earth was the female element and water the male element, and from the fire and the æther they received their spirits, and Nature produced bodies after the species and shapes of men. And man received the Life and Light of the Great Dragon, and of the Life was made his Soul and of the Light his Mind. And so, all these composite creatures containing immortality, but partaking of mortality, continued in this state for the duration of a period. They reproduced themselves out of themselves, for each was male and female. But at the end of the period the knot of Destiny was untied by the will of God and the bond of all things was loosened.

"Then all living creatures, including man, which had been hermaphroditical, were separated, the males being set apart by themselves and the females likewise, according to the dictates of Reason.

"Then God spoke to the Holy Word within the soul of all things, saying: 'Increase in increasing and multiply in multitudes, all you, my creatures and workmanships. Let him that is endued with Mind know himself to be immortal and that the cause of death is the love of the body; and let him learn all things that are, for he who has recognized himself enters into the state of Good.'

A GREEK FORM OF HERMES.

From *Bryant's Mythology*.

The name Hermes is derived from "Herm," a form of *Chiram*, the Personified Universal Life Principle, generally represented by fire. The Scandinavians worshiped Hermes under the name of *Odin*; the Teutons as *Wotan*, and certain of the Oriental peoples as *Buddha*, or *Fo*. There are two theories concerning his demise. The first declares that Hermes was translated like Enoch and carried without death into the presence of God, the second states that he was buried in the Valley of Ebron and a great treasure placed in his tomb--not a treasure of gold but of books and sacred learning.

The Egyptians likened humanity to a flock of sheep. The Supreme and Inconceivable Father was the Shepherd, and Hermes was the shepherd dog. The origin of the shepherd's crook in religious symbolism may be traced to the Egyptian rituals. The three scepters of Egypt include the shepherd's crook, symbolizing that by virtue of the power reposing in that symbolic staff the initiated Pharaohs guided the destiny of their people.

"And when God had said this, Providence, with the aid of the Seven Governors and Harmony, brought the sexes together, making the mixtures and establishing the generations, and all things were multiplied according to their kind. He who through the error of attachment loves his body, abides wandering in darkness, sensible and suffering the things of death, but he who realizes that the body is but the tomb of his soul, rises to immortality."

Then Hermes desired to know why men should be deprived of immortality for the sin of ignorance alone. The Great Dragon answered:, To the ignorant the body is supreme and they are incapable of realizing the immortality that is within them. Knowing only the body which is subject to death, they believe in death because they worship that substance which is the cause and reality of death."

Then Hermes asked how the righteous and wise pass to God, to which Poimandres replied: "That which the Word of God said, say I: 'Because the Father of all things consists of Life and Light, whereof man is made.' If, therefore, a man shall learn and understand the nature of Life and Light, then he shall pass into the eternity of Life and Light."

Hermes next inquired about the road by which the wise attained to Life eternal, and Poimandres continued: "Let the man endued with a Mind mark, consider, and learn of himself, and with the power of his Mind divide himself from his not-self and become a servant of Reality."

Hermes asked if all men did not have Minds, and the Great Dragon replied: "Take heed what you say, for I am the Mind--the Eternal Teacher. I am the Father of the *Word*--the Redeemer of all men--and in the nature of the wise the Word takes flesh. By means of the Word, the world is saved. I, *Thought* (Thoth)--the Father of the Word, the Mind--come only unto men that are holy and good, pure and merciful, and that live piously and religiously, and my presence is an inspiration and a help to them, for when I come they immediately know all things and adore the Universal Father. Before such wise and philosophic ones die, they learn to renounce their senses, knowing that these are the enemies of their immortal souls.

"I will not permit the evil senses to control the bodies of those who love me, nor will I allow evil emotions and evil thoughts to enter them. I become as a porter or doorkeeper, and shut out evil, protecting the wise from their own lower nature. But to the wicked, the envious and the covetous, I come not, for such cannot understand the mysteries of *Mind*; therefore, I am unwelcome. I leave them to the avenging demon that they are making in their own souls, for evil each day increases itself and torments man more sharply, and each evil deed adds to the evil deeds that are gone before until finally evil destroys itself. The punishment of desire is the agony of unfulfillment."

Hermes bowed his head in thankfulness to the Great Dragon who had taught him so much, and begged to hear more concerning the ultimate of the human soul. So Poimandres resumed: "At death the material body of man is returned to the elements from which it came, and the invisible divine man ascends to the source from whence he came, namely the *Eighth Sphere*. The evil passes to the dwelling place of the demon, and the senses, feelings, desires, and body passions return to their source, namely the Seven Governors, whose natures in the lower man destroy but in the invisible spiritual man give life.

"After the lower nature has returned to the brutishness, the higher struggles again to regain its spiritual estate. It ascends the seven Rings upon which sit the Seven Governors and returns to each their lower powers in this manner: Upon the first ring sits the Moon, and to it is returned the ability to increase and diminish. Upon the second ring sits Mercury, and to it are returned machinations, deceit, and craftiness. Upon the third ring sits Venus, and to it are returned the lusts and passions. Upon the fourth ring sits the Sun, and to this Lord are returned ambitions. Upon the fifth ring sits Mars, and to it are returned rashness and profane boldness. Upon the sixth ring sits Jupiter, and to it are returned the sense of accumulation and riches. And upon the seventh ring sits Saturn, at the Gate of Chaos, and to it are returned falsehood and evil plotting.

"Then, being naked of all the accumulations of the seven Rings, the soul comes to the Eighth Sphere, namely, the ring of the fixed stars. Here, freed of all illusion, it dwells in the Light and sings praises to the Father in a voice which only the pure of spirit may understand. Behold, O Hermes, there is a great mystery in the Eighth Sphere, for the Milky Way is the seed-ground of souls, and from it they drop into the Rings, and to the Milky Way they return again from the wheels of Saturn. But some cannot climb the seven-runged ladder of the Rings. So they wander in darkness below and are swept into eternity with the illusion of sense and earthiness.

"The path to immortality is hard, and only a few find it. The rest await the Great Day when the wheels of the universe shall be stopped and the immortal sparks shall escape from the sheaths of substance. Woe unto those who wait, for they must return again, unconscious and unknowing, to the seed-ground of stars, and await a new beginning. Those who are saved by the light of the mystery which I have revealed unto you, O Hermes, and which I now bid you to establish among men, shall return again to the Father who dwelleth in the White Light, and shall deliver themselves up to the Light and shall be absorbed into the Light, and in the Light they shall become Powers in God. This is the Way of *Good* and is revealed only to them that have wisdom.

"Blessed art thou, O Son of Light, to whom of all men, I, Poimandres, the Light of the World, have revealed myself. I order you to go forth, to become as a guide to those who wander in darkness, that all men within whom dwells the spirit of *My Mind* (The Universal Mind) may be saved by My Mind in you, which shall call forth My Mind in them. Establish My Mysteries and they shall not fail from the earth, for I am the Mind of the Mysteries and until Mind fails (which is never) my Mysteries cannot fail." With these parting words, Poimandres, radiant with celestial light, vanished, mingling with the powers of the heavens. Raising his eyes unto the heavens, Hermes blessed the Father of All Things and consecrated his life to the service of the Great Light.

Thus preached Hermes: "O people of the earth, men born and made of the elements, but with the spirit of the Divine Man within you, rise from your sleep of ignorance! Be sober and thoughtful. Realize that your home is not in the earth but in the Light. Why have you delivered yourselves over unto death, having power to partake of immortality? Repent, and *change your minds*. Depart from the dark light and forsake corruption forever. Prepare yourselves to climb through the Seven Rings and to blend your souls with the eternal Light."

Some who heard mocked and scoffed and went their way, delivering themselves to the Second Death from which there is no salvation. But others, casting themselves before the feet of Hermes, besought him to teach them the Way of Life. He lifted them gently, receiving no approbation for himself, and staff in hand, went forth teaching and guiding mankind, and showing them how they might be saved. In the worlds of men, Hermes sowed the seeds of wisdom and nourished the seeds with the Immortal Waters. And at last came the evening of his life, and as the brightness of the light of earth was beginning to go down, Hermes commanded his disciples to preserve his doctrines inviolate throughout all ages. The *Vision of Poimandres* he committed to writing that all men desiring immortality might therein find the way.

In concluding his exposition of the *Vision*, Hermes wrote: "The sleep of the body is the sober watchfulness of the Mind and the shutting of my eyes reveals the true Light. My silence is filled with budding life and hope, and is full of good. My words are the blossoms of fruit of the tree of my soul. For this is the faithful account of what I received from my true Mind, that is Poimandres, the Great Dragon, the Lord of the Word, through whom I became inspired by God with the Truth. Since that day my Mind has been ever with me and in my own soul it hath given birth to the Word: the Word is Reason, and Reason hath redeemed me. For which cause, with all my soul and all my strength, I give praise and blessing unto God the Father, the Life and the Light, and the Eternal Good.

"Holy is God, the Father of all things, the One who is before the First Beginning.

"Holy is God, whose will is performed and accomplished by His own Powers which He hath given birth to out of Himself.

"Holy is God, who has determined that He shall be known, and who is known by His own to whom He reveals Himself.

"Holy art Thou, who by Thy Word (Reason) hast established all things.

"Holy art Thou, of whom all Nature is the image.

"Holy art Thou, whom the inferior nature has not formed.

"Holy art Thou, who art stronger than all powers.

"Holy art Thou, who art greater than all excellency.

"Holy art Thou, who art better than all praise.

"Accept these reasonable sacrifices from a pure soul and a heart stretched out unto Thee.

"O Thou Unspeakable, Unutterable, to be praised with silence!

"I beseech Thee to look mercifully upon me, that I may not err from the knowledge of Thee and that I may enlighten those that are in ignorance, my brothers and Thy sons.

"Therefore I believe Thee and bear witness unto Thee, and depart in peace and in trustfulness into Thy Light and Life.

"Blessed art Thou, O Father! The man Thou hast fashioned would be sanctified with Thee as Thou hast given him power to sanctify others with Thy Word and Thy Truth."

The *Vision of Hermes*, like nearly all of the Hermetic writings, is an allegorical exposition of great philosophic and mystic truths, and its hidden meaning may be comprehended only by those who have been "raised" into the presence of the True Mind."

The Secret Teachings of all Ages, Manly P. Hall, 1928

CHAPTER TWO
The Divine Pymander (in its entirety) Translated by John Everard, 1650

"HERMES TRISMEGISTUS, HIS FIRST BOOK

"1. O MY SON, write this First Book, both for Humanity's sake, and for Piety towards god.

2. For there can be no Religion more true or just, than to know the things that are; and to acknowledge thanks for all things, to Him that made them, which thing I shall not cease continually to do.

3. What then should a man do, O Father, to lead his life well; seeing there is nothing here true?

4. Be Pious and Religious, O my Son; for he that doth so, is the best and highest Philosopher, and without Philosophy it is impossible ever to attain to the height and exactness of Piety and Religion.

5. But he that shall learn and study the things that are, and how they are ordered and governed, and by whom, and for what cause, or to what end. Will acknowledge thanks to the *Workman*, as to a good *Father*, an excellent *Nurse*, and a faithful *Steward*, and he that gives thanks shall be Pious or Religious, and he that is Religious shall know both where the truth is, and what it is, and learning that he will be yet more and more Religious.

6. For never, O my Son, shall, or can that soul, which, while it is in the body, lightens and lifts up itself to know and comprehend that which is good and true, slide back to the contrary. For it is infinitely enamoured thereof, and forgetteth all evils; and when it hath learned and known its *Father* and *Progenitor*, it can no more apostatize or depart from that good.

7. And let this, O Son, be the end of Religion and Piety; whereunto thou art once arrived, thou shalt both live well and die blessedly, whilst thy soul is not ignorant wither it must return, and fly back again.

8. For this only, O Son, is the way to *Truth*, which our *Progenitors* travelled in; and by which making their journey, they at length attained to the good. It is a venerable way and plain, but hard and difficult for the soul to go in that is in the body.

9. For first must it war against its own self, and after much strife and dissention, it must be overcome of the part; for the contention is of one against two, whilst it flies away, and they strive to hold and detain it.

10. But the victory of both is not like, for the one hasteth to that which is Good, but the other is a neighbour to the things that are Evil; and that which is Good desireth to be set at liberty, but the things that are Evil love bondage and Slavery.

11. And if the two parts be overcome, they become quiet, and are content to accept of it as their *Ruler*; but if the one be overcome of the two, it is by them led

and carried to be punished by its being and continuance here.

12. This is, O Son, the Guide in the way that leads thither; for thou must first forsake the Body before thy end, and get the victory in this contention and strifeful life, and when thou hast overcome, return.

13. But now, O my Son, I will by Heads run through the things that are. Understand thou what I say, and remember what thou hearest.

14. All things that are moved, only that which is not is immoveable.

15. Every body is changeable.

16. Not every body is dissolveable.

17. Some bodies are dissolveable.

18. Every living being is not mortal.

19. Nor every living thing is immortal.

20. That which may be dissolved is also corruptible.

21. That which abides always is unchangeable.

22. That which is unchangeable is eternal.

23. That which is always made is always corrupted.

24. That which is made but once is never corrupted, neither becomes any other thing.

25. Firstly, God; secondly, the World; thirdly, Man.

26. The World for Man; Man for God.

27. Of the Soul; that part which is sensible is mortal, but that part which is reasonable is immortal.

28. Every Essence is immortal.

29. Every Essence is unchangeable.

30. Everything that is, is double.

31. None of the things that are stand still.

32. Not all things are moved by a soul, but everything that is, is moved by a soul.

33. Everything that suffers is sensible; everything that is sensible, suffereth.

34. Everything that is sad, rejoiceth also; and is a mortal living creature.

35. Not everything that joyeth is also sad, but is an eternal living thing.

36. Not every body is sick; every body that is sick is dissolveable.

37. The mind in God.

38. Reasoning (or disputing or discoursing) in Man.

39. Reason in the Mind.

40. The Mind is void of suffering.

41. No thing in a body true.

42. All that is incorporeal, is void of Lying.

43. Everything that is made is corruptible.

44. Nothing good upon Earth; nothing evil in Heaven.

45. God is good; Man is evil.

46. Good is voluntary, or of its own accord.

47. Evil is involuntary, or against its will.

48. The gods choose good things, as good things.

49. Time is a Divine thing.

50. Law is humane.

51. Malice is the nourishment of the World.

52. Time is the corruption of Man.

53. Whatsoever is in Heaven is unalterable.

54. All upon Earth is alterable.

55. Nothing in Heaven is servanted; nothing upon Earth free.

56. Nothing unknown in Heaven; nothing known upon Earth.

57. The things upon Earth communicate not with those in Heaven.

58. All things in Heaven are unblameable; all things upon Earth are subject to reprehension.

59. That which is immortal is not mortal; that which is mortal is not immortal.

60. That which is sown is not always begotten; but that which is begotten always is sown.

61. Of a dissolveable body, there are two times; one for sowing to generation, one from generation to death.

62. Of an everlasting Body, the time is only from the Generation.

63. Dissolveable Bodies are increased and diminished.

64. Dissolveable matter is altered into contraries; to wit, Corruption and Generation, but Eternal matter into itself, and its like.

65. The Generation of Man is corruption; the Corruption of Man is the beginning of Generation.

66. That which offsprings or begetteth another, is itself an offspring or begotten by another.

67. Of things that are, some are in bodies, some in their IDEAS.

68. Whasoever things belong to operation or working, are in a body.

69. That which is immortal, partakes not of that which is mortal.

70. That which is mortal cometh not into a Body immortal; but that which is immortal cometh into that which is mortal.

71. Operation or Workings are not carried upwards, but descend downwards.

72. Things upon Earth, do nothing advantage those in Heaven; but all things in Heaven do profit and advantage all things upon Earth.

73. Heaven is capable, and a fit receptacle of everlasting Bodies; the Earth of corruptible Bodies.

74. The Earth is brutish; the Heaven is reasonable or rational.

75. Those things that are in Heaven are subjected or placed under it, but the things on earth are placed upon it.

76. Heaven is the first element.

77. Providence is Divine order.

78. Necessity is the Minister or Servant of Providence.

79. Fortune is the carriage or effect of that which is without order; the Idol of operation, a lying Fantasie or opinion.

80. What is God? The immutable or unalterable good.

81. What is man? An unchangeable evil.

82. If thou perfectly remember these Heads, thou canst not forget those things which in more words I have largely expounded unto thee; for these are the contents or Abridgment of them.

83. Avoid all conversation with the multitude or common people; for I would not have thee subject to Envy, much less to be ridiculous unto the many.

84. For the like always takes to itself that which is like, but the unlike never agrees with the unlike. Such discourses as these have very few Auditors, and peradventure very few will have, but they have something peculiar unto themselves.

85. They do rather sharpen and whet evil men to their maliciousness; therefore, it behoveth to avoid the multitude, and take heed of them as not understanding the virtue and power of the things that are said.

86. *How does thou mean, O Father?*

87. This O Son: the whole nature and Composition of those living things called Men, is very prone to Maliciousness, and is very familiar, and as it were nourished with it, and therefore is delighted with it; now this wight, if it shall come to learn or know that the world was once made, and all things are done according to Providence or Necessity, Destiny or Fate, bearing rule over all, will he not be much worse than himself, despising the whole, because it was made? *And if he may lay the cause of Evil upon Fate or Destiny*, he will never abstain from any evil work.

88. *Wherefore we must look warily to such kind of people, that being in ignorance they may be less evil for fear of that which is hidden and kept secret.*

The End of THE FIRST BOOK OF HERMES..."

THE SECOND BOOK, CALLED, POEMANDER

"MY THOUGHTS being once seriously busied about things that are, and my Understanding lifted up, all my bodily Senses being exceedingly holden back, as it is with them that are heavy of sleep, by reason either of fulness of meat, or of bodily labour: Methought I saw one of an exceeding great stature, and of an infinite greatness, call me by my name, and say unto me, *What wouldst thou hear and see?* Or what wouldst thou understand to learn and know?

2. Then said I, *Who are Thou?* I am, quoth he, *Poemander*, the mind of the great Lord, the most

mighty and absolute *Emperor*: I know what thou wouldst have, and I am always present with thee.

3. Then I said, *I would learn the things that are, and understand the nature of them, and know God.* How? said he. I answered that I would gladly hear. Then said he, Have me again in they mind, and whasoever though wouldst learn, I will teach thee.

4. When he had thus said, he was changed in his *Idea* or *Form*, and straightway, in the twinkling of an eye, all things were opened unto me. And I saw an infinite sight, all things were become light, both sweet and exceeding pleasant; and I was wonderfully delighted in the beholding it.

5. But after a little while, there was a darkness made in part, coming down obliquely, fearful and hideous, which seemed unto me to be changed *into a certain moist nature*, unspeakably troubled, which yielded a smoke as from Fire; and from whence proceeded a voice unutterable, and very mournful, but inarticulate, inasmuch as it seemed to have come from the Light.

6. Then from that Light, a certain *holy Word joined itself unto Nature,* and outflew the pure and unmixed Fire from the moist nature upwards on high; it was exceeding *Light*, and *sharp*, and *operative* withal. And the *Air*, which was also light, followed the *Spirit* and mourned up to *Fire* (from the Earth and the Water), insomuch that it seemed to hang and depend upon it.

7. And the Earth and the Water stayed by themselves so mingled together, that the Earth could not be seen for the Water, but they were moved because of the *Spiritual word* that was carried upon them.

8. Then said *Poemander* unto me, Dost thou understand this *vision*, and what it meaneth? I shall know, said I. Then said he, *I am that Light, the Mind, thy God, who am before that moist nature that appeared out of darkness; and that bright and lightful Word from the mind is the Son of God.*

9. How is that, quoth I? Thus, replied he, understand it: That which in thee seeth and heareth, the Word of the Lord, and the Mind the Father, God, differ not one from the other; and the union of these is Life. *Trismeg.*--I thank thee.

Pimand.--But first conceive well the Light in they mind, and know it.

10. When he had said thus, for a long time we looked steadfastly one upon the other, insomuch that I trembled at his *Idea* or *Form*.

11. But when he nodded to me, I beheld in my mind the Light that is in innumerable, and the truly indefinite *ornament* or *world*; and that the *Fire* is comprehended or contained in, or by a great moist Power, and constrained to keep its station.

12. These things I understood, seeing the word, or *Pimander*; and when I was mightily amazed, he said again unto me, Hast thou seen in thy mind that

Archetypal Form which was before the interminated and infinite Beginning? Thus *Pimander* to me. But whence, quoth I, or whereof are the Elements of Nature made?

Pimander.--Of the Will and counsel of God; which taking the Word, and beholding the beautiful World (in the Archetype thereof) imitated it, and so made this World, by the principles and vital seeds or Soul-like productions of itself.

13. For the *Mind* being God, *Male and Female, Life and Light*, brought forth by His *Word* another *Mind* or *Workman*; which being God of the *Fire*, and the *Spirit*, fashioned and formed seven other Governors, which in their circles contain the *Sensible World*, whose Government or disposition is called *Fate* or *Destiny*.

14. *Straightway* leaped out, or exalted itself from the downward Elements of God, *The Word of God*, into the clean and pure Workmanship of Nature, and was united to the *Workman, Mind*, for it was *Consubstantial*; and so the downward born elements of Nature were left without Reason, that they might be the only Matter.

15. But the *Workman, Mind*, together with the *Word*, containing the circles, and whirling them about, turned round as a wheel, his own Workmanships; and suffered them to be turned from an indefinite Beginning to an indeterminable end, for they always begin where they end.

16. And the *Circulation* or running round of these, as the mind willeth, out of the lower or downward-born Elements, brought forth unreasonable or brutish Creatures, for they had no reason, the Air flying things, and the Water such as swim.

17. And the Earth and the Water were separated, either from the other, as the *Mind* would; and the Earth brought forth from herself, such living creatures as she had, four-footed and creeping beasts, wild and tame.

18. But the Father of all things, the *Mind* being *Life* and *Light*, brought forth *Man* like unto himself, whom he loved his proper *Birth*; for he was all beauteous, having the image of his *Father*.

19. For indeed God was exceedingly enamoured of his own form or shape, and delivered unto it all his own Workmanships. But he, seeing and understanding the *Creation* of the Workman in the whole, would needs also himself *fall to work*, and so was separated from the Father, being in the sphere of Generation or Operation.

20. Having all Power, he considered the Operations or Workmanships of the *Seven*; but they loved him, and everyone made him partaker of his own order.

21. And he learning diligently, and understanding their Essence, and partaking their Nature, resolved to pierce and break through the *Circumference* of the Circles, and to understand the power of him that sits upon the Fire.

22. And having already all power of mortal things, of the Living, and of the unreasonable creatures of the World, stooped down and peeped through the *Harmony*, and breaking through the strength of the Circles, so showed and made manifest the downward-born Nature, the fair and beautiful Shape or Form of God.

23. Which, when he saw, having in itself the unsatiable Beauty, and all the operations of the *Seven Governors*, and the Form or Shape of God, he*smiled* for love, as if he had seen the shape or likeness in the Water, or the shadow upon the Earth, of the fairest Human form.

24. And seeing in the Water a Shape, a Shape like unto himself, in himself he loved it, and would cohabit with it, and immediately upon the resolution ensued the operation, and brought forth the unreasonable Image or Shape.

25. Nature presently laying hold of what it so much loved, did wholly wrap herself about it, and they were mingled, for they loved one another.

26. And from this cause *Man* above all things that live upon earth is double: *Mortal*, because of his body, and *Immortal*, because of the substantial Man. For being immortal, and having power of all things, he yet suffers mortal things, and such as are subject to Fate or Destiny.

27. And therefore being above all *Harmony*, he is made and become a servant to *Harmony*, he

is *Hermaphrodite*, or Male and Female, and watchful, he is governed by and subjected to a Father, that is both Male and Female, and watchful.

28. After these things, I said, *Thou art my mind, and I am in love with Reason.*

29. Then said *Pimander*, This is the *Mystery* that to this day is hidden and kept secret; for Nature being mingled with man, brought forth a Wonder most Wonderful; for he having the nature of the *Harmony* of the *Seven*, from him whom I told thee, the Fire and the Spirit, Nature continued not, but forthwith brought forth seven Men, all *Males* and *Females*, and sublime, or on high, according to the Natures of the seven Governors.

30. And after these things, O *Pimander*, quoth I, I am now come into a great desire and longing to hear; do not digress or run out.

31. But he said, Keep silence, for I have not yet finished the first speech.

32. *Trism.* Behold, I am silent.

33. *Pim.* The Generation therefore of these Seven was after this manner:--The *Air* being *Feminine* and the Water desirous of Copulation, took from the Fire its ripeness, and from the aether Spirit, and so Nature produced Bodies after the species and shape of men.

34. And man was made of *Life* and *Light*, into *Soul* and *Mind*; of *Life* the soul, of *Light* the *Mind*.

35. And so all the members of the *Sensible World,* continued unto the period of the end, bearing rule and generating.

36. Hear now the rest of that speech thou so much desireth to hear.

37. When that *period* was fulfilled, the bond of all things was loosed and untied by the will of God; for all living *Creatures* being Hermaphroditical, or *Male* and *Female,* were loosed and untied together with man; and so the Males were apart by themselves and the Females likewise.

38. And straightways God said to the Holy Word, *Increase in increasing and multiplying in multitude all you my Creatures and Workmanships. And let him that is endued with mind, know himself to be immortal; and that the cause of death is the love of the body, and let him learn all things that are.*

39. When he had thus said, *Providence by Fate of Harmony,* made the mixtures and established the Generations, and all things were multiplied according to their kind. And he that knew himself, came at length to the *Superstantial* of every way substantial good.

40. But he that thro' the error of Love loved the *Body,* abideth wandering in darkness, sensible, suffering the things of death.

41. *Trism.* But why do they that are ignorant, sin so much, that they should therefore be deprived of immortality?

42. *Pim.* Thou seemest not to have understood what thou hast heard.

43. *Trism.* Peradventure I seem so to thee; but I both understand and remember them.

44. *Pim.* I am glad for thy sake if thou understoodest them.

45. *Trism.* Tell me why are they worthy of death, that are in death?

46. *Pim.* Because there goeth a sad and dismal darkness before its body; of which darkness is the moist nature, of which moist nature the Body consisteth in the sensible world, from whence death is derived. Has thou understood this aright?

47. *Trism.* But why, or how doth he that understands himself, go or pass into God?

48. *Pim.* That which the Word of God said, say I: Because the Father of all things consists of Life and Light, whereof man is made.

49. *Trism.* Thou sayest very well.

50. *Pim.* God and the Father is Light and Life, of which Man is made. If therefore thou learn and

believe thyself to be of the Life and Light, thou shalt again pass into Life.

51. *Trism.* But yet tell me more, O my Mind, how I shall go into Life.

52. *Pim.* God saith, Let man, endued with a mind, mark, consider, and know himself well.

53. *Trism.* Have not all men a mind?

54. *Pim.* Take heed what thou sayest, for I the mind come unto men that are holy and good, pure and merciful, and that live piously and religiously; and my presence is a help unto them. And forthwith they know all things, and lovingly they supplicate and propitiate the Father; and blessing him, they give him thanks, and sing hymns unto him, being ordered and directed by filial Affection and natural Love. And before they give up their bodies to the death of them, they hate their senses, knowing their Works and Operations.

55. Rather I that am the Mind itself, will not suffer the operations or Works, which happen or belong to the body, to be finished and brought to perfection in them; but being the *Porter* or *Doorkeeper*, I will shut up the entrances of Evil, and cut off the thoughtful desires of filthy works.

56. But to the foolish, and evil, and wicked, and envious, and covetous, and murderous, and profane, I am far off, giving place to the revenging *Demon*, which applying unto him the sharpness of fire,

tormenteth such a man sensible, and armeth him the more to all wickedness, that he may obtain the greater punishment.

57. And such an one never ceaseth, having unfulfiled desires, and unsatisfiable concupiscences, and always fighting in darkness; for the *Demon* always afflicts and tormenteth him continually, and increaseth the fire upon him more and more.

58. *Trism.* Thou hast, O Mind, most excellently taught me all things, as I desired; but tell me, moreover, after the return is made, what then?

59. *Pim.* First of all, in the resolution of the material body, the Body itself is given up to alteration, and the form which it had becometh invisible; and the idle manners are permitted, and left to the *Demon*, and the senses of the body return into their Fountains, being parts, and again made up into Operations.

60. And Anger, and concupiscence, go into the brutish or unreasonable nature; and the rest striveth upward by Harmony.

61. And to the first *Zone* it giveth the power it had of increasing and diminishing.

62. To the second, the machinations or plotting of evils, and one effectual deceit or craft.

63. To the third, the idle deceit of Concupiscence.

64. To the fourth, the desire of Rule, and unsatiable Ambition.

65. To the fifth, profane Boldness, and the headlong rashness of confidence.

66. To the sixth, Evil and ineffectual occasions of Riches.

67. To the seventh *Zone*, subtle Falsehood, always lying in wait.

68. And then being made naked of all the Operations of *Harmony*, it cometh to the Eighth Nature, having its proper power, and singeth praises to the father with the things that are, and all they that are present rejoice, and congratulate the coming of it; and being made like to them with whom it converseth, it heareth also the Powers that are above the Eighth Nature, singing Praise to God in a certain voice that is peculiar to them.

69. And then in order they return unto the Father, and themselves deliver themselves to the Powers, and becoming Powers they are in God.

70. This is the Good, and to them that know, to be desired.

71. Furthermore, why sayest thou, What resteth, but that understanding all men thou become a guide, and way-leader to them that are worthy; that the kind of *Humanity*, or *Mankind*, may be saved by God?

72. When *Pimander* had thus said unto me, he was mingled among the Powers.

73. But I, giving thanks, and blessing the father of all things, rose up, being enabled by him, and taught the Nature of the Nature of the whole, and having seen the greatest sight or spectacle.

74. And I began to Preach unto men, the beauty and fairness of Piety and Knowledge.

75. *O ye people, men, born and made of the earth, which have given yourselves over to drunkenness and sleep, and to the ignorance of God, be sober and cease your surfeit, whereunto you are allured and visited by brutish and unreasonable sleep.*

76. And they that heard me come willingly and with one accord; and then I said further:

77. *Why, O Men of the Offspring of Earth, why have you delivered yourselves over unto Death, having power to partake of Immortality? Repent and change your minds, you that have together walked in Error, and have been darkened in ignorance.*

78. Depart from that dark light, be partakers of Immortality, and leave or forsake corruption.

79. And some of *them that heard me*, mocking and scorning went away, and delivered themselves up to the way of Death.

80. But others casting themselves down before my feet, besought me that they might be taught; but I, causing them to rise up, became a guide of mankind, teaching them the reasons how, and by what means they may be saved. And I sowed in them the Words of Wisdom, and nourished them with *Ambrozian* Water of *Immortality*.

81. And when it was evening and the brightness of the same began wholly to go down, I commanded them to go down, I commanded them to give thanks to God; and when they had finished their thanksgiving, everyone returned to his own lodging.

82. But I wrote in myself the bounty and benevolence of *Pimander*; and being filled with what I most desired, I was exceedingly glad.

83. For the sleep of the body was the sober watchfulness of the mind; and the shutting of my eyes the true sight, and my silence great with child and full of good; and the pronouncing of my words the blossoms and fruits of good things.

84. And thus it came to pass or happened unto me, which I received from my mind, that is *Pimander*, the Lord of the Word; whereby I became inspired by God with the Truth.

85. For which cause, with my soul and whole strength, I give praise and blessing unto God the Father.

86. *Holy is God, the Father of all things.*

87. *Holy is God, whose will is performed and accomplished by his own powers.*

88. *Holy is God, that determineth to be known, and is known by his own, or those that are his.*

89. *Holy art thou, that by thy Word has established all things.*

90. *Holy art thou, of whom all Nature is the Image.*

91. *Holy art thou, whom Nature hath not formed.*

92. *Holy art thou, that art stronger than all power.*

93. *Holy art thou, that art stronger than all excellency.*

94. *Holy art thou, that art better than all praise.*

95. *Accept these reasonable sacrifices from a pure soul, and a heart that stretched out unto thee.*

96. *O unspeakable, unutterable, to be praised with silence!*

97. *I beseech thee, that I may never err from the knowledge of thee; look mercifully upon me, and enable me, and enlighten with this Grace those that are in Ignorance, the brothers of my kind, but thy Sons.*

98. *Therefore I believe thee, and bear witness, and go into the Life and Light.*

99. *Blessed art thou, O Father; thy man would be sanctified with thee, as thou hast given him all power."*

The Divine Pymander of Hermes, Hermes Trismegistus, Translated by John Everard, 1650

"THE THIRD BOOK, THE HOLY SERMON

THE glory of all things, God, and that which is Divine, and the Divine Nature, the beginning of things that are.

2. God, and the Mind, and Nature, and Matter, and Operation or Working, and Necessity, and Matter, and Operation or Working, and Necessity, and the End, and Renovation.

3. For there were in the *Chaos* an infinite darkness in the Abyss or bottomless Depth, and Water, and a subtle in Spirit intelligible in Power; and there went out the Holy Light, and the Elements were coagulated from the Sand out of the moist substance.

4. And all the Gods distinguished the Nature full of Seeds.

5. And when all things were interminated and unmade up, the light things were divided on high. And the heavy things were founded upon the moist Sand, all things being Terminated or Divided by Fire, and being sustained or hung up by the Spirit, they were so carried, and the Heaven was seen in *Seven Circles.*

6. And the Gods were seen in their *Ideas* of the Stars, with all their signs, and the Stars were numbered with the Gods in them. And the Sphere was all lined with *Air*, carried about in a circular motion by the Spirit of God.

7. And every God, by his internal power, did that which was commanded him; and there were made four-footed things, and creeping things, and such as live in the water, and such as fly, and every fruitful seed, and Grass, and the Flowers of all Greens, all which had sowed in themselves the Seeds of Regeneration.

8. As also the Generations of Men, to the Knowledge of the Divine Works, and a lively or working Testimony of Nature, and a multitude of men, and the dominion of all things under Heaven, and the Knowledge of good things, and to be increased in increasing, and multiplied in multitude.

9. And every Soul in Flesh, by the wonderful working of the Gods in the Circles, to the beholding of Heaven, the Gods Divine Works, and the operations of Nature; and for signs of good things, and the Knowledge of the Divine Power, and to find out every cunning Workmanship of good things.

10. So it beginneth to live in them, and to be wise according to the operation of the course of the circular Gods; and to be resolved into that which shall be great Monuments and Rememberances of the cunning Works done upon earth, leaving them to be read by the darkness of times.

11. And every Generation of living Flesh, of Fruit, Seed, and all Handicrafts, though they be lost, must of necessity be renewed by the renovation of the Gods, and of the Nature of a Circle, moving in number; for it is a Divine thing that every worldly temperature should be renewed by Nature; for in that which is Divine is Nature also established.

The End of the Fragments of the Third Book, THE HOLY SERMON...."

"THE FOURTH BOOK, CALLED THE KEY

YESTERDAY'S Speech, O *Asclepius*, I dedicated to thee; this day it is fit to dedicate to Tat, because it is an Epitome of those general Speeches which were spoken to him.

2. God therefore, and the Father, and the Good, *O Tat*, have the same Nature, or rather also the same Act and operation.

3. For there is one name or appellation of Nature or Increase, which concerneth things changeable, and another about things unchangeable, and about things unmoveable, that is to say, Things Divine and Humane; every one of that which himself will have so to be; but action or operation is of another thing, or elsewhere, as we have taught in other things, Divine and Humane, which must here also be understood.

4. *For his Operation or Act is his will, and his Essence, to will all things to be.*

5. For what is God, and the Father, and the Good, but the Being of all things that yet are not, and the existence itself of those things that are?

6. This is God, this is the Father, this is the Good, whereunto no other thing is present or approacheth.

7. For the *World*, and the *Sun*, which is also a *Father* by *Participation*, is not for all that equally the cause of Good, and of Life, to living creatures. And if this be so, he is altogether constrained by the Will of the Good, without which it is not possible either to be, or to be begotten or made.

8. But the Father is the cause of his Children, who hath a will both to sow and nourish that which is good by the Sun.

9. For Good is always active or busy in making; and this cannot be in any other but in him that taketh nothing, and yet willeth all things to be; for I will not say, O *Tat*, making them; for he that maketh is defective in much time, in which sometimes he maketh not, as also of quantity and quality; for sometimes he maketh those things that have quantity and quality, and sometimes the contrary.

10. But God is the Father, and the Good, in being all things; for he both will be this and is it, and yet all this for himself (as is true) in him that can see it.

11. For all things else are for this, it is the property of Good, to be known. This is the Good, O *Tat*.

12. *Tat.* Thou hast filled us, O *Father*, with a sight both good and fair, and the eye of my mind is almost become more holy by the sight or Spectacle.

13. *Trism.* *I wonder not at it*, for the *sight of Good* is not like the beam of the *Sun*, which being of a fiery shining brightness, maketh the eye blind by his excessive Light, that gazeth upon it; rather the contrary, for it enlighteneth, and so much increaseth the light of the eye, as any man is able to receive the influence of this intelligible clearness.

14. For it is more swift and sharp to pierce, and innocent or harmless withal, and full of immortality; and they are capable, and can draw any store of this spectacle and sight, do many times fall asleep from the Body, into this most fair and beauteous Vision; which thing *Celius* and Saturn our Progenitors obtained unto.

15. *Tat.* I would we also, O Father, could do so.

16. *Trism.* I would we could, O Son; but for the present we are less intent to the Vision, and cannot yet open the eyes of our mind to behold the incorrputible and incomprehensible Beauty of that Good; but then we shall see it, when we have nothing at all to say of it.

17. For the knowledge of it is a Divine Silence, and the rest of all the senses; for neither can he that understands that, understand anything else, nor he that sees that, see anything else, nor hear any other thing, nor in sum move the Body.

18. For shining steadfastly upon and round the whole mind, it enlighteneth all the Soul; and loosing it from the Bodily senses and motions, it draweth it from the Body, and changeth it wholly into the Essence of God.

19. *For it is possible for the Soul, O Son, to be deified while yet it lodgeth in the Body of Man, if it contemplate the beauty of the Good.*

20. *Tat.* How does thou mean deifying, *Father?*

21. *Trism.* There are differences, O Son, of every Soul.

22. *Tat.* But how dost thou again divide the changes?

23. *Trism.* Hast thou not heard in the general Speeches, that from one Soul of the universe are all those Souls which in the world are tossed up and down, as it were, and severally divided? Of these Souls there are many changes, some into a more fortunate estate, and some quite the contrary; for they which are of creeping things are changed into those of watery things; and those of things living in the water, to those of things living upon the Land; and Airy ones are changed into men, and human Souls, that lay hold of immortality, are changed intoDemons.

24. And so they go on into the Sphere or Region of the fixed Gods; for there are two choirs or companies of Gods, one of them that wander, and another of them that are fixed; And so this is the perfect glory of the Soul.

25. But the Soul entering into the body of a Man, if it continue evil, shall neither taste of immortality, nor is partaker of the Good.

26. But being drawn back the same way, it returneth into creeping things; And this is the condemnation of an Evil Soul.

27. And the wickedness of a Soul is ignorance; for the Soul that knows nothing of the things that are, neither the Nature of them, nor that which is good, but is blinded, rusheth and dasheth against the bodily passions; and unhappy as it is, and not knowing itself, it serveth strange bodies and evil ones, carrying the Body as a burden, and not ruling but ruled: And this is the mischief of the Soul.

28. On the contrary, the virtue of the soul is Knowledge; for he that knows is both good and religious, and already Divine.

29. *Tat.* But who is such a one, O Father?

30. *Trism.* He that neither speaks nor hears many things; for he, O Son, that heareth two speeches, or hearings, fighteth in the shadow.

31. For God, and the Father, and Good, is neither spoken nor heard.

32. This being so in all things that are, are the *Senses*, because they cannot be without them.

33. But Knowledge differs much from Sense; for Sense is of things that surmount it, but Knowledge is the end of Sense.

34. Knowledge is the gift of God; for all Knowledge is unbodily, but useth the Mind as an instrument, as the Mind useth the Body.

35. Therefore, both intelligible and material things, go both of them into bodies; for, of contraposition, *that is, setting one against another,* and *contrariety, all things must consist.* And it is impossible it should be otherwise.

36. *Tat.* Who, therefore, is this Material God?

37. *Trism.* The fair and beautiful World, and yet it is not good; for it is material, and easily passible, nay, it is the first of all passible things; and the second of the things that are, and needy or wanting somewhat else. And it was once made, and is always, and is ever in generation, and made, and continually makes, or generates things that have quantity and quality.

38. For it is moveable, and every material motion is generation; but the intellectual stability moves the material motion after this manner.

39. Because the World is a Sphere, that is, a head, and above the head there is nothing material, as beneath the feet there is nothing intellectual.

40. The whole Universe is material: The Mind is the head, and it is moved spherically, that is, like a head.

41. Whatsoever, therefore, is joined or united to the Membrane or Film of the head, wherin the Soul is, is immortal, and as in the Soul of a made Body, hath its Soul full of the Body; but those that are further from that Membrane, have the Body full of Soul.

42. The whole is a living wight, and therefore consisteth of material and intellectual.

43. And the World is the first and Man the second living wight after the World, but the first of things that are mortal; and therefore hath whatsoever benefit of the Soul all the other have: And yet for all this, he is not only not good, but flatly evil, as being mortal.

44. For the World is not good, as it is moveable; nor evil, as it is immortal.

45. But man is evil, both as he is moveable, and as he is mortal.

46. But the Soul of Man is carried in this manner, *The Mind is in Reason, Reason in the Soul, The Soul in the Spirit, The Spirit in the Body.*

47. The Spirit being diffused and going through the veins, and arteries, and blood, both moveth the living creature, and after a certain manner beareth it.

48. Wherefore some also have thought the Soul to be blood, being deceived in Nature, not knowing that first the spirit must return into the Soul, and then the blood is congealed, and the veins and arteries

emptied, and then the living thing dieth: And this is the death of the Body.

49. All things depend of one beginning, and the beginning depends of that which is one and alone.

50. And the beginning is moved, that it may again be a beginning; but that which is one, standeth and abideth, and is not moved.

51. There are therefore, these three, *God the Father, and the Good, the World, and Man*. God hath the World, and the World hath Man; and the World is the Son of God, and Man as it were the offspring of the World.

52. For God is not ignorant of Man, but knows him perfectly, and will be known by him. This only is healthful to man, the knowledge of God: This is the return of *Olympus*; by this only the soul is made good, and not sometimes good, and sometimes evil, but of necessity Good.

53. *Tat.* What meaneth thou, O Father?

54. *Trism.* Consider, O Son, the Soul of a Child, when as yet it hath as yet received no dissolution of its body, which is not yet grown, but is very small: how then if it look upon itself, it sees itself beautiful, as not having been as yet spotted with the Passions of the Body, but as it were depending yet upon the soul of the World.

55. But when the Body is grown, and distracteth the Soul, it engenders forgetfulness, and partakes no

more of the *Fair and the Good,* and Forgetfulness is evilness.

56. The like also happeneth to them that go out of the Body: For when the soul runs back into itself, the Spirit is contracted into the blood, and the Soul into the Spirit. But the Mind being made pure, and free from these clothings; and being Divine by Nature, taking a fiery body, rangeth abroad in every place, leaving the soul to judgment, and to the punishment it hath deserved.

57. *Tat.* Why dost thou say so, O Father, that the Mind is separated from the Soul, and the Soul from the Spirit? When even now thou saidst that the Soul was the clothing or apparel of the Mind, and the Body of the Soul.

58. *Trism.* O Son, he that hears must co-understand, and conspire in thought with him that speaks; yea, he must have his hearing swifter and sharper than the voice of the speaker.

59. The disposition of these clothings or Covers is done in an Earthly Body; for it is impossible that the Mind should establish or rest itself, naked, and of itself in an Earthly Body; neither is the Earthly Body able to bear such immortality: and therefore, that it might suffer so great virtue, the Mind compacted, as it were, and took to itself the passable Body of the Soul, as a covering or clothing. And the Soul being also in some sort Divine, useth the Spirit as her Minister or Servant; and the Spirit governeth the living things.

60. When therefore the Mind is separated, and departeth from the Earthly Body, presently it puts on its Fiery Coat, which it could not do, having to dwell in an Earthly Body.

61. For the Earth cannot suffer fire, for it is all burned of a small spark; therefore is the water poured round about the Earth, as a wall or defence, to withstand the flame of fire.

62. But the Mind being the most sharp or swift of all the Divine Cogitations, and more swift than all the Elements, hath the fire for its Body.

63. For the Mind, which is the Workman of all, useth the fire as his Instrument in his Workmanship; and he that is the Workman of all useth it to the making of all things, as it is used by Man to the making of Earthly things only, for the Mind that is upon Earth, void or naked of fire, cannot do the business of men, nor that which is otherwise the affairs of God.

64. But the Soul of Man, and yet not everyone, but that which is pious and religious, is Angelic and Divine. And such a soul, after it is departed from the body, having striven the strife of Piety, becomes either Mind or God.

65. And the strife of piety is to know God, and to injure no Man; and this way it becomes Mind.

66. But the impious Soul abideth in its own offence, punished of itself, and seeking an earthly and humane body to enter into.

67. For no other Body is capable of a Humane Soul, neither is it lawful for a Man's Soul to fall into the Body of an unreasonable living thing: For it is the Law or Decree of God to preserve a Human Soul from so great a contumely and reproach.

68. *Tat.* How then is the Soul of Man punished, O Father, and what is its greatest torment?

69. *Herm.* Impiety, O my Son; for what Fire hath so great a flame as it? Or what biting Beast doth so tear the Body as it doth the Soul?

70. Or dost thou not see how many Evils the wicked Soul suffereth, roaring and crying out, *I am burned, I am consumed, I know not what to say or do, I am devoured, unhappy wretch, of the evils that compass and lay hold upon me; miserable that I am, I neither hear nor see anything.*

71. These are the voices of a punished and tormented Soul, and not as many; and thou, O Son, thinkest that the Soul going out of the Body grows brutish or enters into a Beast; which is a very great error, for the Soul punished after this manner.

72. For the Mind, when it is ordered or appointed to get a Fiery Body for the services of God, coming down into the wicked soul, torments it with the whips of Sins, wherewith the wicked Soul, being scorged, turns itself to Murders and Contumelies, and Blasphemies, and divers violences, and other things by which men are injured.

73. But into a pious soul, the mind entering, leads it into the Light of Knowledge.

74. And such a Soul is never satisfied with singing praise *to God*, and speaking well of all men; and both in words and deeds always doing good, in imitation of her Father.

75. Therefore, O Son, we must give thanks and pray that we may obtain a good mind.

76. The Soul therefore may be altered or changed into the better, but into the worse it is impossible.

77. But there is a communion of souls, and those of Gods, communicate with those men, and those of Men with those of Beasts.

78. And the better always take of the worse, Gods of Men; Men of brute Beasts, but God of all: For He is the best of all, and all things are less than He.

79. Therefore is the World subject unto God, Man unto the World, and unreasonable things to Man.

80. But God is above all and about all; and the beams of God are operations; and the beams of the World are Natures; and the beams of Man are *Arts and Sciences*.

81. And operations do act by the World, and upon Man by the natural beams of the World, but Natures work by the Elements, and Man by *Arts and Sciences*.

82. And this is the Government of the whole, depending upon the Nature of the *One*, and piercing or coming down by the *one Mind*, than which nothing is more Divine and more efficacious or operative; and nothing more uniting, or nothing is more *One*. The Communion of Gods to Men, and of Men to Gods.

83. This is the *Bonas Genius*, or good *Demon*: blessed soul that is fullest of it! And unhappy soul that is empty of it.

84. *Tat.* And wherefore, Father?

85. *Trism.* Know, Son, that every Soul hath the *Good Mind*; for of that it is we now speak, and not of that Minister of whom we said before, that he was sent from the Judgment.

86. For the Soul without the Mind can neither say nor do anything; for many times the Mind flies away from the Soul, and in that hour the Soul neither seeth nor heareth, but is like an unreasonable thing; so great is the power of the Mind.

87. But neither brooketh it an idle or lazy Soul, but leaves such an one fastened to the Body, and by it is pressed down.

88. And such a Soul, O Son, hath no Mind; wherefore neither must such a one be called a Man.

89. For Man is a Divine living thing, and is not to be compared to any brute Beast that lives upon Earth,

but to them that are above in Heaven, that are called Gods.

90. Rather, if we shall be bold to speak the truth, he that is a Man indeed is above them, or at least they are equal in power, one to the other. For none of the things in Heaven will come down upon Earth, and leave the limits of Heaven, but a Man ascends up into Heaven, and measures it.

91. And he knoweth what things are on high, and what below, and learneth all other things exactly.

92. And that which is the greatest of all, he leaveth not the Earth, and yet is above: So great is the greatness of his Nature.

93. Wherefore we must be bold to say, *That an Earthly Man is a mortal God, and that the Heavenly God is an immortal Man.*

94. Wherefore, by these two are all things governed, the World and Man; but they and all things else of that which is *One*.

THE END OF THE FOURTH BOOK, Called THE KEY..."

"THE FIFTH BOOK, THAT GOD IS NOT MANIFEST, AND YET MOST MANIFEST

THIS Discourse, I will also make to thee, *O Tat*, that thou mayest not be ignorant of the more excellent name of God.

2. But do thou contemplate in thy Mind how that which to many seems hidden and unmanifest may be most manifest to thee.

3. For it were not all, if it were apparent, for whatsoever is apparent is generated or made; for it was made manifest, but that which is not manifest is ever.

4. For it needeth not be manifested, for it is always.

5. And he maketh all other things manifest, being unmanifest, as being always, and making other things manifest, he is not made manifest.

6. Himself is not made, yet in fantasie he fantasieth all things, or in appearance he maketh them appear; for appearance is only of those things that are generated or made, for appearance is nothing but generation.

7. But he that is *One*, that is not made nor generated, is also unapparent and unmanifest.

8. But making all things appear, he appeareth in all, and by all; but especially he is manifested to or in those things wherein himself listeth.

9. Thou, therefore, *O Tat*, my Son, pray first to the *Lord and Father*, and to the *Alone*, and to the *One*, from whom is one to be merciful to thee, that thou mayest know and understand so great a God; and that he would shine one of his beams upon thee in thy understanding.

10. For only the Understanding see that which is not manifest, or apparent, as being itself not manifest or apparent; and if thou canst, *O Tat*, it will appear to the eyes of thy Mind.

11. For the Lord, void of envy, appeareth through the whole world. Thou mayest see the intelligence, and take it into they hands, and contemplate the image of God.

12. But if that which is in thee, be not known or apparent unto thee, how shall he in thee be seen, and appear unto thee by the eyes?

13. But if thou will see him, consider and understand the *Sun*, consider the course of the *Moon*, consider the order of the *Stars*.

14. Who is he that keepeth order? For all order is circumscribed or terminated in number and place.

15. The Sun is the greatest of the Gods in Heaven, to whom all the Heavenly Gods give place, as to a King and Potentate; and yet he being such an one, greater than the Earth or the Sea, is content to suffer infinite lesser stars to walk and move above himself: whom doth he fear the while, O Son?

16. Every one of these Stars that are in Heaven do not make the like, or an equal course; who is it that hath prescribed unto every one the manner and the greatness of their course?

17. This Bear that turns round about its own self, and carries round the whole World with her, who possessed and made such an Instrument?

18. Who hath set the bounds to the Sea? Who hath established the Earth? For there is somebody, *O Tat*, that is the Maker and Lord of these things.

19. For it is impossible, O Son, that either place, or number, or measure, should be observed without a maker.

20. For no order can be made by disorder or disproportion.

21. I would it were possible for thee, O my Son, to have wings, and to fly into the Air, and being taken up in the midst, between Heaven and Earth, to see the stability of the Earth, the fluidness of the Sea, the courses of the Rivers, the largeness of the Air, the sharpness and swiftness of the Fire, the motion of the Stars, and the speediness of the Heaven, by which it goeth round about all these.

22. O Son, what a happy sight it were, at one instant, to see all these; that which is immoveable moved, and that which is hidden appear and be manifest!

23. And if thou wilt see and behold this Workman, even by mortal things that are upon earth, and in the deep, consider, O Son, how Man is made and framed in the Womb; and examine diligently the skill and cunning of the Workman, and learn who it was that wrought and fashioned the beautiful and Divine shape of *Man*; who circumscribed and marked out his eyes? who bored his nostrils and ears? who opened his mouth? who stretched out and tie together his sinews? who channelled the veins? who hardened and made strong the bones? who clothed the flesh with skin? who divided the fingers and joints? who flatted and made broad the soles of the feet? who digged the pores? who stretched out the spleen? who made the Heart like a *Pyramis*? who made the Liver broad? who made the Lights spungy, and full of holes? who made the belly large and capacious? who set to outward view the more honorable parts, and hid the filthy ones?

24. See how many arts in one Matter, and how many Works in one Superscription, and all exceedingly beautiful and all done in measure, and yet all differing.

25. Who hath made all these things? What Mother? What Father? Save only god that is not manifest; that made all things by his own will.

26. And no man says that a statue or an image is made without a Carver or a Painter, and was this Workmanship made without a Workman? O Great Blindness! O Great Impiety! O Great Ignorance!

27. Never, *O Son Tat*, canst thou deprive the Workmanship of the Workman; rather, it is the best Name of all the Names of God, to call him the *Father* of all, for so he is alone; and this is his work to be the Father.

28. And if thou will force me to say anything more boldly, it is his Essence to be pregnant, or great with all things, and to make them.

29. And as without a maker it is impossible that anything should be made, so it is that he should not always be, and always be making all things in Heaven, in the Air, in the Earth, in the Deep, in the whole World, and in every part of the whole, that is or that is not.

30. For there is nothing in the whole World that is not himself; both the things that are, and the things that are not.

31. For the things that are he hath made manifest, and the things that are not he hath hid in himself.

32. This is God that is better than any name; this is he that is secret; this is he that is most manifest; this is he that is to

be seen by the Mind; this is he that is visible to the Eye; this is he that hath no body; and this is he that hath many bodies; rather, there is nothing of any body which is not *he*.

33. For he alone is all things.

34. *And for this cause he hath many Names, because he is the One Father; and therefore he hath no Name, because he is the Father of all.*

35. Who therefore can bless thee, or give thanks for thee, or to thee?

36. Which way shall I look when I praise thee? upward? downward? outward? inward?

37. For about these there is no manner nor place, nor anything else of all things that are.

38. But all things are in thee; all things from thee; thou givest all things, and takest nothing; for thou hast all things; and there is nothing that thou hast not.

39. When shall I praise thee, *O Father*, for it is neither possible to comprehend thy hour, nor they time?

40. For what shall I praise thee? For what thou hast made, or for what thou hast not made? for those things thou hast manifested, or for those things thou hast hidden?

41. Wherefore shall I praise thee, as being of myself, or having anything of mine own, or rather being anothers?

42. For thou art what I am, thou art what I do, thou art what I say.

43. *Thou art all things, and there is nothing else thou art not.*

44. *Thou are thou, all that is made, and all that is not made.*

45. The Mind that understandeth.

46. The Father that maketh and frameth.

47. The Good that worketh.

48. The Good that doth all things.

49. Of the matter, the most subtle and slender is *Air*; of the Air the *Soul*; of the soul the *Mind*; of the mind *God*.

The End of the Fifth Book....
THAT GOD IS NOT MANIFEST, AND YET MOST
MANIFEST..."

"THE SIXTH BOOK, THAT IN GOD ALONE IS GOOD

GOD, *O Asclepius*, is in nothing but in God alone, or rather God himself is the Good always.

2. And if it be so, then must he be an Essence or Substance, void of all Motion and Generation; but nothing is void or empty of him.

3. And this Essence hath about or in himself a *Stable* and firm *Operation*, wanting nothing, most full and giving abundantly.

4. One thing is the Beginning of all things, for it giveth all things; and when I name the Good, I mean that which is altogether and always Good.

5. This is present to none, but God alone; for he wanteth nothing that he should desire to have it, nor can anything be taken from him; the loss whereof may grieve him; for sorrow is a part of evilness.

6. Nothing is stronger than he, that he should be opposed by it; nor nothing equal to him, that he should be in love with it; nothing unheard of to be angry, with nothing wiser to be envious at.

7. And none of these being in his Essence, what remains but only the Good?

8. For as in this, being such an Essence, there is none of the evils; so in none of the other things shall the Good be found.

9. For in all other things, are all those other things, as well in the small as the great, and as well in the particulars as in this living Creature; the greater and mightiest of all.

10. For all things that are made or generated, are full of passion, Generation itself being a passion; and where Passion is, there is not the Good; where the Good is, there is no Passion; where it is day, it is not Night; where it is night, it is not Day.

11. Wherefore it is impossible that in Generation should be the Good, but only in that which is not generated or made.

12. Yet as the Participation of all things is in the Matter bound, so also of that which is Good. After this manner is the World Good, as it maketh all things, and in the part of making or doing … it is Good, but in all other things not good.

13. For it is passable and moveable, and the Maker of passable things.

14. In Man also the Good is ordered (or *taketh denomination*) in comparison of that which is evil; for that which is not very Evil, is here Good; and that which is here called Good, is the least particle, or proportion of Evil.

15. It is impossible, therefore, that the Good should be here pure from Evil; for here the Good groweth Evil, and growing Evil, it doth not still abide Good; and not abiding Good, it becomes Evil.

16. Therefore in God alone is the Good, or rather God is the Good.

17. Therefore, *O Asclepius*, there is nothing in men (or *among men*) but the name of Good, the thing itself is not, for it is impossible; for a material Body receiveth (or *comprehendeth*), is not as being on every side encompassed and coacted with evils, and labours, and griefs, and desires, and wrath, and deceits, and foolish opinions.

18. And in that which is the worst of all, *Asclepius*, every one of the forenames things, is here believed to be the greatest Good, especially that supreme mischief ... the pleasures of the Belly, and the ringleader of all evils. Error is here the absence of the Good.

19. And I give thanks unto God, that, concerning the knowledge of good, put this assurance in my Mind, that it is impossible it should be in the World.

20. For the World is the fulness of Evilness; but God is the fulness of Good, or good of God.

21. For the eminencies of all appearing Beauty, are in the Essence more pure, and more sincere, and peradventure they are also the Essences of it.

22. For we must be bold to say, *Asclepius*, that the Essence of God, if he have an Essence, is ... that which is fair or beautiful; but no good is comprehended in this World.

23. For all things that are subject to the eye, are Idols, and as it were Shadows; but those things that are not subject to the eye, are ever, especially the *Essence* of the Fair and the Good.

24. And as the Eye cannot see God, so neither the Fair and the Good.

25. For those are the parts of God, that partake the Nature of the whole, proper, and familiar unto him

alone, inseparable, most lovely, whereof either God is enamoured, or they are enamoured of God.

26. If thou canst understand God, thou shall understand the *Fair*, and the Good, which is most shining, and enlightening, and most enlightened by God.

27. For that Beauty is above Comparison, and that Good is inimitable, as God himself.

28. As, therefore, thou understandest God, so understand the Fair and the Good; for these are incommunicable to any other living creatures, because they are inseparable from God.

29. If thou seek concerning God, thou seekest or asketh also of the Fair, for there is one way which leadeth to the same thing, that is *Piety*, with *Knowledge*.

30. Wherefore, they that are ignorant, and go not in the way of *Piety*, dare call Men Fair and Good, never seeing so much as in a dream, what good is; but being infolded and wrapped upon all evil, and believing that the Evil is the Good, they, by that means, both use it insatiable, and are afraid to be deprived of it; and therefore they strive, by all possible means, that they may not only have it, but also increase it.

31. Such, *O Asclepius*, are the good and fair things of Men, which we can neither love nor hate; for this is the hardest thing of all, that we have need of them, and cannot live without them.

The End of the Sixth Book....
THAT IN GOD ALONE IS GOOD...."

"THE SEVENTH BOOK, HIS SECRET SERMON IN THE MOUNT OF REGENERATION, AND THE PROFESSION OF SILENCE

TO HIS SON *TAT.*

Tat.
IN the general speeches, O Father, discoursing of the *Divinity*, thou speakest enigmatically, and didst not clearly reveal thyself, saying, That no man can be saved before *Regeneration*.

2. And when I did humbly entreat thee, at the going up to the Mountain, after thou hadst discoursed to me, having a great desire to learn this *Argument of Regeneration*; because among all the rest, I am ignorant only of this, thou toldst me thou wouldst impart it to me, when I would estrange myself from the world; whereupon I made myself ready, and have vindicated the understanding that is in me, from the deceit of the World.

3. Now, then fulfil my defect, and as thou saidst, instruct me of *Regeneration*, either by word of mouth or secretly; for I know not, O *Trismegistus*, of what Substance, or what Seed, or what Womb, a man is thus born.

4. *Herm.* O Son, this wisdom is to be understood in silence, and the seed is the true Good.

5. *Tat.* Who soweth it, O Father? for I am utterly ignorant and doubtful.

6. *Herm.* The Will of God, O Son.

7. And what manner of Man is he that is thus born? for in this point, I am clean deprived of the Essence that understandeth in me.

8. *Herm.* The Son of God will be another. God made the universe, that in everything consisteth of all powers.

9. *Tat.* Thou tellest me a Riddle, Father, and dost not speak as a Father to a Son.

10. *Herm.* Son, things of this kind are not taught, but are by God, when he pleaseth, brought to remembrance.

11. *Tat.* Thou speakest of things strained, or far fetched, and impossible, Father; and therefore I will directly contradict them.

12. *Herm.* Wilt thou prove a Stranger, Son, to thy Father's kind?

13. *Tat.* Do not envy me, Father, or pardon me, I am thy Natural Son; discourse unto me the manner of *Regeneration.*

14. *Herm.* What shall I say, O my Son? I have nothing to say more than this, That I see in myself an unstrained sight or spectacle, made by the mercy of

God; and I am gone out of myself into an immortal body, and am not now, what I was before, but was begotten in Mind.

15. This thing is not taught, nor is it to be seen in this formed element; for which the first compounded form was neglected by me, and that I am now separated from it; for I have both the touch and the measure of it, yet am I now estranged from them.

16. Thou seest, O Son, with thine eyes; but though thou never look so steadfastly upon me, with the Body, and the Bodily sight, thou canst not see nor understand what I am now.

17. *Tat.* Thou hast driven me, O Father, into no small fury and distraction of mind, for I do not now see myself.

18. *Herm.* I would, O Son, that thou also wert gone out of thyself, like them that Dream in their sleep.

19. *Tat.* Then tell me this, who is the Author and Maker of Regeneration?

20. *Herm.* The Child of God, one Man by the Will of God.

21. *Tat.* Now, O Father, thou hast put me to silence for ever, and all my former thoughts have quite left and forsaken me; for I see the greatness and shape of things here below, and nothing but falsehood in them all.

22. And so thence this mortal form is daily changed, and turned by time into increase or diminution, as being falsehood: What therefore is true, O Trismegistus?

23. *Trism.* That, O my Son, which is not troubled, nor bounded; not coloured, not figured, not changed, that which is naked, high. Comprehensible only of itself, unalterable, unbodily.

24. *Tat.* Now I am mad indeed, O Father, for when I thought me to have been made a wise man by thee, with these thoughts, thou hast quite dulled all my senses.

25. *Herm. Yet is it so as I say, O Son, He that looketh only upon* that which is carried upward as Fire, that which is carried downward as Earth, that which is moist as Water, and that which bloweth, or is subject to blast, as Air; how can he sensibly understand that which is neither hard nor moist, nor tangible, nor perspicuous, seeing it is only understood in power and operation? But I beseech and pray to the Mind, which alone can understand the*Generation* which is in God.

26. *Tat.* Then am I, O Father, utterly unable to do it.

27. *Herm.* God forbid, Son, rather draw or pull him unto thee *(or study to know him)* and he will come, *be but willing and it shall be done;* quite (or make idle) the senses of the Body, purging thyself from the unreasonable brutish torments of matter.

28. *Tat.* Have I any (revengers or) tormentors in myself, *Father*?

29. *Herm.* Yea, and those not a few, but many, and fearful ones.

30. *Tat.* I do not know them, Father.

31. *Herm.* One Torment, Son, is *Ignorance*: a second, *Sorrow*; a third, *Intemperance*; a fourth, *Concupiscence*; a fifth, *Injustice*; a sixth, *Covetousness*; a seventh, *Deceit*; an eighth, *Envy*; a ninth, *Fraud* or *Guile*; a tenth, *Wrath*; an eleventh, *Rashness*; a twelfth, *Maliciousness*.

32. They are in number twelve, and under these many more; some which through the prison of the Body do force the inwardly placed man to suffer sensibly.

33. And they do not suddenly or easily depart from him that hath obtained mercy of God; and herein consists both the manner and the reason of *Regeneration*.

34. For the rest, O Son, hold thy peace, and praise God in silence, and by that means the mercy of God will not cease, or be wanting unto us.

35. Therefore, rejoice, my Son, from henceforward, being purged by the powers of God, to the Knowledge of the Truth.

36. For the revelation of God is come to us, and when that came, all ignorance was cast out.

37. The Knowledge of Joy is come unto us. And when that comes, Sorrow shall fly away to them that are capable.

38. I call unto Joy the power of Temperance, a power whose Virtue is most sweet; let us take her unto ourselves, O son, most willingly, for how at her coming hath she put away Intemperance?

39. Now I call forth, Continence, the power which is over Concupiscence. This, O Son, is the stable and firm foundation of Justice.

40. For see how without labour she hath chased away Injustice; and we are justified, O Son, when Injustice is away.

41. The sixth Virtue, which comes into us, I call *Communion*, which is against Covetousness.

42. And when that (Covetousness) is gone, I call Truth, and when she cometh, Error and Deceit vanisheth.

43. See, O Son, how the Good is fulfilled by the access of Truth; for by this means Envy is gone from us; for Truth is accompanied with the Good, together also with Life and Light.

44. And there came no more any torment of Darkness, but being overcome, they all fled away suddenly and tumultuously.

45. Thou hast understood, O Son, the manner of regeneration; for upon the coming of these Ten, the Intellectual Generation is perfected, and then it driveth away the Twelve; and we have seen it in the Generation itself.

46. Whoseoever therefore hath of Mercy obtained this Generation, which is according to God, he leaving all bodily sense, knoweth himself to consist of divine things, and rejoiceth, being made by god Stable and immutable.

47. *Tat.* O Father, I conceive and understand, not by the sight of mine eyes, but by the Intellectual operation, which is by the Powers. I am in Heaven, in the Earth, in the Water, in the Air; I am in Living Creatures, in Plants, in the Womb, everywhere.

48. Yet tell me, further, this one thing, How are the Torments of Darkness, being in number Twelve, driven away and expelled by the Ten Powers? What is the manner of it, *Trismegistus*?

49. This Tabernacle, O Son, consists of the Zodiacal Circle; and this consisting of Twelve numbers, the *Idea* of one; but all formed Nature admit divers Conjugations to the deceiving of Man.

50. And though they be different in themselves, yet are they united in practice (as, for example, Rashness is inseparable from Anger), and they are also indeterminate. Therefore, with good reason do they make their departure, being driven away by the Ten Powers; that is to say, by the dead.

51. For the number of Ten, O Son, is the begetter of Souls. And there Life and Light are united, where the number of *Unity* is born of the spirit.

52. Therefore, according to Reason, Unity hath the number of Ten, and the number of Ten hath Unity.

53. *Tat.* O Father, I now see the Universe and myself in the Mind.

54. *Herm.* This is *Regeneration*, O Son, that we should not any longer fix our imagination upon this Body, subject to the three dimensions, according to this, according to this speech which we have now commented, that we may not at all caluminate the Universe.

55. *Tat.* Tell me, O Father, This body that consists of Powers, shall it ever admit of Dissolution?

56. *Herm.* Good words, Son, and speak not things impossible; for so thou shalt sin, and the eye of thy mind grow wicked.

57. The sensible body of Nature is far from the Essential Generation, for that is subject to dissolution, but this is not; and that is mortal, but this immortal. Dost thou not know that thou art born a God, and the Son of the One, as I am?

58. *Tat.* How feign would I, O Father, hear that praise given by a Hymn, which thou saidst thou heardest from the Powers, when I was in the *Octonary*?

59. *Herm.* As *Pimander* said, by way of Oracle to the *Octonary*: Thou dost well, O Son, to desire the Solution of the *Tabernacle*, for thou art purified.

60. Pimander, the Mind of Absolute Power and Authority, hath delivered no more unto me, than those that are written; knowing that of myself, I can understand all things, and hear, and see what I will. And he commanded me to do those things that are good; and therefore all the powers that are in me sing.

61. *Tat.* I would hear thee, O Father, and understand these things.

62. *Herm.* Be quiet, O Son, and now hearken to that harmonious blessing and thanksgiving; the hymn of*Regeneration*, which I did not determine to have spoken of so plainly, but to thyself in the end of all.

63. Wherefore, this is not taught, but hid in silence.

64. So then, O son, do thou, standing in the open Air, worship, looking to the North Wind, about the going down of the Sun; and to the South, when the Sun ariseth. And now keep silence, Son.

THE SECRET SONG.
The Holy Speech.

65. Let all the Nature of the World entertain the hearing of this Hymn.

66. Be opened, O Earth, and let all the Treasure of the Rain be opened.

67. You Trees, tremble not, for I will sing and praise the Lord of the Creation, and the *All*, and the *One*.

68. Be opened, you Heavens; ye Winds, stand still, and let the immortal Circle of God receive these words.

69. For I will sing and praise him that created all things, that fixed the earth, and hung up the Heavens, and commanded the sweet water to come out of the *Ocean*, into all the World, inhabited and not inhabited, to the use and nourishment of all things or men.

70. That commanded the fire to shine for every action, both to Gods and Men.

71. Let us altogether give him blessing, which rideth upon the Heavens, the Creator of all Nature.

72. This is he that is the Eye of the Mind, and will accept the praise of my Powers.

73. O all ye Powers that are in me, praise the *One*, and *All*.

74. Sing together with my Will, all you Powers that are in me.

75. O Holy knowledge, being enlightened by thee, I magnify the intelligible Light, and rejoice in the joy of the Mind.

76. All my Powers sing praise with me, and now, my Continence, sing, praise my Righteousness by me; praise that which is righteous.

77. O Communion which is in me; praise the *All*.

78. By me the *Truth* sings praise to the *Truth*, the Good praiseth the Good.

79. O Life, O Light, from us, unto you, comes this praise and thanksgiving.

80. I give thanks unto thee, O Father, the operation or act of my Powers.

81. I give thanks unto thee, O God, the Power of my operations.

82. By me the Word sings praise unto thee; receive by me this reasonable (or verbal) Sacrifice in words.

83. The powers that are in me cry these things, they praise the *All*, they fulfil thy Will; thy Will and counsel is form thee unto thee.

84. *O All*, receive a reasonable sacrifice from all things.

85. *O Life*, save all that is in us; *O Light*, enlighten, *O God*, the *Spirit*; for the Mind guideth (or feedeth) the Word; O Spirit-bearing Workman.

86. Thou are *God*, thy *Man* cryeth these things unto thee through, by the Fire, by the Air, by the Earth, by the Water, by the Spirit, by thy Creatures.

87. From eternity I have found (means to) bless and praise thee, and I have what I seek; for I rest in thy Will.

88. *Tat.* O Father, I see thou hast sung this song of praise and blessing, with thy whole Will; and therefore have I put and placed it in my World.

89. *Herm.* Say *in thy Intelligible World,* O Son.

90. *Tat.* I do mean in my Intelligible world; for by thy Hymn and song of praise my mind is enlightened, and gladly would I send from my Understanding, a Thanksgiving unto God.

91. *Herm.* Not rashly, O Son.

92. *Tat.* In my Mind, O Father.

93. *Herm.* Those things that I see and contemplate, I infuse them into thee, and therefore say, thou Son, *Tat,* the author of thy succeeding Generations, I send unto god these reasonable sacrifices.

94. *O God, thou art the Father, thou art the Lord, thou art the Mind, accept these reasonable sacrifices which thou requirest of me.*

95. For all things are done as the Mind willeth.

96. Thou, O Son, send this acceptable Sacrifice to god, the Father of all things; but propound it also, O Son, by word.

97. *Tat.* I thank thee, Father, thou hast advised and instructed me thus to give thanks and praise.

98. *Herm.* I am glad, O Son, to see the Truth bring forth the Fruits of Good things, and such immortal Branches.

99. And learn this from me: Above all other Virtues entertain Silence, and impart unto no man, O Son, the tradition of *Regeneration*, lest we be reputed Calumniators; for we both have now sufficiently meditated, I in speaking, thou in hearing. And now thou dost intellectually know thyself and our Father.

The End of the Seventh Book....HIS SECRET SERMON IN THE MOUNT OF REGENERATION, AND THE PROFESSION OF SILENCE."

"THE EIGHTH BOOK, THE GREATEST EVIL IN MAN IS THE NOT KNOWING GOD

WHITHER are you carried, O Men, drunken with drinking strong Wine of Ignorance? which seeing you cannot bear, why do you vomit it up again?

2. Stand, and be sober, and look up again with the Eyes of your heart, and if you cannot all do so, yet do so many as you can.

3. For the malice of Ignorance surroundeth all the Earth, and corrupteth the Soul, shut up in the Body, not suffering it to arrive at the Havens of Salvation.

4. Suffer not yourselves to be carried with the Great Stream, but stem the tide you that can lay hold of the Haven of Safety, and make your full course towards it.

5. Seek on that may lead you by the hand, and conduct you to the door of Truth and Knowledge, where the clear Light is that is pure from Darkness, where there is not one drunken, but all are sober, and in their heart look up to him, whose pleasure it is to be seen.

6. For he cannot be heard with ears, nor seen with eyes, nor expressed in words; but only in mind and heart.

7. But first thou must tear to pieces, and break through the garment thou wearest, the web of Ignorance; the foundation of all Mischief; the bond of Corruption; the dark Coverture; the living Death; the sensible Carcass; the Sepulchre, carried about with us; the domestical Thief, which in what he loves us, hates us, envies us.

8. Such is the hurtful Apparel, wherewith thou art clothed, which draws and pulls thee downward by its own self, lest looking upward and seeing the beauty of Truth, and the Good that is reposed therein, thou shouldst hate the wickedness of this Garment and

understand the traps and ambushes which it had laid for thee.

9. Therefore doth it labour to make good those things that seem, and are by the senses, judged and determined; and the things that are truly, it hides, and envelopeth in much matter, filling what it presents unto thee, with hateful pleasure, that thou canst neither hear what thou shouldst hear, nor see what thou shouldst see.

The End of the Eighth Book,
THE GREATEST EVIL IN MAN IS
THE NOT KNOWING GOD."

"THE NINTH BOOK, A UNIVERSAL SERMON TO ASCLEPIUS

Herm.
ALL that is moved, O *Asclepius*, is it not moved in something and by something?

2. *Asclep.* Yes, indeed.

3. Herm. Must not that in which a thing is moved, of necessity be greater than the thing that is moved?

4. Of necessity.

5. And that which moveth, is it not stronger than that which is moved?

6. *Asclep.* It is stronger.

7. *Herm.* That in which a thing is moved, must it not needs have a Nature contrary to that of the thing that is moved?

8. Asclep. It must needs.

9. *Herm.* Is not this great World a Body, than which there is no greater?

10. *Asclep.* Yes, confessedly.

11. *Herm.* And is it not solid, as filled with many great bodies, and indeed with all the Bodies that are?

12. *Asclep.* It is so.

13. *Herm.* And is not the World a Body, and a Body that is moved?

14. *Asclep.* It is.

15. *Herm.* Then what a kind of place must it be, wherein it is moved, and of what Nature? Must it not be much bigger, that it may receive the continuity of Motion? And lest which is moved, should for want of room, be stayed, and hindered in the Motion?

16. *Asclep.* It must needs be an immense thing, *Trismegistus,* but of what Nature?

17. *Herm.* Of a contrary Nature, O *Asclepius.* But is not the Nature of things unbodily, contrary to a Body?

18. *Asclep.* Confessedly.

19. *Herm.* Therefore the place is unbodily; but that which is unbodily is either some Divine thing, or God himself. And by something Divine, I do not mean that which was made or begotten.

20. If therefore it be Divine, it is an Essence or Substance; but if it be God, it is above Essence; but he is otherwise intelligible.

21. For the first, God is intelligible, not to himself, but to us; for that which is intelligible is subject to that which understandeth by Sense.

22. Therefore, God is not intelligible to himself; for not being any other thing from that which is understood, he cannot be understood by himself.

23. But he is another thing from us, and therefore he is understood by us.

24. If therefore Place be intelligible, it is not Place but God; but if God be intelligible, he is intelligible not as Place, but as a capable Operation.

25. Now, everything that is moved, is moved not in or by that which is moved, but in that which standeth or resteth, and that which moveth standeth or resteth; for it is impossible it should be moved with it.

26. *Asclep.* How, then, O *Trismegistus,* are those things that are here moved with the things that are moved? for thou sayest that the Spheres that wander, are moved by the sphere that wanders not.

27. *Herm.* That, O *Asclepius,* is not a moving together, but a counter motion; for they are not moved after a like manner, but contrary one to the other; and contrariety hath a standing resistance of motion, for the ..., or resistance, is a staying of Motion.

28. Therefore, the wandering spheres being moved contrarily to that Sphere which wandereth not, shall have one from another contrarily standing of itself.

29. For this Bear thou seest neither rise nor go down, but turning always about the same; dost thou think it moveth or standeth still?

30. *Asclep.* I think it moves, Trismegistus.

31. What motion, O *Asclepius?*

32. *Asclep.* A motion that is always carried about the same.

33. But the Circulation which is about the same, and the motion bout the same, are both hidden by Station; for that which is about the same, forbids that which is above the same, if it stand to that which is about the same.

34. And so the contrary motion stands fast always, being always established by the contrariety.

35. But I will give thee concerning this matter, an Earthly Example, that may be seen with eyes.

36. Look upon any of these living Creatures upon Earth, as Man, for example, and see him swimming; for as the Water is carried one way, the reluctation or resistance of his feet and hands is made a station to the Man, that he should not be carried with the Water, nor sink underneath it.

37. *Asclep.* Thou hast laid down a very clear example, *Trismegistus.*

38. *Herm.* Therefore, every motion is in station, and is moved of station.

39. The motion, then, of the World, and of every material living thing, happeneth not to be done by those things that are without the World, but by those things within it, a Soul, or Spirit, or some other unbodily thing, to those things that are without it.

40. For an inanimate Body doth not know, much less a Body if it be wholly inanimate.

41. *Asclep.* What meaneth thou by this, O *Trismegistus,* wood and stones, and all other inanimate things, are they not moving Bodies?

42. *Herm.* By no means, O *Asclepius,* for that within the Body, which moves the inanimate thing, is not the Body, that moves both as well the Body of that which beareth, as the Body of that which is born; for one dead or inanimate thing cannot move another; that which moveth, must needs be alive if it move.

43. Thou seest therefore how the Soul is surcharged, when it carrieth two Bodies.

44. And now it is manifest that the things that are moved in something, and by something.

45. *Asclep.* The things that are moved, O *Trismegistus*, must needs be moved in that which is void, or empty vacuum, ….

46. Be advised, O *Asclepius*, for all the things that are, there is nothing empty, only that which is not, is empty and a stranger to existence or being.

47. But that which is could not be if it were not full of existence; for that which is in being or existence, can never be made empty.

48. *Asclep.* Are there not therefore some things that are empty, O *Trismegistus*, as an empty Barrel, an empty Hogshead, an empty Will, an empty Wine-press, and many such like?

49. *Herm.* O the grossness of thy error, O *Asclepius*; those things that are most full and replenished, dost thou account them void and empty?

50. *Asclep.* What may be thy meaning, *Trismegistus*?

51. *Herm.* Is not the Air a Body?

52. *Asclep.* It is a Body.

53. *Herm.* Why then this Body, does it not pass through all things that are? And passing through them, fill them? and that Body, doth it not consist of the mixture of the four? therefore, all those things which thou callest empty are full of Air.

54. Therefore, those things thou callest empty, thou oughtest to call them hollow, not empty; for they exist and are full of Air and Spirit.

55. *Asclep.* This reason is beyond all contradiction, O *Trismegistus,* but what shall we call the place in which the whole Universe is moved?

56. *Herm.* Call it incorporeal, O *Asclepius.*

57. *Asclep.* What is that, incorporeal or unbodily?

58. *Herm.* The Mind and Reason, the whole, wholly comprehending itself, free from all Body, undeceivable, invisible, impassible from a Body itself, standing fast in itself, capable of all things, and that Savour of the things that are.

59. Whereof the *Good,* the *Truth,* the *Archetypal Light,* the Archetype of the Soul, are, as it were, Beams.

60. *Asclep.* Why, then, what is God?

61. *Herm.* That which is none of these things, yet is, and is the cause of being to all, and every one of the things that are; for he left nothing destitute of Being.

62. And all things are made of things that are, and not of things that are not; for the things that are not, have not the nature to be able to be made; and again, the things that are, have not the nature never to be, or not to be at all.

63. *Asclep.* What dost thou then say at length that God is?

64. *Herm.* God is not a Mind, but the Cause that the Mind is; not a spirit, but the Cause that the Spirit is; not Light, but the Cause that Light is.

65. Therefore, we must worship God by these two Appellations, which are proper to him alone, and to no other.

67. And this he is and nothing else; but all other things are separable from the nature of Good.

68. For the Body and the Soul have no place that is capable of or can contain the Good.

69. For the greatness of Good is as great as the Existence of all things that are, both bodily and unbodily, both sensible and intelligible.

70. This is the Good, even God.

71. See, therefore, that thou do not at any time call ought else Good, for so thou shalt be impious; or any else God, but only the Good, for so thou shalt again be impious.

72. In Word it is often said by all men the Good, but all men do not understand what it is; but through Ignorance they call both the Gods, and some men, Good, that can never be, or be made so.

73. Therefore all the other Gods are honoured with the title or appellation of God, but God is the Good, not according to Heaven, but Nature.

74. For there is one Nature of God, even the Good, and one kind of them both, from whence all are kinds.

75. For he that is Good, is the giver of all things, and takes nothing; and, therefore, God gives all things, and receives nothing.

76. The other title and appellation, is the Father, because of his making all things; for it is the part of a Father to make.

77. Therefore, it hath been the greatest and most Religious care in this life, to them that are Wise, and well-minded, to beget children.

78. As likewise it is the greatest misfortune and impiety, for any to be separated from men, without children; and this man is punished after Death by the *Demons*, and the punishment is this: To have the Soul of this childless man, adjudged and condemned, to a Body that neither hath the nature of a man, nor of a woman, which is an accursed thing under the Sun.

79. Therefore, O *Asclepius*, never congratulate any man that is childless; but on the contrary pity his

misfortune, knowing what punishment abides, and is prepared for him.

80. Let so many, and such manner of things, O *Asclepius,* be said as a certain precognition of all things in Nature.

The End of the Ninth Book,
A UNIVERSAL SERMON TO ASCLEPIUS."

"THE TENTH BOOK, THE MIND TO HERMES

FORBEAR thy Speech, *O Hermes Trismegistus,* and call to mind to those things that are said; but I will not delay to speak what comes into my mind, sithence many men have spoken many things, and those very different, concerning the Universe, and Good; but I have not learned the Truth.

2. Therefore, the Lord make it plain to me in this point; for I will believe thee only, for the manifestation of these things.

3. Then said the Mind how the case stands.

4. God and All.

5. God, Eternity, the World, Time, Generation.

6. God made Eternity, Eternity the World, the world Time, and Time Generation.

7. Of God, as it were, the Substance, is the *Good,* the *Fair, Blessedness, Wisdom.*

8. Of Eternity, Identity, or Selfness.

9. Of the World, Order.

10. Of Time, Change.

11. Of Generation, Life and Death.

12. But the Operation of God, is Mind and Soul.

13. Of Eternity, Permanence, or Long-lasting, and Immortality.

14. Of the World, Restitution, and Decay, or Destruction.

15. Of Time, Augmentation and Diminution.

16. And of Generation qualities.

17. Therefore, Eternity is in God.

18. The World in Eternity.

19. Time in the World.

20. And Generation in Time.

21. And Eternity standeth about God.

22. The World is moved in Eternity.

23. Time is determined in the World.

24. Generation is done in Time.

25. Therefore, the Spring and Fountain of all things is God.

26. The Substance Eternity.

27. The Matter is the World.

28. The Power of God is Eternity.

29. And the Work of Eternity, is the World not yet made, and yet ever made by Eternity.

30. Therefore, shall nothing be at any time destroyed, for Eternity is incorruptible.

31. Neither can anything perish, or be destroyed in the World, the World being contained and embraced by Eternity.

32. But what is the Wisdom of God? Even the *Good* and the *Fair*, and *Blessedness*, and every Virtue, and Eternity.

33. Eternity, therefore, put into the Matter Immortality and Everlastingness; for the Generation of that depends upon Eternity, even as Eternity doth of God.

34. For Generation and Time, in Heaven and in Earth, are of a double Nature; in Heaven they are unchangeable and incorruptible; but on Earth they are changeable and corruptible.

35. And the Soul of Eternity is God; and the Soul of the World, Eternity; and of the Earth, Heaven.

36. God is in the Mind, the Mind in the Soul, the Soul in the Matter, all things by Eternity.

37. All this Universal Body, in which are all Bodies, is full of Soul, the Soul full of Mind, the Mind full of God.

38. For within he fills them, and without he contains them, quickening the Universe.

39. Without, he quickens this perfect living thing the World, and within all living Creatures.

40. And above in Heaven he abides in Identity or Selfness, but below upon Earth he changeth Generation.

41. Eternity comprehendeth the World either by necessity, or Providence, or Nature.

42. And if any man shall think any other thing, it is God that actuateth, or operateth this All.

43. But the operation or Act of God, is Power insuperable, to which none may compare anything, either Humane or Divine.

44. Therefore, O *Hermes,* think none of these things below, or the things above, in anywise like unto God; for if thou dost, thou errest from the Truth.

45. For nothing can be like the unlike, and only, and One; nor mayest thou think that he hath given of his Power to any other thing.

46. For who after him can make anything, either of Life or Immortality: of Change or of Quality? and himself, what other things should he make?

47. For God is not idle, for then all things would be idle; for all things are full of God.

48. But there is not anywhere in the World, such a thing as Idleness; for Idleness is a name that implieth a thing void or empty, both of a Doer, and a thing done.

49. But all things must necessarily be made or done both always, and according to the nature of every place.

50. For he that maketh or doth, is in all things, yet not fastened or comprehended in anything; nor making or doing one thing, but all things.

51. For being an active or operating Power, and sufficient of himself for the things that are made, and the things that are made are under him.

52. Look upon, through me, the World is subject to thy sight, and understand exactly the Beauty thereof.

53. A Body perpetual, than the which there is nothing more ancient, yet always vigorous and young.

54. See also the Seven Worlds set over us, adorned with an everlasting order, and filling Eternity with a different course.

55. For all things are full of Light, but the Fire is nowhere.

56. For the friendship and commixture of contraries and unlike, become Light shining from the Act or Operation of God, the Father of all Good, the Prince of all Order, and the Ruler of the Seven Worlds.

57. Look also upon the Moon, the forerunner of them all, the Instrument of Nature, and which changeth the matter here below.

58. Behold the Earth the middle of the Whole, the firm and stable Foundation of the Fair World, the Feeder and Nurse of Earthly things.

59. Consider, moreover, how great the multitude is of immortal living things, and of mortal ones also; and see the Moon going about in the midst of both, to wit, of things immortal and mortal.

60. But all things are full of Soul, and all things are properly moved by it; some things about the Heaven, and some things about the Earth; and neither of those on the right hand to the left; nor those on the left hand to the right; nor those things that are above, downward; nor those things that are below, upwards.

61. And that all these things are made, O beloved *Hermes,* thou needst not learn of me.

62. For they are Bodies, and have a Soul, and are moved.

63. And that all these should come together into one, it is impossible without something to gather them together.

64. Therefore, there must be some such ones, and he altogether One.

65. For seeing that the motions are divers, and many, and the Bodies not alike, and yet one ordered swiftness among them all; It is impossible there should be two or more Makers.

66. For one order is not kept by many.

67. But in the weaker there would be jealousy of the stronger, and thence also contentions.

68. And if there were one Maker, of mutable mortal living Wights, he would desire also to make immortal ones, as he that were the Maker of immortal ones, would do to make mortal.

69. Moreover, also, if there were two, the Matter of being one, who should be chief, or have the disposing of the future?

70. Or if both of them, which of them the greater part?

71. But thinks thus that every living Body hath its consistence of Matter and soul; and of that which is immortal, and that which is mortal and unreasonable.

72. For all living Bodies have a Soul; and those things that are not living, are only matter by itself.

73. And the Soul likewise of itself drawing near her Maker, is the cause of Life and Being, and Being the cause of Life is, after a manner, the cause of immortal things.

74. How then are mortal Wights other from immortal?

75. Or how cannot he make living Wights, that causeth immortal things and immortality?

76. That there is some Body that doth these things it is apparent, and that he is also one, it is most manifest.

77. For there is one Soul, one Life, and one matter.

78. Who is this? who can it be, other than the *One God*?

79. For whom else can it benefit to make living things, save only God alone?

80. There is therefore One God.

81. For it is a ridiculous thing to confess the World to be one, one Sun, one Moon, one Divinity, and yet to have, I know not how many gods.

82. He therefore being One, doth all things in many things.

83. And what great thing is it for God, to make Life, and Soul, and Immortality, and Change, when thyself dost so many things?

84. For thou both seest, speaketh, and hearest, smellest, tastest, and touchest, walkest, understandest, and breathest.

85. And it is not one that sees, and another that heareth, and another that speaketh, and another that toucheth, and another that smelleth, and another that walketh, and another that understandeth, and another that breatheth; but one that doth all these things.

86. Yet neither can these things possibly be without God.

87. For as thou, if thou shouldest cease from doing these things, were not a living wight, so if God should cease from those, he were not (which is not lawful to say) any longer God.

88. For if it be already demonstrated that nothing can be idle or empty, how much more may be affirmed of God?

89. For if there be anything which he doth not do, then is he (if it were lawful to say so) imperfect.

90. Whereas, seeing he is not idle, but perfect, certainly he doth all things.

91. Now give thyself unto me, O *Hermes*, for a little while, thou shalt the more easily understand, that it is the necessary work of God, that all things should be made or done that are done, or were once done, or shall be done.

92. And this, O best beloved, is Life.

93. And this is the *Fair*.

94. And this is the *Good*.

95. And this is *God*.

96. And if thou will understand this by work also, mark what happens to thyself when thou will generate.

97. And yet this is not like unto him, for he is not sensible of pleasure, for neither hath he any other Fellow Workman.

98. But being himself the only Workman, he is always in the work, himself being that which he doth or maketh.

99. For all things, if they were separate from him, must needs fall and die, as there being no life in them.

100. And again, if all things be living wights, both which are in heaven, and upon earth, and that there be one Life in all things which are made by God, and that is God, then certainly all things are made or done by God.

101. Life is the union of the Mind and the Soul.

102. But death is not the destruction of those things that were gathered together, but a dissolving of the Union.

103. The Image therefore of God, is Eternity; of Eternity, the World; of the World, the Sun: of the Sun, Man.

104. But the people say, That changing is Death, because the body is dissolved, and the Life goeth into that which appeareth not.

105. By this discourse, my dearest *Hermes*, I affirm as thou hearest. That the World is changed, because every day part thereof becomes invisible, but that it is never dissolved.

106. And these are the Passions of the World, Revolutions and Occultations, and Revolution is a turning, but Occultation is Renovation.

107. And the World being all formed, hath not the forms lying without it, but itself changeth in itself.

108. Seeing then the World is all formed, what must he be that made it! for without form, he cannot be.

109. And if he be all formed, he will be kept like the World, but if he have but one form, he shall be in this regardless of the world.

110. What do we then say that he is? We will not raise any doubts by our speech, for nothing that is doubtful concerning God is yet known.

111. He hath therefore one *Idea*, which is proper to him, which, because it is unbodily, is not subject to the sight, and yet shows all forms by the Bodies.

112. And do not wonder if there be an incorruptible *Idea*.

113. For they are like the Margents of the Speech, which is in writing; for they seem to be high and swelling, but they are by nature smooth and even.

114. But understand well this that I say, more boldly, for it is more true: As man cannot live without life, so neither can God live not doing good.

115. For this is, as it were, the Life and Motion of God, to Move all things, and Quicken them.

116. But some of the things I have said, must have a particular explanation; Understand then what I say.

117. All things are in God, not as lying in a place, for Place is both a body and immoveable, and those things that are placed, have no motion.

118. For they lie otherwise in that which is unbodily, than in the fantasie, or to appearance.

119. Consider him that contains all things, and understand that nothing is more capacious, than that

which is incorporeal, nothing more swift, nothing more powerful, but it is most capacious, most swift, and most strong.

120. And judge of this by thyself, command thy Soul to go into *India*, and sooner than thou canst bid it, it will be there.

121. Bid it likewise pass over the *Ocean*, and suddenly it will be there; not as passing from place to place, but suddenly it will be there.

122. Command it to fly into Heaven, and it will not need no wings, neither shall anything hinder it, not the fire of the Sun, not the *Aether*, not the turning of the Spheres, not the bodies of any other Stars, but cutting through all, it will fly up to the last and furthest body.

123. And if thou wilt even break the whole, and see those things that are without the world (if there be anything without), thou mayest.

124. Behold, how great power, how great swiftness thou hast! Canst thou do all thee things, and cannot God?

125. After this manner, therefore, contemplate God to have all the whole world to himself, as it were, all thoughts, or intellections.

126. If therefore thou wilt not equal thyself to God, thou canst not understand God.

127. For the like is intelligible by the like.

128. Increase thyself unto an immeasureable greatness, leaping beyond every Body, and transcending all Time, become Eternity, and thou shalt understand God: If thou believe in thyself, that nothing is impossible, but accountest thyself immortal, and that thou canst understand all things, every Art, every Science, and the manner and custom of every living thing.

129. Become higher than all height, lower than all depths, comprehend in thyself the qualitites of all the Creatures, of the Fire, the Water, the Dry, and Moist, and conceive likewise, that thou canst at once be everywhere, in the Sea, in the Earth.

130. Thou shalt at once understand thyself, not yet begotten in the Womb, young, old, to be dead, the things after death, and all these together, as also times, places, deeds, qualities, quantities, or else thou canst not yet understand God.

131. But if thou shut up thy Soul in the Body, and abuse it, and say, I understand nothing, I can do nothing, I am afraid of the Sea, I cannot climb up to Heaven, I know not who I am, I cannot tell what I shall be: What hast thou to do with god? for thou canst understand none of those Fair and Good things, and be a lover of the body and Evil.

132. For it is the greatest Evil, not to know God.

133. But to be able to know, and to will, and to hope, is the straight way, and Divine way, proper to the Good, and it will everywhere meet thee, and everywhere be seen of thee, plain and easy, when thou dost not expect or look for it; it will meet thee waking, sleeping, sailing, travelling, by night, by day, when thou speakest, and when thou keepest silence.

134. For there is nothing which is not the Image of God.

135. And yet thou sayest, God is invisible; but be advised, for who is more manifest than He?

136. For therefore hath he made all things, that thou by all things mayest see Him.

137. This is the Good of God, this is the Virtue, to appear, and to be seen in all things.

138. There is nothing invisible, no, not of those things that are incorporeal.

139. The Mind is seen in understanding, and God is seen in doing or making.

140. Let these things thus far forth, be made manifest unto thee, O *Trismegistus*.

141. Understand in like manner, all other things by thyself, and thou shalt not be deceived.

The End of the Tenth Book,
THE MIND TO HERMES."

"THE ELEVENTH BOOK OF THE COMMON MIND, TO TAT

THE Mind, O *Tat*, is of the very Essence of God, if yet there be any Essence of God.

2. What kind of Essence that is, he alone knows himself exactly.

3. The Mind therefore is not cut off, or divided from the essentiality of God, but united as the light of the Sun.

4. And this Mind in men, is God, and therefore are some men Divine, and their Humanity is near Divinity.

5. For the good *Demon* called the Gods, immortal Men, and men mortal Gods.

6. But in the brute Beast, or unreasonable living Wights, the Mind is their Nature.

7. For where there is a Soul, there is the Mind, as where there is Life there is also a Soul.

8. In living Creatures, therefore, that are without Reason, the Soul is Life, void of the operations of the Mind.

9. For the Mind is the Benefactor of the Souls of men, and worketh to the proper Good.

10. And in unreasonable things it co-operateth with the nature of everyone of them, but in men it worketh against their Natures.

11. For the Soul being in the body, is straightway made Evil by Sorrow, and Grief, and Pleasure, or Delight.

12. For Grief and Pleasure, flow like juices from the compound Body, whereinto when the Soul entereth or descendeth, she is moistened and tinctured with them.

13. As many Souls, therefore, as the Mind governeth, or overruleth, to them it shows its own Light, resisting their prepossessions or presumptions.

14. As a good Physician grieveth the Body, prepossessed of a disease, by burning or lancing it for health's sake;

15. After the same manner also the Mind grieveth the Soul, by drawing it out of Pleasure, from whence every disease of the Soul proceedeth.

16. But the Great Disease of the Soul is *Atheism*, because that opinion followeth to all Evil, and no Good.

17. Therefore, the Mind resisting, it procureth Good to the Soul, as a Physician to the Body.

18. But as many Souls of Men, as do not admit or entertain the Mind for their Governor, do suffer the

same thing that the Soul of unreasonable living things.

19. For the Soul being a *Co-operator* with them, permits or leaves them to their concupiscences, whereunto they are carried by the torrent of their Appetite, and so tend to brutishness.

20. And as brute Bests, they are angry without reason, and they desire without reason, and never cease, nor are satisfied with evil.

21. For unreasonable Angers and Desires are the most exceeding Evils.

22. And therefore hath God set the Mind over there, as a Revenger and Reprover of them.

23. *Tat.* Here, O Father, that discourse of Fate of Destiny, which thou madest to me, is in danger of being overthrown; for if it be fatal for any man to commit *Adultery* or *Sacrilege*, or do any evil, he is punished also, though he, of necessity, do the work of the Fate or Destiny.

24. *Herm.* All things, O Son, are the work of Fate, and without it can no bodily thing, either Good or Evil, be done.

25. For it is decreed by Fate, that he that doth any evil, should also suffer for it.

26. And therefore he doth it, that he may suffer that which he suffereth because he did it.

27. But for the present, let alone that speech, concerning Evil and Fate, for at other times we have spoken of it.

28. Now, our discourse is about the Mind, and what it can do, and how it differs, and is in men such a one, but in brute Beasts changed.

29. And again in brute Beasts it is not beneficial, but in men by quenching both their Anger and Concupiscences.

30. And of man, thou must understand, some to be rational, or governed by reason, and some irrational.

31. But all men are subject to Fate, and to Generation, and Change, for these are the beginning and end of Fate or Destiny

32. And all men suffer those things that are decreed by Fate.

33. But rational men, over whom, as we said, the mind bears rule, do not suffer like unto other men; but being free from viciousness, and being not evil, they do suffer evil.

34. *Tat.* How sayest thou this again, Father?
An *Adulterer*, is he not evil? A *Murderer*, is he not evil? and so of others.

35. *Herm.* But the rational man, O Son, will not suffer for Adultery, but as the Adulterer not for Murder, but as the Murderer.

36. And it is impossible to escape the Quality of change as of Generation, but the Viciousness, he that hath the Mind, may escape.

37. And therefore, O Son, I have always heard the good *Demon* say, and if he had delivered it in writing, he had much profited all mankind. For he alone, O So, as the first born, God seeing all things, truly spake Divine words. *I have heard him sometimes, That all things are one thing, especially intelligible Bodies, or that all especially intelligible Bodies are one.*

38. We live in Power, in Act, and in Eternity.

39. Therefore, a good mind is that which the soul of him is.

40. And if this be so, then no intelligible thing differs from intelligible things.

41. As, therefore, it is possible that the Mind, the Prince of all things; so likewise, that the soul that is of God, can do whatsoever it will.

42. But understand thou well, for this Discourse I have made to the Question which thou askest of me before, I man concerning Fate and the Mind.

43. First, if, O Son, thou shalt diligently withdraw thyself from all contentious speeches, thou shalt find that in Truth, the Mind, the Soul of God bears rule over all things, both over Fate, and Law, and all other things.

44. And nothing is impossible to him, no, not of the things that are of Fate.

45. Therefore, though the Soul of Man be above it, let it not neglect the things that happen to be under Fate.

46. And these, thus far, were the excellent sayings of the good *Demon*.

47. *Tat.* Most divinely spoken, O Father, and truly and profitably, yet clear this one thing unto me.

48. Thou sayest, that in brute Beasts the Mind worketh or acteth after the manner of Nature, co-operating also with their)... impetus) inclinations.

49. Now, the impetuous inclinations of brute Beasts, as I conceive, are Passions. If, therefore, the Mind do co-operate with these impetuous Inclinations, and that they are the Passions in brute Beasts, certainly the Mind is also a Passion, conforming itself to Passions.

50. *Herm.* Well done, Son, thou askest nobly, and yet it is just that I should answer thee.

51. All incorporeal things, O Son, that are in the Body, are passible, nay, they are properly Passions.

52. Everything that moveth is incorporeal; everything that is moved is a Body; and it is moved into the Bodies by the Mind. Now, Motion is passion, and there they both suffer; as well that which moveth, as that which is moved, as well that which ruleth, as that which is ruled.

53. But being freed from the Body, it is freed likewise from Passion.

54. But especially, O Son, there is nothing impassible, but all things are passible.

55. But Passion differs from that which is passible; for that (Passion) acteth, but this suffers.

56. Bodies also of themselves do act; for either they are unmoveable, or else are moved; and which soever it be, it is a Passion.

57. But incorporeal things do always act, or work, and therefore they are passible.

58. Let not, therefore, the appellations or names trouble thee, for Action and Passion are the same thing, but that it is not grievous to use the more honorable name.

59. *Tat.* O Father, thou hast delivered this discourse most plainly.

60. *Herm.* Consider this also, O Son, that God hath freely bestowed upon man, above all other living things, these two, to wit, Mind and Speech, or Reason ..., equal to immortality.

61. These, if any man use, or employ upon what he ought, he shall differ nothing from the Immortals.

62. Yea, rather going out of the Body, he shall be guided and led by them, both into the Choir and Society of the God, and blessed ones.

63. *Tat.* Do not other living creatures use speech, O Father?

64. *Herm.* No, Son, but only voice. Now, speech and voice do differ exceeding much; for speech is common to all men, but voice is proper unto every kind of living thing.

65. *Tat.* Yea, but the Speech of men is different, O Father; every man according to his Nation.

66. *Herm.* It is true, O Son, they do differ: yet as Man is one, so is Speech one also, and it is interpreted and found the same, both in *Egypt*, *Persia*, and *Greece*.

67. But thou seemest unto me, Son, to be ignorant of the Vertue, or Power and greatness of Speech.

68. For the blessed God, the good *Demon* said or commanded the Soul to be in the Body, the Mind in the Soul ..., the Word, or Speech, or Reason in the Mind, and the Mind in God, and that God is the Father of them all.

69. Therefore, the Word is the Image of the Mind, and the Mind of God, and the Body of the *Idea*, and the *Idea* of the Soul.

70. Therefore, of the Matter, the subtilest or smallest part is Air, of the Air the Soul, of the Soul the Mind, of the Mind God.

71. And God is about all things, and through all things, but the Mind about the Soul, the Soul about the Air, and the Air about the Matter.

72. But Necessity, and Providence, and Nature, are the Organs or Instruments of the World, and of the Order of Matter.

73. For of those things that are intelligible, everyone is; but the essence of them is Identity.

74. But of the Bodies of the whole, or universe, every one is many things.

75. For the Bodies that are put together, and that have, and make their changes into other, having this Identity, do always and preserve the incorruption of the Identity.

76. But in every one of the compound Bodies there is a Number

77. For without Number it is impossible there should be consistence or constitution, or composition, or dissolution.

78. But Unities do both beget and increase Numbers, and again being dissolved, come into themselves.

79. And the Matter is One.

80. But this whole World, the great God, and the Image of the Greater, and united unto him, and concerning the Order, and Will of the Father, is the fulness of Life.

81. And there is nothing therein, through all the Eternity of the Revolution, neither of the whole, nor of the parts which doth not live.

82. For there is nothing dead, that either hath been, or is, or shall be in the World.

83. For the Father would have it, as long as it lasts, to be a living thing; and therefore it must needs be God also.

84. How, therefore, O Son, can there be in God in the image of the Universe, in the fulness of Life, any dead things?

85. For dying is Corruption, and corruption is destruction.

86. How, then, can any part of the incorruptible be corrupted, or of God be destroyed?

87. *Tat.* Therefore, O Father, do not the living things in the World die, though they be parts thereof?

88. *Herm.* Be wary in thy speech, O Son, and not deceived in the names of things.

89. For they do not die, O Son, but as Compound bodies they are dissolved.

90. But dissolution is not death; and they are dissolved, not that they may be destroyed, but that they may be made new.

91. *Tat.* What, then, is the operation of Life? Is it not Motion?

92. *Herm.* And what is there in the World unmoveable? Nothing at all, O Son.

93. *Tat.* Why, doth not the Earth seem immoveable to thee, O Father?

94. *Herm.* No, but subject to many Motions, though after a manner, it alone be stable.

95. What a ridiculous thing it were that the nurse of all things should be immoveable which beareth and bringeth forth all things.

96. For it is impossible that anything that bringeth forth, should bring forth without Motion.

97. And a ridiculous question it is, whether the fourth part of the whole, be idle; for the word immoveable, or without motion, signifies nothing else, but idleness.

98. Know generally, O Son, that whatsoever is in the World is moved either according to Augmentation or Diminution.

99. But that which is moved, liveth also, yet it is not necessary that a living thing should be or continue the same.

100. For while the whole world is together, it is unchangeable, O Son, but all the parts thereof are changeable.

101. Yet nothing is corrupted or destroyed, and quite abolished, but the names trouble men.

102. For Generation is not Life, but Sense, neither is Change Death, but Forgetfulness, or rather Occultation, and lying hid. Or better thus:--

103. *For Generation is not a Creation of Life, but a production of things to Sense, and making them manifest. Neither is Change Death, but an Occultation of hiding of that which was.*

104. These things being so, all things are Immortal, Matter, Life, Spirit, Soul, Mind, whereof every living thing consisteth.

105. Every living thing therefore is Immortal, because of the Mind, but especially Man, who both receiveth God, and converseth with him.

106. For with this living wight, alone is God familiar; in the night by dreams, in the day by Symbols or Signs.

107. And by all things doth he foretell him of things to come, by Birds, by Fowls, by the Spirit, or Wind, and by an Oak.

108. Wherefore, also, Man professeth to know things that have been, things that are present, and things to come.

109. Consider this also, O Son, that every other living Creature goeth upon one part of the World, Swimming things in the Water, Land wights upon the Earth, Flying Fowls in the Air.

110. But Man useth all these, the Earth, the Water, the Air, and the Fire, nay, he seeth and toucheth Heaven by his senses.

111. But God is both about all things, and through all things, for he is both Act and Power.

112. And it is no hard thing, O Son, to understand God.

113. And if thou wilt also see him, look upon the Necessity of things that appear, and the Providence of things that have been, and are done.

114. See the Matter being most full of Life, and so great a God moved, with all good, and Fair, both Gods, and*Demons*, and Men.

115. *Tat.* But these, O Father, are wholly Acts, or Operations.

116. *Herm.* If they be, therefore, wholly acts or operations, O Son, by whom are they acted or operated, but by God?

117. Or art thou ignorant, that as parts of the World, are Heaven, and Earth, and Water, and Air; after the same manner, the Members of God, are Life, and Immortality, and Eternity, and Spirit, and Necessity, and Providence, and Nature, and Soul, and Mind, and the Continuance or Perseverance of all these which is called Good.

118. And there is not anything of all that hath been, and all that is, where God is not.

119. *Tat.* What, in Matter, O Father?

120. *Herm.* The Matter, Son, what is it without God, that thou shouldst ascribe a proper place to it?

121. Or what dost thou think it to be? Peradventure, some heap that is not actuated or operated.

122. But if it be actuated, by whom is it actuated? for we have said, that Acts or Operations, are the parts of God.

123. By whom are all living things quickened? and the Immortal, by whom are they immortalized? the things that are changeable, by whom are they changed?

124. Whether thou speak of Matter or Body, or Essence, know that all these are Acts of God.

125. And that the Act of Matter is materiality, and of the Bodies corporality, and of essence essentiality, and this is God the whole.

126. And in the whole, there is nothing that is not God.

127. Wherefore, about God, there is neither Greatness, Place, Quality, Figure, or time, foe he is All, and the All, through all, and about all.

128. This Word, O Son, worship and adore. And the only service of God, is not to be evil.

The End of the Eleventh Book
OF THE COMMON MIND, TO TAT."

"THE TWELFTH BOOK, HIS CRATER OR MONAS

THE Workman made this Universal World, not with his Hands, but his Word.

2. Therefore thus think of him, as present everywhere, and being always, and making all things; and one above, that by his Will hath framed the things that are.

3. For that is his Body, not tangible, nor visible, nor measurable, nor extensible, nor like any other body.

4. For it is neither Fire, nor Water, nor Air, nor Wind, but all these things are of him; for being Good, he hath dedicated that name unto himself alone.

5. But he would also adorn the Earth, but with the Ornament of a Divine Body.

6. And he sent Man, an Immortal, and a mortal wight.

7. And Man had more than all living Creatures, and the World; because of his Speech, and Mind.

8. For Man became the Spectator of the Works of God, and wondered, and acknowledged the Maker.

9. For he divided Speech among all Men, but not Mind, and yet he envied not any; for Envy comes not thither, but is abode here below in the Souls of men, that have not the Mind.

10. *Tat.* But wherefore, Father, did not God distribute the Mind to all men?

11. *Herm.* Because it pleased him, O Son, to set that in the middle among all souls, as a reward to strive for.

12. *Tat.* And where hath he set it?

13. *Herm.* Filling a large Cup or Bowl therewith, he sent it down, giving also a Cryer or Proclaimer.

14. And he commanded him to proclaim these things to the souls of men.

15. Dip and wash thyself, thou that art able in this Cup or Bowl: Thou that believeth that thou shalt return to him that sent this Cup; thou that acknowledgest whereunto thou wert made.

16. As many, therefore, as understood the Proclamation, and were baptized, or dowsed into the

Mind, these were made partakers of knowledge, and became perfect men, receiving the Mind.

17. But as many as missed of the Proclamation, they received Speech, but not Mind; being ignorant whereunto they were made, or by whom.

18. But their Senses are just like to brute Beasts, and having their temper in Anger and Wrath, they do not admire the things worthy of looking on.

19. But wholly addicted to the pleasures and desires of the Body, they believe that man was made for them.

20. But as many as partake of the gift of God; these, O *Tat*, in comparison of their works, are rather immortal, than mortal men.

21. Comprehending all things in their Mind, which are upon Earth, which are in Heaven, and if there be anything above Heaven.

22. And lifting up themselves so high, they see the Good, and seeing it, they account it a miserable calamity to make their abode here.

23. And despising all things bodily and unbodily, they make haste to the *One and Only*.

24. Thus, O *Tat*, is the knowledge of the Mind, the beholding of Divine things, and the Understanding of God, the Cup itself, being Divine.

25. *Tat.* And I, O Father, would be baptized and drenched therein.

26. Herm. Except thou first hate thy body, O Son, thou canst not love thyself, but loving thyself, thou shalt have the Mind, and having the Mind, thou shalt also partake the Knowledge or Science.

27. *Tat.* How meanest thou, O Father?

28. *Herm.* Because it is impossible, O Son, to be conversant about things Mortal and Divine.

29. For the things that are, being two Bodies, and things incorporeal, wherein is the Mortal and the Divine, the Election or Choice of either is left to him that will choose: For no man can choose both.

30. And of which soever the choice is made, the other being diminished or overcome, magnifieth the act or operation of the other.

31. The choice of the better, therefore, is not only best for him that chooseth it, by deifying man, but it also shewth Piety and Religion towards God.

32. But the choice of the worst destroys a man, but doth nothing against God, save that as *Pomps* or *Pageants*, when they come abroad, cannot do anything themselves but hinder; after the same manner also do these make*Pomps* and *Pageants* in the World, being seduced by the pleasures of the Body.

33. These Things being so, O *Tat*, that things have been, and are so plenteously ministered to us from God, let them proceed also from us, without any scarcity or sparing.

34. For God is innocent or guiltless, but we are the causes of Evil, preferring them before the Good.

35. Thou seest, O Son, how many Bodies we must go beyond, and how many Choirs of *Demons*, and what continuity and courses of Stars, that we may make haste to the One, and only God.

36. For the Good is not to be transcended, it is unbounded and infinite, unto itself, without beginning, but unto us, seeming to have a beginning, even our knowledge of it.

37. For our Knowledge is not the beginning of it, but shews us the beginning of its being known unto us.

38. Let us, therefore, lay hold of the beginning, and we shall quickly go through all things.

39. It is indeed a difficult thing to leave those things that are accustomable and present, and turn us to those things that are ancient, and according to the original.

40. For these things that appear, delight us, but make the things that appear not, hard to believe, *or the things that appear not, are hard to believe.*

41. The things most apparent are Evil, but the Good is secret, or hid in, or to the things that appear, for it hath neither Form nor Figure.

42. For this cause it is like to itself, but unlike everything else, for it is impossible that anything incorporeal should be made know, or appear to a Body.

43. For this is the difference between the like and the unlike, and the unlike wanteth always somewhat of the like.

44. For the Unity, Beginning, and Root of all things, as being the Root and Beginning.

45. Nothing is without a beginning, but the Beginning is of nothing, but of itself, for it is the Beginning of all other things.

46. Therefore it is, seeing it is not from another beginning.

47. Unity therefore being the Beginning, containeth very number, but itself is contained of none, and begetteth every number, itself being begotten of no other number.

48. Everything that is begotten (or made), is imperfect, and may be divided, increased, diminished.

49. But to the perfect, there happeneth none of these.

50. And that which is increased, is increased by Unity, but is consumed and vanished through weakness, being not able to receive the Unity.

51. This Image of God, have I described to thee, *O Tat,* as well as I could, which if thou do diligently consider, and view by the eyes of they Mind, and hear, believe me, Son, thou shalt find the way to things above, or, rather, the Image itself will lead thee.

52. But the spectacle or sight, hath this peculiar and proper: Them that can see, and behold it, it holds fast and draws unto it, as they say, the Loadstone doth Iron.

The End of the Twelfth Book,
HIS CRATER OR MONAS."

"THE THIRTEENTH BOOK, OF SENSE AND UNDERSTANDING

YESTERDAY, *Asclepius,* I delivered a perfect Discourse, but now I think it necessary, in suite of that, to dispute also of Sense.

2. For Sense and Understanding seem to differ, because the one is material and the other essential.

3. But unto me, they appear to be both one, or united, and not divided in men, I mean.

4. For in other living Creatures, Sense is united into Nature, but in men to Understanding.

5. But the Mind differs from Understanding, as much a God from Divinity.

6. For Divinity is... from under God, and Understanding from the Mind, being the Sister of the Word or Speech, and they the Instruments one of another.

7. For neither is the Word pronounced without Understanding, neither is Understanding manifested without the Word.

8. Therefore, Sense and Understanding do both flow together into a man, as if they were infolded one within another.

9. For neither is it possible without Sense to Understand, nor can we have Sense without Understanding.

10. And yet it is possible (*for the time being*), that the Understanding may understand without Sense, as they that fancy visions in their Dreams.

11. But it seems unto me, that both the operations are in the Visions of Dreams, and that the Sense is stirred up out of sleep, into awakening.

12. For Man is divided into a Body and a Soul, when both parts of the Sense accord one with another, then is the Understanding childed, or brought forth by the Mind pronounced.

13. For the Mind brings forth all Intellections or Understandings, Good ones when it receiveth good seed from God, and the contrary, when it receives them from Devils.

14. For there is not part of the World void of the Devil, which entering in privately, sowed the seed of his own*proper* operation, and the mind did make pregnant, or did bring forth that which was sown. *Adulteries, Murders, Striking of Parents, Sacrileges, Impieties, Stranglings,* throwing down headlong, and all other things, which are the works of Evil *Demons.*

15. And the seeds of God are few, but great and Fair, and Good, Virtue, and Temperance, and Piety.

16. And the Piety is the knowledge of God, whom whosoever knoweth, being full of all good things, hath Divine Understanding, and not like the many.

17. And therefore they that have that knowledge, neither please the multitude, nor the multitude them, but they seem to be mad, and to move laughter, hated and despised, and many times also murdered.

18. For we have already said, That wickedness must dwell here, being in her own region.

19. For her region is the Earth, and not the World, as some will sometimes say, Blaspheming.

20. But the Godly or God-worshipping Man, laying hold on knowledge, will despise or tread under all

these things, for though they be evil to other men, yet to him all things are good.

21. And upon mature consideration, he refers all things to knowledge, and that which is most to be wondered at, he alone makes Evil things good.

22. But I return again to my Discourse of Sense.

23. It is, therefore, a thing proper to man, to communicate and conjoin Sense and Understanding.

24. But every man, as I said before, doth not enjoy Understanding, for one man is material, another Essential.

25. And he that is material with wickedness, as I said, received from the Devils the seed of Understanding, but they that are with the Good essentially, are eared with God.

26. For God is the workman of all things, and when he worketh, he useth Nature.

27. He maketh all things good like himself.

28. But these things that are made good, are in the use of operation, unlawful.

29. For the Motion of the World, stirring up Generations, makes Qualities; infesting some with evilness, and purifying some with good.

30. And the World, *Asclepius*, hath a peculiar Sense and Understanding, not like to Man's, nor so various or manifold, but a better and more simple.

31. For the Sense and Understanding of the World is *One*, in that it makes all things, and unmakes them again into itself, for it is the Organ of Instrument of the Will of God.

32. And it is so organized or framed, and made for an Instrument by God, that receiving all Seeds into itself from God, and keeping them in itself, it maketh all things effectually, and dissolving them, reneweth all things.

33. And therefore like a good Husbandman of Life, when things are dissolved or loosened, he affords, by the casting of Seed, renovation to all things that grow.

34. There is nothing that it (the World) doth not beget or bring forth alive, and by its Motion, it makes all things alive.

35. And it is at once, both the Place and the Workman of Life.

36. But the Bodies are from the Matter, in a different manner, for some are of Earth, some of Water, some of Air, some of Fire, and all are compounded, but some are more compounded, and some are more simple.

37. They that are compounded, are the heavier, and they that are less, are the higher.

38. And the swiftness of the Motion of the World, makes the varieties of the qualities of Generation, for the Spiration of Influence being most frequent, extendeth unto the Bodies' qualities, with infulness, which is of Life.

39. Therefore, God is the Father of the World, but the World is Father of the things in the World.

40. And the World is the Son of God, but things in the World, are the Sons of the World.

41. And, therefore, it is well called ... the World, that is, an Ornament, because it adorneth and beautifieth all things with the Variety of Generation, and indeficiency of Life, which the unweariedness of Operation, and the swiftness of Necessity, with the mingling of Elements, and the order of things done.

42. Therefore, it is necessarily and proper called ... the World.

43. For all living things, both the sense and the Understanding, cometh into them from without, inspired by that which compasseth them about, and continueth them.

44. And the World receiving it once from God as soon as it was made, has it still, *whatever it once had.*

45. But God is not as it seems to some who Blaspheme through superstition, without Sense, and without Mind, or Understanding.

46. For all things that are, O *Asclepius,* are in God, and made by him, and depend of him, some working by bodies, some moving by a Soul, like Essence, some quickening by a Spirit, and some receiving the things that are weary, and all very fitly.

47. Or rather, I say, that he hath them not, but I declare the Truth, *he is all things,* not receiving them from without, but exhibiting them outwardly.

48. And this is the Sense and Understanding of God, to move all things always.

49. And there shall never be any time, when any of these things that are, shall fail, or be wanting.

50. When I say the things that are, I mean God, for the things that are, God hath, and neither is there anything without him, nor he without anything.

51. These things, O *Asclepius,* will appear to be true, if thou understand them, but if thou understand them not, incredible.

52. For to understand, is to believe, but not to believe, is not to understand; For my speech or words reach not unto the Truth, but the Mind is great, and being led or conducted for a while by Speech, is able to attain to the Truth.

53. And understanding all things round about, and finding them consonant, and agreeable to those things that were delivered, and interrupted by Speech, believeth, and in that good belief resteth.

54. To them, therefore, that understand the things that have been said of God, they are credible, but to them that understand them not, incredible.

55. And let these, and thus many things, be spoken concerning *Understanding* and *Sense*.

The End of the Thirteenth Book,
OF SENSE AND UNDERSTANDING."

"THE FOURTEENTH BOOK, OF OPERATION AND SENSE

Tat.
THOU has well explained these things, Father. Teach me furthermore these things, for thou sayest, that *Science* and *Art* were the operations of the Rational, but now thou sayest, that Beasts are unreasonable, and for want of Reason, both are, and are called Brutes, so that by this reason, it must needs follow, that unreasonable Creatures partake not of Science, or Art, because they come short of Reason.

2. *Herm.* It must needs be so, Son.

3. *Tat.* Why then, O Father, do we see some unreasonable living Creatures use both Science and Art; as the *Pismires* treasure up for themselves food against Winter, and Fowls of the Air likewise make them Nests, and four-footed Beasts know their own Dens?

4. These things they do, O Son, not by Science or Art, but by Nature; For Science and Art are things that are

taught, but none of these Brute Beasts are taught any of these things.

5. But these things being Natural unto them, are wrought by Nature, whereas, Art and Science do not happen unto all, but unto some.

6. As Men are Musitians, but not all; neither are all Archers, or Huntsmen, or the rest, but some of them have learned something by the working of Science, or Art.

7. After the same manner also, if some *Pismires* did so, and some not, thou mightest well say, they gather their Food according to Science and Art.

8. But being, they are all led by Nature, to the same thing, even against their Wills, it is manifest they do not do it by Science or Art.

9. For operations, O *Tat*, being unbodily are in Bodies, and work by bodies.

10. Wherefore, O *Tat*, in as much as they are unbodily, thou must needs say, they are immortal.

11. But inasmuch as they cannot act without Bodies, I say they are always in a Body.

12. For those things that are to anything, or for the cause of anything made subject to Providence or Necessity, cannot possibly remain idle of their own proper operation.

13. For that which is, shall ever be, for both the Body, and the Life of it, is the same.

14. And by this reason, it follows, that the Bodies also are always, because I affirm: That this corporeity is always by the Act and Operation, or for them.

15. For although Earthly Bodies be subject to dissolution, yet these bodies must be the Places, and the Organs, and Instruments of Acts or Operations.

16. But acts or Operations are immortal, and that which is Immortal is always in Act, and therefore also*Corporification* if it be always.

17. Acts or operations do follow the Soul, yet come not suddenly or promiscuously; but some of them come together with being made man, being about brutish or unreasonable things.

18. But the purer operations do insensibly in the change of time, work with the oblique part of the Soul.

19. And these operations depend upon Bodies, and truly they that are *Corporifying*, come from the Divine Bodies into Mortal ones.

20. But every one of them acteth both about the Body and the Soul, and are present with the Soul, even without the Body.

21. And they are always Acts or operations, but the Soul is not always in a Mortal Body, for it can be

without a Body, but Acts or Operations cannot be without Bodies.

22. This is a sacred Speech, Son; *the Body cannot consist without a Soul.*

23. *Tat.* How meanest thou that, Father?

24. *Herm.* Understand it thus, O *Tat*: When the Soul is separated from the Body, there remaineth that same body.

25. And this same Body, according to the time of its abode, is actuated, or operated in that it is dissolved and becomes invisible.

26. And these things the Body cannot suffer without act or operation, and consequently there remaineth with the Body, the same act or operation.

27. This then is the difference between an Immortal Body and a Mortal one, that the Immortal one consists of one Matter, and so doth not the Mortal one, and the immortal one doth, but this suffereth.

28. And every thing that acteth or operateth is stronger, and ruleth, but that which is actuated or operated, is ruled.

29. And that which ruleth, directeth, and governeth as free, but the other is rules, a servant.

30. Acts or Operations, do not only act or operate, living or breathing, or insouled ... Bodies, but also

Breathless Bodies, or without Souls, Wood and Stones, and such like, encreasing and bearing fruit, ripening, corrupting, rotting, putrifying and breaking, or working such like things, and whatsoever inanimate Bodies can suffer.

31. Act or Operation, O Son, is called, whatsoever is, or is made or done, and there are always many things made, or rather all things.

32. For the World is never widowed or forsaken of any of those things that are, but being always carried or moved in itself, it is in labour to bring forth the things that are, which shall never be left by it to corruption.

33. Let, therefore, every act or operation be understood to be always immortal, in what manner of Body soever it be.

34. But some Acts or Operations be of Divine, some of corruptible bodies, some universal, some peculiar, and some of the generals, and some of the parts of everything.

35. Divine Acts or Operations, therefore, there be, and such as work or operate upon their proper Bodies, and these also are perfect, and being upon or in perfect Bodies.

36. Particular are they which work by any of the living Creatures.

37. Proper be they that work upon any of the things that are.

38. By this Discourse, therefore, O Son, it is gathered that all things are full of Acts or Operations.

39. For if necessarily they be in every Body, and that there be many Bodies in the World, I may very well affirm, that there be many other Acts or Operations.

40. For many items in one Body, there if one, and a second, and a third, besides these universal ones that follow.

41. And universal operations, I call them that are indeed bodily, and are done by the Senses and Motions.

42. For without these, it is impossible that the Body should consist.

43. But other operations are proper to the Souls of Men, by Arts, Sciences, Studies, and Actions.

44. The Senses also follow these Operations, or rather are the effects or perfections … of them.

45. Understand, therefore, O Son, the difference of Operations, it is sent from above.

46. But Sense being in the Body, and having its essence from it, when it receiveth Act or Operation, manifesteth it, making it as it were corporeal.

47. Therefore, I say, that the Senses are both corporeal and mortal, having so much existence as the Body, for they are born with the Body, and die with it.

48. But mortal things themselves have not Sense, as *not* consisting of such an Essence.

49. For Sense can be of no other than a corporeal apprehension, either of Evil or Good, that comes to the Body.

50. But to External Bodies there is nothing comes, nothing departs, therefore there is no Sense in them.

51. *Tat.* Doth the Sense therefore perceive or apprehend in every Body?

52. *Herm.* In every Body, O Son.

53. *Tat.* And do the Acts or Operations work in all things?

54. *Herm.* Even in things inanimate, O Son, but there are differences of Senses.

55. For the Senses of things rational, are with Reason, of things unreasonable, Corporeal only; but the Senses of things inanimate, are passive only, according to Augmentation and Diminution.

56. But Passion and Sense depend both upon one head, or hight, and are gathered together into the same, by Acts or Operations.

57. But in living Wights, there be two other Operations that follow the Senses and Passions, to wit, *Grief* and *Pleasure*.

58. And without these, it is impossible that a living Wight, especially a reasonable one, should perceive or apprehend.

59. And, therefore, I say, that these are the *Ideas* of Passions that bear rule, especially in reasonable living wights.

60. The Operations work indeed, but the Senses do declare and manifest the operations, and they being bodily, are moved by the brutish parts of the Soul; therefore, I say, they are both malificial, or doers of evil.

61. For that which affords the Sense to rejoice with Pleasure, is strightway the cause of many evils, happening to him that suffers it.

62. But sorrow gives stronger torments and Anguish, therefore, doubtless, are they both malificial.

63. The same may be said of the Sense of the Soul.

64. *Tat.* Is not the soul incorporeal, and the sense a Body, Father? Or is it rather in the Body?

65. *Herm.* If we put it in a Body, O So, we shall make it like the Soul, or the Operations; for these being unbodily, we say are in Bodies.

66. But Sense is neither Operation, nor Soul, nor anything else that belongs to the Body, but as we have said, and, therefore, it is not incorporeal.

67. And if it be not incorporeal, it must needs be a Body, for we always say, that of things that are, some are Bodies, and some incorporeal.

The End of The Fourteenth Book,
OF OPERATION AND SENSE."

THE FIFTEENTH BOOK, OF TRUTH TO HIS SON TAT

Herm.

OF TRUTH, O *Tat*, it is not possible that man, being an imperfect Wight, compounded of Imperfect members, and having his Tabernacle, consisting of different, and many Bodies, should speak with any Confidence.

2. But as far as it is possible and just (I say). That Truth is only in Eternal Bodies, whose very Bodies are also True.

3. The Fire is fire itself only, and nothing else; the Earth is earth itself, and nothing else; the Air is air itself, and nothing else; the Water, water itself, and nothing else.

4. But our Bodies consist of all these, for they have of the Fire, they have of the Earth, they have of the

Water, and Air, and yet there is neither Fire, nor Earth, nor Water, nor Air, nor anything true.

5. And if at the beginning, our Constitution had not Truth, how could men either see the Truth, or speak it, or understand it, only except God would?

6. All things, therefore, upon Earth, O *Tat*, are not Truth, but imitations of the Truth, and yet not all things neither, for they are but few that are so.

7. But the other things are Falsehood and Deceit, O *Tat*, and opinions, like the Images of the fancy of appearance.

8. And when the fancy hath an influence from above, then it is an imitation of Truth, but without the operations from above, it is left a lie.

9. And as an Image shews the Body described, and yet it is not the Body of that which is seen, as it seems to be, and it is seen to have eyes, but it sees nothing, and ears, but it hears nothing at all, and all other things hath the picture, but they are false, deceiving the eyes of the beholder, whilst they think they see the Truth, and yet they are indeed but lies.

10. As many, therefore, as see not falsehood, see the Truth.

11. If, therefore, we do so understand, and see every one of those things as it is, then we see and understand true things.

12. But if we see or understand anything besides, or otherwise, than that which is, we shall neither understand, nor know the Truth.

13. *Tat.* Is Truth, therefore, upon Earth, O Father?

14. *Herm.* Thou dost not miss the mark, O Son; Truth indeed is nowhere at all upon Earth, O *Tat*, for it cannot be generated, or made.

15. But concerning the Truth, it may be that some men, to whom God will give the Good seeing power, may understand it.

16. So that unto the Mind and Reason, there is nothing true indeed upon earth.

17. But unto the true Mind and Reason, all things are fancies, or appearances, and opinions.

18. *Tat.* Must we not, therefore, call it Truth, to understand and speak the things that are?

19. *Herm.* But there is nothing true upon Earth.

20. *Tat.* How then is this true: that we do not know anything true? How can that be done here?

21. *Herm.* O Son, Truth is the most perfect Virtue, and the highest Good itself, not troubled by Matter, not encompassed by a Body, naked, clear, unchangeable, venerable, unalterable Good.

22. But the things that are here, O Son, are visible, incapable of Good, corruptible, passible, dissolvable, changeable, continually altered, and made of another.

23. The things therefore that are not true to themselves, how can they be true?

24. For everything that is altered, is a lie, not abiding in what it is, but being changed it shews us always, other and other appearances.

25. *Tat.* Is not man true, O Father?

26. *Herm.* As far forth as he is a man, he is not true, Son, for that which is true, hath of itself alone its constitution, and remains and abides according to itself, such as it is.

27. But man consists of many things, and doth not abide of himself, but is turned and changed, age after age, *Idea* after *Idea*, or form after form, and this while he is yet in the Tabernacle.

28. And many have not known their own children after a little while, and many children likewise have not known their own Parents.

29. Is it then possible, O *Tat*, that he who is so changed, as is not to be known, should be true? No, on the contrary, he is Falsehood, being in many Appearance of changes.

30. But do thou understand the True to be that which abides the Same, and is Eternal, but man is not ever,

therefore not True, but man is a certain appearance, and Appearance is the highest Lie or Falsehood.

31. *Tat.* But these eternal bodies, Father, are they not true, though they be changed?

32. *Herm.* Everything that is begotten, or made, and changed, is not true; but being made by our Progenitor, they might have had true matter.

33. But these also have in themselves, something that is false, in regard to their change.

34. For nothing that remains not in itself, is true.

35. *Tat.* What shall one say then, Father, that only the sun, which besides the Nature of other things, is not changed, but abides in itself, is Truth?

36. *Herm.* It is Truth, and therefore is he only intrusted with the Workmanship of the World, ruling and making all things, whom I do both honour, and adore his Truth; and after the *One*, and First, I acknowledge him the Workman.

37. *Tat.* What, therefore, dost thou affirm to be the first Truth, O Father?

38. *Herm.* The *One* and *Only*, O *Tat*, that is not of Matter, that is not in a Body, that is without colour, without Figure, or Shape, Immutable, Unalterable, which always is, but Falsehood, O Son, is corrupted.

39. And corruption hath laid hold upon all things on Earth, and the Providence of the *True* encompasseth, and will encompass them.

40. For without corruption there can no generation consist.

41. For corruption followeth every generation, that it may again be generated.

42. For those things that are generated, must of necessity be generated of those things that are corrupted, and the things generated must needs be corrupted, that the Generation of things being, may not stand still or cease.

43. Acknowledge, therefore, the first Workman, by the Generation of things.

44. Consequently the things that are generated of Corruption are false, as being sometimes one thing, sometimes another: For it is impossible, they should be made the same things again, and that which is not the same, how is it true?

45. Therefore, O Son, we must call these things fancies or appearances.

46. And if we will give a man his right name, we must call him the appearance of Manhood; and a child, the fancy or appearance of a child; an old man, the fancy or appearance of an old man; a young man, the appearance of a young man; and a man of ripe age, the appearance of a man of ripe age.

47. For neither is a man, a man, nor a child, a child, nor a young man, young man, nor an old man, an old man.

48. But the things that pre-exist, and that are, being changed, are false.

49. These things, understand thus, O Son, as these false operations, having their dependence from above, even of the Truth itself.

50. Which being so, I do affirm, that Falsehood is the Work of the Truth.

The End of the Fifteenth Book,
OF TRUTH TO HIS SON TAT."

"THE SIXTEENTH BOOK, THAT NONE OF THE THINGS THAT ARE CAN PERISH

Herm.

WE must now speak of the Soul and body, O Son, after what manner the soul is Immortal, and what operation that is, which constitutes the Body, and dissolves it.

2. But in none of these is Death, for it is a conception of a name, which is either an empty word, or else it is wrongly called Death ..., by taking away the first letter, instead of Immortal ....

3. For Death is destruction, but there is nothing in the whole World that is destroyed.

4. For if the World be a second God, and an Immortal living Wight, it is impossible that any part of an Immortal living Wight should die.

5. But all things that are in the World, are members of the World, especially man, the reasonable living Wight.

6. For the first of all is God, the Eternal, the Unmade, and the Workman of all things.

7. The second is the World, made by him, after his own Image, and by him holden together, and nourished, and immortalized, and as from its own Father, ever living.

8. So that as Immortal, it is ever living, and ever immortal.

9. For that which is ever living, differs from that which is eternal.

10. For the Eternal was not begotten, or made by another, and if it were begotten or made, yet it was made by itself, not by any other, but it is always made.

11. For the Eternal, as it is Eternal, is the Universe.

12. For the Father himself, is Eternal of himself, but the World was made by the Father, ever living, and immortal.

13. And as much Matter as there was laid up by him, the Father made it all into a Body, and swelling it, made it round like a Sphere, endued it with Quality, being itself immortal, and having Eternal Materiality.

14. The Father being full of *Ideas*, sowed qualities in the Spheres, and shut them up as in a Circle, deliberating to beautify with every Quality, that which afterwards should be made.

15. Then clothing the Universal Body with Immortality, lest the Matter, if it would depart from this Composition, should be dissolved into its own disorder.

16. For when the Matter was Incorporated, O Son, it was disordered, and it hath here the same confusion daily revolved about other little things, endued with Qualities, in point of Augmentation, and Diminution, which men call Death, being indeed a disorder happening about earthly living Wights.

17. For the Bodies of Heavenly things, have one order, which they have received from the Father at the beginning, and is by the instauration of each of them, kept indissolveable.

18. But the instauration of earthly Bodies is their consistence, and their dissolution restores them into indissolveable, that is, Immortal.

19. And so there is made a privation of Sense, but not a destruction of Bodies.

20. Now the third living Wight is Man, made after the Image of the World, and having by the will of the Father, an mind above other earthly Wights.

21. And he hath not only a sympathy with the second God, but also an understanding of the first.

22. For the Second God, he apprehends as a Body, but the first, he understands as Incorporeal, and the Mind of the Good.

23. *Tat.* And doth not this living Wight perish?

24. *Herm.* Speak advisedly, O Son, and learn what God is, what the World, what an Immortal Wight, and what a dissolveable one is.

25. And understand that the World is of God, and in God, but Man of the World, and in the World.

26. The Beginning, and End, and Consistence of all, is God.

The End of the Sixteenth Book,
THAT NONE OF THE THINGS THAT ARE CAN
PERISH."

"THE SEVENTEENTH BOOK, TO ASCLEPIUS, TO BE TRULY WISE

BECAUSE, my Son, *Tat*, in thy absence, would needs learn the Nature of the things that are, he would not suffer me to give over (as coming very young to the knowledge of every individual), till I was forced to discourse to him many things at large, that his contemplation might, from point to point, be more easy and successful.

2. But to thee, I have thought good to write in few words, choosing out the principal heads of the things then spoken, and to interpret them more mystically, because thou hast both more years, and more knowledge of Nature.

3. All things that appear, were made, and are made.

4. Those things that are made, are not made by themselves, but by another.

5. And there are many things made, but especially all things that appear, and which are different, and not like.

6. If the things that be made and done, be made and done by another, there must be one that must make, and do them, and he, unmade, and more ancient than the things that are made.

7. For I affirm the things that are made, to be made by another, and it is impossible, that of the things that are made, any should be more ancient than all, but only that which is not made.

8. He is stronger, and one, and only knowing all things indeed, as not having anything more ancient than himself.

9. For he bears rule, both over multitude and greatness, and the diversity of the things that are made, and the continuity of the Facture, and of the Operation.

10. Moreover, the things that are made, are visible, but he is invisible, and for this cause, he maketh them, that he may be visible, and therefore he makes them always.

11. Thus, it is fit to understand, and understanding to admire, and admiring to think thyself happy, that knowest thy natural Father.

12. For what is sweeter than a natural Father?

13. Who, therefore, is this, or how shall we know him?

14. Or is it just to ascribe unto him alone, the Title and Appellation of God, or of the Maker or of the Father, or all Three? That of God because of his Power; the Maker, because of his Working and Operation; and the Father because of his Goodness.

15. For Power is different from the things that are made, but Act or Operation in that all things are made.

16. Wherefore, letting go all much and vain talking, we must understand these two things: *That which is made*, and *him which is the Maker*; for there is nothing in the Middle, between these Two, nor is there any third.

17. Therefore, understanding All things, remember these Two; and think that these are All things, putting nothing into doubt; neither of the things above, nor of the things below; neither of things changeable, nor things that are in darkness or secret.

18. For All things, are but Two things, *That which maketh*, and *that which is made*; and the One of them cannot depart, or be divided from the other.

19. For neither is it possible that the Maker should be without the thing made, for either of them is the self-same thing; therefore cannot the one of them be separated from the other, no more than a thing can be separated from itself.

20. For if he that makes be nothing else but that which makes alone, *simple, uncompounded*, it is of necessity, that he makes the same thing to himself, to whom it is the Generation of him that maketh to be also All that is made.

21. For that which is Generated or made, must necessarily be generated or made by another, but without the maker, that which is made, neither is made, nor is; for the one of them without the other, has lost his proper Nature by the privation of the other.

22. So if these Two be confessed, That which maketh, and that which is made, then they are One in Union, this going before, and that following.

23. And that which goeth before, is, God the Maker; and that which follows, is, that which is made, be it what it will.

24. And let no man be afraid because of the variety of things that are made or done, lest he should case an aspersion of baseness, or infamy upon God; for it is the only Glory of him to do, or make all things.

25. And this making, or Facture, is as it were the Body of God; and to him that maketh, or doth, there is nothing evil or filthy to be imputed, or *there is nothing thought evil, or filthy.*

26. For these are Passions that follow Generation, as Rust doth Copper, or as Excrements do the Body.

27. But neither did the Coppersmith make the Rust, nor the Maker of the Filth, nor God the Evilness.

28. But the vicissitude of Generation doth make them, as it were, to blossom out; and for this cause did make change to be, as one should say, The Purgation of Generation.

29. Moreover, is it lawful for the same Painter to make both Heaven, and the Gods, and the Earth, and the Sea, and Men, and brute Beasts, and inanimate things, and Trees; and is it impossible for God to make these things? O the great madness, and ignorance of men in things that concern God!

30. For men that think so, suffer that which is most ridiculous of all; for professing to bless, and praise

God, yet in not ascribing to him the making or doing of All things, they know him now.

31. And besides their not knowing him, they are extremely impious against him, attributing unto him Passions, as*Pride*, or *Oversight*, or Weakness, or Ignorance, or Envy.

32. For if he do not make, or do all things, he is either proud, or not able, or ignorant, or envious, which is impious to affirm.

33. For god hath only one Passion, namely, Good; and he that is good, is neither proud, nor impotent, nor the rest, but God is Good itself.

34. For *Good* is all *Power*, to do or make all things, and everything that is made, is made by God, that is, by the Good, and that can make or do all things.

35. See, then, how he maketh all things, and how the things are done, that are done, and if thou wilt learn, thou mayest see an Image thereof, very beautiful and like.

36. Look upon the Husbandman, how he casteth seeds into the Earth, here wheat, there barley, and elsewhere some other seeds.

37. Look upon the same Man, planting a vine, or an apple tree, or a fig tree, or some other tree.

38. So doth God in Heaven sow Immortality in the Earth, Change in the whole Life and Motion.

39. And these things are not many, but few, and easily numbered; for they are all but four, God and Generation, in which are all things."

The End of the Seventeenth Book,
TO ASCLEPIUS, TO BE TRULY WISE.
(End of the Divine Pymander--1650)"

The Divine Pymander of Hermes, Hermes Trismegistus, Translated by John Everard, 1650

CHAPTER THREE
The Emerald Tablet of Hermes

The Emerald Tablet of Thoth/Hermes

THE EMERALD TABLET

Truly, without deceit, certain, and most veritable.

That which is Below corresponds to that which is Above,
and that which is Above corresponds to that which is Below
to accomplish the miracles of the One Thing.
And just as all things come from this One Thing
through the meditation of One Mind,
so do all created things originate from this One Thing
through Transformation.

Its father is the Sun;
its mother the Moon.
The Wind carries it in its belly.
Its nurse is the Earth.
It is the origin of all,
the consecration of the Universe.
Its inherent Strength is perfected,
if it is turned into Earth.

Separate the Earth from Heaven,
the Subtle from the Gross,
gently and with great ingenuity.
It rises from Earth to Heaven
and descends again to Earth,
thereby combining within its
the powers of both the Above and the Below.

Thus will you obtain the Glory of the Whole Universe.
All Obscurity will be clear to you.
This is the greatest Force of all powers,
because it overcomes every Subtle thing
and penetrates every Solid thing.

In this way was the Universe created.
From this will come many wondrous Applications,
because this is the Pattern.

Therefore am I called Thrice Greatest Hermes,
having all three parts of the wisdom of the Whole Universe.
Herein have I completely explained the Operation of the Sun.

The Emerald Tablet of Thoth/Hermes Translation

(Marilynn's Explanation) The Emerald Tablet has been known by many names, among them the Smaragdine Table, Tabula Smaragdina, or The Secret of Hermes. It is an ancient text which was inscribed upon a stone which is not of this earth and cannot be destroyed. The text purports to reveal the secret of the primordial substance and its *transmutations*. Hermes Trismegistus ("Hermes the Thrice-Greatest"), who shares his identity with the Egyptian deity Thoth, is believed to be its author. The whereabouts of this ancient relic are at this time unknown . . .

"History of the Tablet

"History of the Tablet (largely summarised from Needham 1980, & Holmyard 1957)

"The Tablet probably first appeared in the West in editions of the psuedo-Aristotlean Secretum Secretorum which was actually a translation of the Kitab Sirr al-Asar, a book of advice to kings which was translated into latin by Johannes Hispalensis c. 1140 and by Philip of Tripoli c.1243. Other translations of the Tablet may have been made during the same period by Plato of Tivoli and Hugh of Santalla, perhaps from different sources. The date of the Kitab Sirr al-Asar is uncertain, though c.800 has been suggested and it is not clear when the tablet became part of this work.

Holmyard was the first to find another early arabic version (Ruska found a 12th centruy recension claiming to have been dictated by Sergius of Nablus) in the Kitab Ustuqus al-Uss al-Thani (Second Book of the Elements of Foundation) attributed to Jabir.

Shortly after Ruska found another version appended to the Kitab Sirr al-Khaliqa wa San`at al-Tabi`a (Book of the Secret of Creation and the Art of Nature), which is also known as the Kitab Balaniyus al-Hakim fi'l-`Ilal (book of Balinas the wise on the Causes). It has been proposed that this book was written may have been written as early as 650, and was definitely finished by the Caliphate of al-Ma'mun (813-33). Scholars have seen similarities between this book and the Syriac Book of Treasures written by Job of Odessa (9th century) and more interestingly the Greek writings of the bishop Nemesius of Emesa in Syria from the mid fourth century. However though this suggests a possible Syriac source, non of these writings contain the tablet.

Balinas is usually identified with Apollonius of Tyna, but there is little evidence to connect him with the Kitab Balabiyus, and even if there was, the story implies that Balinas found the tablet rather than wrote it, and the recent discoveries of the dead sea scrolls and the nag hamamdi texts suggest that hiding texts in caves is not impossible, even if we did not have the pyramids before us.

Ruska has suggested an origin further east, and Needham has proposed an origin in China. Holmyard, Davis and Anon all consider that this Tablet may be one of the earliest of all alchemical works we have that survives.

It should be remarked that apparantly the Greeks and Egyptians used the termtranslated as `emerald' for emeralds, green granites, "and perhaps green jasper". In medieval times the emerald table of the Gothic kings of Spain, and the Sacro catino- a dish said to have belonged to the Queen of Sheba, to have been used at the last supper, and to be made of emerald, were made of green glass [Steele and Singer: 488]."

"Translations

"From Jabir ibn Hayyan.

0) Balinas mentions the engraving on the table in the hand of Hermes, which says:
1) Truth! Certainty! That in which there is no doubt!
2) That which is above is from that which is below, and that which is below is from that which is above, working the miracles of one.
3) As all things were from one.
4) Its father is the Sun and its mother the Moon.
5) The Earth carried it in her belly, and the Wind nourished it in her belly,
7) as Earth which shall become Fire.
7a) Feed the Earth from that which is subtle, with the greatest power.
8) It ascends from the earth to the heaven and becomes ruler over that which is above and that which is below.
14) And I have already explained the meaning of the whole of this in two of these books of mine.
[Holmyard 1923: 562.]

Another Arabic Version (from the German of Ruska, translated by 'Anonymous').

0) Here is that which the priest Sagijus of Nabulus has dictated concerning the entrance of Balinas into the hidden chamber... After my entrance into the chamber, where the talisman was set up, I came up to an old man sitting on a golden throne, who was holding an emerald table in one hand. And behold the following - in Syriac, the primordial language- was written thereon:

1) Here (is) a true explanation, concerning which there can be no doubt.

2) It attests: The above from the below, and the below from the above -the work of the miracle of the One.

3) And things have been from this primal substance through a single act. How wonderful is this work! It is the main (principle) of the world and is its maintainer.

4) Its father is the sun and its mother the moon; the

5) wind has borne it in its body, and the earth has nourished it.

6) the father of talismen and the protector of miracles

6a) whose powers are perfect, and whose lights are confirmed (?),

7) a fire that becomes earth.

7a) Separate the earth from the fire, so you will attain the subtle as more inherent than the gross, with care and sagacity.

8) It rises from earth to heaven, so as to draw the lights of the heights to itself, and descends to the earth; thus within it are the forces of the above and the below;

9) because the light of lights within it, thus does the darkness flee before it.

10) The force of forces, which overcomes every subtle thing and penetrates into everything gross.

11) The structure of the microcosm is in accordance with the structure of the macrocosm.

12) And accordingly proceed the knowledgeable.

13) And to this aspired Hermes, who was threefold graced with wisdom.

14) And this is his last book, which he concealed in the chamber.

[Anon 1985: 24-5]

Twelfth Century Latin

0) When I entered into the cave, I received the tablet zaradi, which was inscribed, from between the hands of Hermes, in which I discovered these words:

1) True, without falsehood, certain, most certain.

2) What is above is like what is below, and what is below is like that which is above. To make the miracle of the one thing.

3) And as all things were made from contemplation of one, so all things were born from one adaptation.

4) Its father is the Sun, its mother is the Moon.

5) The wind carried it in its womb, the earth breast fed it.

6) It is the father of all 'works of wonder' (Telesmi) in the world.

6a) Its power is complete (integra).

7) If cast to (turned towards- versa fuerit) earth,

7a) it will separate earth from fire, the subtile from the gross.

8) With great capacity it ascends from earth to heaven. Again it descends to earth, and takes back the power of the above and the below.

9) Thus you will receive the glory of the distinctiveness of the world. All obscurity will flee from you.

10) This is the whole most strong strength of all strength, for it overcomes all subtle things, and penetrates all solid things.

11a) Thus was the world created.

12) From this comes marvelous adaptions of which this is the proceedure.

13) Therefore I am called Hermes, because I have three parts of the wisdom of the whole world.

14) And complete is what I had to say about the work of the Sun, from the book of Galieni Alfachimi.

[From Latin in Steele and Singer 1928: 492.]

Translation from Aurelium Occultae Philosophorum..Georgio Beato

1) This is true and remote from all cover of falsehood

2) Whatever is below is similar to that which is above. Through this the marvels of the work of one thing are procured and perfected.

3) Also, as all things are made from one, by the condsideration of one, so all things were made from this one, by conjunction.

4) The father of it is the sun, the mother the moon.

5) The wind bore it in the womb. Its nurse is the earth, the mother of all perfection.

6a)Its power is perfected.

7) If it is turned into earth,

7a) separate the earth from the fire, the subtle and thin from the crude and course, prudently, with modesty and wisdom.

8) This ascends from the earth into the sky and again descends from the sky to the earth, and receives the power and efficacy of things above and of things below.

9) By this means you will acquire the glory of the whole world, and so you will drive away all shadows and blindness.

10) For this by its fortitude snatches the palm from all other fortitude and power. For it is able to penetrate and subdue everything subtle and everything crude and hard.

11a) By this means the world was founded

12) and hence the marvelous cojunctions of it and admirable effects, since this is the way by which these marvels may be brought about.

13) And because of this they have called me Hermes Tristmegistus since I have the three parts of the wisdom and Philsosphy of the whole universe.

14) My speech is finished which i have spoken concerning the solar work

[Davis 1926: 874.]

Translation of Issac Newton c. 1680.

1) Tis true without lying, certain & most true.

2) That wch is below is like that wch is above & that wch is above is like yt wch is below to do ye miracles of one only thing.

3) And as all things have been & arose from one by ye mediation of one: so all things have their birth from this one thing by adaptation.
4) The Sun is its father, the moon its mother,
5) the wind hath carried it in its belly, the earth its nourse.
6) The father of all perfection in ye whole world is here.
7) Its force or power is entire if it be converted into earth.
7a) Seperate thou ye earth from ye fire, ye subtile from the gross sweetly wth great indoustry.
8) It ascends from ye earth to ye heaven & again it desends to ye earth and receives ye force of things superior & inferior.
9) By this means you shall have ye glory of ye whole world & thereby all obscurity shall fly from you.
10) Its force is above all force. ffor it vanquishes every subtile thing & penetrates every solid thing.
11a) So was ye world created.
12) From this are & do come admirable adaptaions whereof ye means (Or process) is here in this.
13) Hence I am called Hermes Trismegist, having the three parts of ye philosophy of ye whole world.
14) That wch I have said of ye operation of ye Sun is accomplished & ended.
[Dobbs 1988: 183-4.]

Translation from Kriegsmann (?) alledgedly from the Phoenician

1) I speak truly, not falsely, certainly and most truly

2) These things below with those above and those with these join forces again so that they produce a single thing the most wonderful of all.

3)And as the whole universe was brought forth from one by the word of one GOD, so also all things are regenerated perpetually from this one according to the disposition of Nature.

4) It has the Sun for father and the Moon for mother:

5) it is carried by the air as if in a womb, it is nursed by the earth.

6) It is the cause, this, of all perfection of all things throughout the universe.

6a) This will attain the highest perfection of powers

7) if it shall be reduced into earth

7a) Distribute here the earth and there the fire, thin out the density of this the suavest (suavissima) thing of all.

8)Ascend with the greatest sagacity of genius from the earth into the sky, and thence descend again to the earth, and recognise that the forces of things above and of things below are one,

9) so as to posses the glory of the whole world- and beyond this man of abject fate may have nothing further.

10)This thing itself presently comes forth stronger by reasons of this fortitude: it subdues all bodies surely, whether tenuous or solid, by penetrating them.

11a) And so everything whatsoever that the world contains was created.

12) Hence admirable works are accomplished which are instituted (carried out- instituuntur) according to the same mode.

13) To me therefor the name of Hermes Trismegistus has been awarded because I am discovered as the Teacher of the three parts of the wisdom of the world.
14) These then are the considerations which I have concluded ought to be written down concerning the readiest operations of the Chymic art.
[Davis 1926: 875 slightly modified.]

From Sigismund Bacstrom (allegedly translated from Chaldean).

0) The Secret Works of CHIRAM ONE in essence, but three in aspect.
1) It is true, no lie, certain and to be depended upon,
2) the superior agrees with the inferior, and the inferior agrees with the superior, to effect that one truly wonderful work.
3) As all things owe their existence to the will of the only one, so all things owe their origin to the one only thing, the most hidden by the arrangement of the only God.
4) The father of that one only thing is the sun its mother is the moon,
5) the wind carries it in its belly; but its nourse is a spirituous earth.
6) That one only thing is the father of all things in the Universe.
6a) Its power is perfect,
7) after it has been united with a spirituous earth.
7a) Separate that spirituous earth from the dense or crude by means of a gentle heat, with much attention.
8) In great measure it ascends from the earth up to heaven, and descends again, newborn, on the earth,

and the superior and the inferior are increased in power.

9) By this wilt thou partake of the honours of the whole world. And Darkness will fly from thee.

10) This is the strength of all powers. With this thou wilt be able to overcome all things and transmute all what is fine and what is coarse.

11a) In this manner the world was created;

12) the arrangements to follow this road are hidden.

13) For this reason I am called Chiram Telat Mechasot, one in essence, but three in aspect. In this trinity is hidden the wisdom of the whole world.

14) It is ended now, what I have said concerning the effects of the sun. Finish of the Tabula Smaragdina. [See Hall 1977: CLVIII,]

From Madame Blavatsky

2) What is below is like that which is above, and what is above is similar to that which is below to accomplish the wonders of the one thing.

3) As all things were produced by the mediation of one being, so all things were produced from this one by adaption.

4) Its father is the sun, its mother the moon.

6a) It is the cause of all perfection throughout the whole earth.

7) Its power is perfect if it is changed into earth.

7a) Separate the earth from the fire, the subtile from the gross, acting prudently and with judgement.

8) Ascend with the greatest sagacity from earth to heaven, and unite together the power of things inferior and superior;

9) thus you will possess the light of the whole world, and all obscurity will fly away from you.

10) This thing has more fortitude than fortitude itself, because it will overcome every subtile thing and penetrate every solid thing.

11a) By it the world was formed.

[Blavatsky 1972: 507.]

From Fulcanelli (translated from the French by Sieveking)

1) This is the truth, the whole truth and nothing but the truth:-

2) As below, so above; and as above so below. With this knowledge alone you may work miracles.

3) And since all things exist in and eminate from the ONE Who is the ultimate Cause, so all things are born after their kind from this ONE.

4) The Sun is the father, the Moon the mother;

5) the wind carried it in his belly. Earth is its nurse and its guardian.

6) It is the Father of all things,

6a) the eternal Will is contained in it.

7) Here, on earth, its strength, its power remain one and undivded.

7a) Earth must be separated from fire, the subtle from the dense, gently with unremitting care.

8) It arises from the earth and descends from heaven; it gathers to itself the strength of things above and things below.

9) By means of this one thing all the glory of the world shall be yours and all obscurity flee from you.

10) It is power, strong with the strength of all power,

for it will penetrate all mysteries and dispel all ignorance.

11a) By it the world was created.

12) From it are born manifold wonders, the means to achieving which are here given

13) It is for this reason that I am called Hermes Trismegistus; for I possess the three essentials of the philosophy of the universe.

14) This is is the sum total of the work of the Sun.

[Sadoul 1972: 25-6.]

From Fulcanelli, new translation

1) It is true without untruth, certain and most true:

2) that which is below is like that which is on high, and that which is on high is like that which is below; by these things are made the miracles of one thing.

3) And as all things are, and come from One, by the mediation of One, So all things are born from this unique thing by adaption.

4) The Sun is the father and the Moon the mother.

5) The wind carries it in its stomach. The earth is its nourisher and its receptacle.

6 The Father of all the Theleme of the universal world is here.

6a) Its force, or power, remains entire,

7) if it is converted into earth.

7a) You separate the earth from the fire, the subtle from the gross, gently with great industry.

8) It climbs from the earth and descends from the sky, and receives the force of things superior and things inferior.

9) You will have by this way, the glory of the world

and all obscurity will flee from you.

10) It is the power strong with all power, for it will defeat every subtle thing and penetrate every solid thing

11a) In this way the world was created.

12) From it are born wonderful adaptations, of which the way here is given.

13) That is why I have been called Hermes Tristmegistus, having the three parts of the universal philosophy.

14) This, that I have called the solar Work, is complete.

[Translated from Fulcanelli 1964: 312.]

From Idries Shah

1) The truth, certainty, truest, without untruth.

2)What is above is like what is below. What is below is like what is above. The miracle of unity is to be attained.

3) Everything is formed from the contemplation of unity, and all things come about from unity, by means of adaptation.

4) Its parents are the Sun and Moon.

5) It was borne by the wind and nurtured by the Earth.

6) Every wonder is from it

6a) and its power is complete.

7) Throw it upon earth,

7a) and earth will separate from fire. The impalbable separated from the palpable.

8) Through wisdom it rises slowly from the world to heaven. Then it descends to the world combining the

power of the upper and the lower.

9)Thus you will have the illumination of all the world, and darkness will disappear.

10) This is the power of all strength- it overcomes that which is delicate and penetrates through solids.

11a) This was the means of the creation of the world.

12) And in the future wonderful developements will be made, and this is the way.

13) I am Hermes the Threefold Sage, so named because I hold the three elements of all wisdom.

14) And thus ends the revelation of the work of the Sun.

(Shah 1964: 198).

Hypothetical Chinese Original

1) True, true, with no room for doubt, certain, worthy of all trust.

2) See, the highest comes from the lowest, and the lowest from the highest; indeed a marvelous work of the tao.

3) See how all things originated from It by a single process.

4) The father of it (the elixir) is the sun (Yang), its mother the moon (Yin).

5) The wind bore it in its belly, and the earth nourished it.

6)This is the father of wondrous works (changes and transformations), the guardian of mysteries,

6a) perfect in its powers, the animator of lights.

7) This fire will be poured upon the earth...

7a) So separate the earth from the fire, the subtle from the gross, acting prudently and with art.

8) It ascends from the earth to the heavens (and orders the lights above), then descends again to the earth; and in it is the power of the highest and the lowest.

9) Thus when you have the light of lights darkness will flee away from you.

10) With this power of powers (the elixir) you shall be able to get the mastery of every subtle thing, and be able to penetrate everything that is gross.

11a) In this way was the great world itself formed.

12) Hence thus and thus marvellous operations will be acheived.

[Slightly altered from Needham 1980: 371.]"

The Emerald Tablet of Hermes

"Glory of the World

"The Emerald Table

"It is true, without any error, and it is the sum of truth; that which is above is also that which is below, for the performance of the wonders of a certain one thing, and as all things arise from one Stone, so also they were generated from one common Substance, which includes the four elements created by God. And among other miracles the said Stone is born of the First Matter. The Sun is its Father, the Moon its Mother, the wind bears it in its womb, and it is nursed by the earth. Itself is the Father of the whole earth, and the whole potency thereof. If it be transmuted into earth, then the earth separates from the fire that which is most subtle from that which is hard, operating gently and with great artifice. Then the Stone ascends from earth to heaven, and again descends from heaven to earth, and receives the choicest influences of both heaven and earth. If you can perform this you have the glory of the world, and are able to put to flight all diseases, and to transmute all metals. It overcomes Mercury, which is subtle, and penetrates all hard and solid bodies. Hence it is compared with the world. Hence I am called Hermes, having the three parts of the whole world of philosophy.

Explanation of the Emerald Table of Hermes.

"Hermes is right in saying that our Art is true, and has been rightly handed down by the Sages; all doubts concerning it have arisen through false interpretation of the mystic language of the philosophers. But, since they are loth to confess their own ignorance, their readers prefer to say that the words of the Sages are imposture and falsehood. The fault really lies with the ignorant reader, who does not understand the style of the Philosophers. If, in the interpretation of our books, they would suffer themselves to be guided by the teaching of Nature, rather than by their own foolish notions, they would not miss the mark so hopelessly. By the words which follow: "That which is above is also that which is below," he describes the Matter of our Art, which, though *one*, is divided into two things, the volatile water which rises upward, and the earth which lies at the bottom, and becomes fixed. But when the reunion takes place, the body becomes spirit, and the spirit becomes body, the earth is changed into water and becomes volatile, the water is transmuted into body, and becomes fixed. When bodies become spirits, and spirits bodies, your work is finished, for then that which rises upward and that which descends downward become one body. Therefore the Sage says that that which is above is that which is below, meaning that, after having been separated into two substances (from being one substance), they are again joined together into one substance, i.e., an union which can never be dissolved, and possesses such virtue and efficacy that it can do in one moment what the Sun cannot accomplish in a thousand years. And this miracle is wrought by a thing which is despised and rejected by the multitude. Again, the Sage tells us that all things were created, and are still generated, from one first substance and consist of the same elementary material; and in this first substance God has appointed the four elements, which represent a common material into which it might perhaps be possible to resolve all things. Its development is brought about by the distillation of the Sun and Moon. For it is operated upon by the natural heat of the Sun Moon, which stirs up its internal action, and multiplies each thing after its kind, imparting to the substance a specific form. The soul, or nutritive principle, is the earth which receives the rays of the Sun and Moon, and therewith feeds her children as with mother's milk. Thus the Sun is the father, the Moon is the mother, the earth the nurse -- and in this substance is that which we require. He who can take it and prepare it is truly to be envied. It is separated by the Sun and Moon in the form of a vapour, and collected in the place where it is found. When Hermes adds that "the air bears it in its womb, the earth is its nurse, the whole world its Father," he means that when the substance of our Stone is dissolved, then the wind bears it in its womb, i.e., the air bears up the substance in the form of water, in which is hid fire, the soul of the Stone, and fire is the Father of the whole world. Thus, the volatile substance rises upward, while that which remains at the bottom, is the "whole world" (seeing that our Art is compared to a "small world "). Hence Hermes calls fire the father of the whole world, because it is the Sun of our Art, and air, Moon, and water ascend from it; the earth is the nurse of the Stone, i.e., when the earth receives the rays of the Sun and Moon, a new body is born, like a new foetus in the mother's womb. The earth receives and digests the light of Sun and Moon, and imparts food to its foetus day by day, till it becomes great and strong, and puts off its blackness and defilement, and is changed to a different colour. This, "child,"which is called "our daughter," represents our Stone, which is born anew of the Sun and Moon, as you may easily see, when the spirit, or the water that ascended, is gradually transmuted into the body, and the body is born anew, and grows and increases in size like the foetus in the mother's womb. Thus the Stone is generated from the first substance, which contains the four elements; it is brought forth by two things, the body and the spirit; the wind bears it in its womb, for it carries the Stone upward from earth to heaven, and down again from heaven to earth. Thus the Stone receives increase from above and from below, and is born a second time, just as every other foetus is generated in the maternal womb; as all created things bring forth their young, even so does the air, or wind, bring forth our Stone. When Hermes adds, "Its power, or virtue, is entire, when it is transmuted into earth," he means that when the spirit is transmuted into the body, it receives its full strength and virtue. For as yet the spirit is volatile, and not fixed, or permanent. If it is to be fixed, we must proceed as the baker does in baking bread. We must impart only a little of the spirit to the body at a time, just as the baker only puts a little leaven to his meal, and with it leavens the whole lump. The spirit, which is our leaven, in like fashion transmutes the whole body into its own substance. Therefore the body must be leavened again and again, until the whole lump is thoroughly pervaded with the power of the leaven. In our Art the body leavens the spirit, and transmutes it into one body, and the spirit leavens the body, and transmutes it into one spirit And the two, when they have become one, receive power to leaven all things, into which they are injected, with their own virtue.

The Sage continues: "If you gently separate the earth from the water, the subtle from the hard, the Stone ascends from earth to heaven, and again descends from heaven to earth, and receives its virtue from above and from below. By this process you obtain the glory and brightness of the whole world. With it you can put to flight poverty, disease, and weariness; for it overcomes the subtle mercury, and penetrates all hard and firm bodies." He means that all who would accomplish this task must separate the moist from the dry, the water from the earth. The water, or fire, being subtle, ascends, while the body is hard, and remains where it is. The separation must be accomplished by gentle heat, i.e., in the temperate bath of the Sages, which acts slowly, and is neither too hot nor too cold. Then the Stone ascends to heaven, and again descends from heaven to earth. The spirit and body are first separated, then again joined together by gentle coction, of a temperature resembling that with which a hen hatches her eggs. Such is the preparation of the substance, which is worth the whole world, whence it is also called a "little world." The possession of the Stone will yield you the greatest delight, and unspeakably precious comfort. It will also set forth to you in a typical form the creation of the world. It will enable you to cast out all disease from the human body, to drive away poverty, and to have a good understanding of the secrets of Nature. The Stone has virtue to transmute mercury into gold and silver, and to penetrate all hard and firm bodies, such as precious stones and metals. You cannot ask a better gift of God than this gift, which is greater than all other gifts. Hence Hermes may justly call himself by the proud title of "Hermes Trismegistus, who holds the three parts of the whole world of wisdom."

Basil Valentine, His Triumphant Chariot of Antimony, with Annotations of Theodore Kirkringus (1678)

From the Secret Works of Chiram One

""*The Genuine Translation (of the Emerald Tablet of Hermes) from the Original Very Ancient Chaldee (Of the Emerald Tablet) is as Follows:*

"THE SECRET WORKS OF *CHIRAM ONE* IN ESSENCE, BUT THREE IN ASPECT.

"(The two first large words mean *the Secret Work.*)

"(The second line in large letters, reads: Chiram Telat Machasot, i.e. *Chiram the Universal Agent, One in Essence but three in aspect.*)

'IT IS TRUE, NO LIE, CERTAIN, AND TO BE DEPENDED UPON, THE SUPERIOR AGREES WITH THE INFERIOR, AND THE INFERIOR WITH THE SUPERIOR, TO EFFECT THAT ONE TRULY WONDERFUL WORK. AS ALL THINGS OWE THEIR EXISTENCE TO THE WILL OF THE *ONLY ONE*, SO ALL THINGS OWE THEIR ORIGIN TO THE *ONE ONLY THING*, THE MOST HIDDEN, BY THE ARRANGEMENT OF *THE ONLY GOD*. THE FATHER OF THAT *ONE ONLY THING* IS *THE SUN*, ITS MOTHER IS *THE MOON*, THE WIND CARRIES IT IN ITS BELLY; BUT ITS COURSE IS *A SPIRITUOUS EARTH*. THAT *ONE ONLY THING* (after God) IS THE FATHER OF ALL THINGS IN THE UNIVERSE. ITS POWER IS PERFECT, AFTER IT HAS BEEN UNITED TO A SPIRITUOUS EARTH.

"(Process--First Distillation.) SEPARATE THAT SPIRITUOUS EARTH FROM THE DENSE OR

CRUDE BY MEANS OF A GENTLE HEAT, WITH MUCH ATTENTION.

"(Last Digestion.) IN GREAT MEASURE IT ASCENDS *FROM THE EARTH* UP TO HEAVEN, AND DESCENDS AGAIN, NEWBORN, ON THE EARTH, AND THE SUPERIOR AND THE INFERIOR ARE INCREASED IN POWER. The Azoth (Mercury or 'One Mind') ascends from the Earth, from the bottom of the Glass, and redescends in Veins and drops into the Earth and by this continual circulation the Azoth is more and more subtilized, *Volatilizes Sol* and carries the volatilized Solar atoms along with it and thereby becomes a *Solar Azoth,* i.e. *our third, and genuine Sophic Mercury* **(Wisdom of the One Mind)**, and this circulation of the Solar Azoth must continue until it ceases of itself, and the Earth has sucked it all in, when it muse become the black pitchy matter, the *Toad* [the substances in the alchemical retort and also the lower elements in the body of man], which denotes complete putrefaction or *Death of the Compound.*

"BY THIS THOU WILT PARTAKE OF THE HONOURS OF THE WHOLE WORLD. Without doubt as the black, pitchy matter will and must of necessity become *White* and *Red,* and the Red having been carried to perfection, *medicinally* and for Metals, is then fully capable to preserve *mentem sanam in corpore sano* **(a healthy mind in a healthy body)** until the natural period of Life and promise us ample means, in infinitum multipliable, to be benevolent and charitable without any diminution of our inexhaustible resources, therefore well may it be called *the Glory* [Honours] *of the Whole World,* as truly the study and contemplation of the L. P. [*Lapis Philosophorum*], harmonising with Divine Truths, elevates the mind to God our Creator and merciful Father, and if He should permit us to possess it practically must eradicate the very principle of Avarice, Envy, and Evil Inclinations, and cause our hearts to melt in gratitude toward Him that has been so kind to us! Therefore the Philosophers say with great Truth, that the L. P. either finds a good man or makes one.

"AND DARKNESS WILL FLY FROM THEE. By invigorating the Organs the Soul makes use of for communicating with exterior objects, the Soul must acquire greater powers not only for conception but also for retention, and therefore if we wish to obtain still more knowledge, the organs and secret springs of physical life being wonderfully strengthened and invigorated, the Soul must acquire new powers for conceiving and retaining, especially if we pray to God for knowledge, and confirm our prayers by faith, all Obscurity must vanish of course. That this has not been the case with all possessors, was their own fault, as they contented themselves merely with the **Transmutation** of Metals.

"(Use.) THIS IS THE STRENGTH OF ALL POWERS. This is a very strong figure, to indicate that the L. P. positively does possess all the Powers concealed in Nature, not for destruction but for exaltation and regeneration of matter, in the three Departments of Nature.

"WITH THIS THOU WILT BE ABLE TO OVERCOME ALL THINGS, AND TO *TRANSMUTE* ALL *WHAT IS*

FINE (☉ ☽) AND WHAT IS *COARSE* (♃♄ ♀ ♂ ☿ 〰)

). It will conquer every subtil Thing, of course, as it refixes the most subtil Oxygen into its own *fiery Nature* and that with more power, penetration and virtue, in a tenfold ratio, at every multiplication, and each time in a much shorter period, until its power becomes incalculable, which multiplied power also penetrates [overcomes] every *Solid Thing*, such as *unconquerable* *Gold* *and* *Silver*, the otherwise *unalterable Mercury*, Crystals and Glass Fluxes, to which it is able to give natural hardness and fixity, as *Philaletha* does attest, and is proved by an artificial Diamond, in my father's time, in possession of *Prince Lichtenstein in Vienna*, valued at Five Hundred Thousand Ducats, fixed by the Lapis [Philosopher's Stone].

"IN THIS MANNER THE WORLD WAS CREATED; THE ARRANGEMENTS TO FOLLOW THIS ROAD ARE HIDDEN. FOR THIS REASON I AM CALLED *CHIRAM TELAT MECHASOT, ONE IN ESSENCE*, BUT *THREE IN ASPECT*. IN THIS TRINITY IS HIDDEN THE WISDOM OF THE WHOLE WORLD (i.e., in *Chiram* and *its Use*). It is thought that *Hermes* was *Moses* or *Zoroaster*, otherwise Hermes signifies a *Serpent*, and the Serpent used to be *an Emblem of Knowledge or Wisdom*. The *Serpent* is met with everywhere amongst the Hieroglyphics of the ancient Egyptians, so is *the Globe with Wings, the Sun* and *Moon, Dragons* and *Griffins*, whereby the Egyptians denoted their sublime knowledge of the Lapis Philosophorum, according to Suidas, the hints in the Scriptures, and even *De Non* where he speaks of the sanctuaries of the ancient Egyptian Temples.

"IT IS ENDED NOW, WHAT I HAVE SAID CONCERNING THE EFFECTS OF THE SUN. FINISH OF THE TABULA SMARAGDINA. What I have said or taught of *the Solar Work*, is now finished. The *perfect Seed*, fit for multiplication.

"This I know is acknowledged to be the genuine *Tabula Smaragdina Hermetis.*"'

The Secret Works of Chiram One, From the Chaldean, Dr. Sigismund Bacstrom's Collection of Manuscripts on the Emerald Tablet, The Emerald Table, the Most Ancient Monument of the Chaldeans concerning the Lapis Philosophorum (the stone of the philosophers)

CHAPTER FOUR
The Emerald Tablet by Doral

From the Emerald Tablet by Doreal

"The History of Thoth, The Atlantean

I, THOTH, the Atlantean, master of mysteries,
keeper of records, mighty king, magician,
living from generation to generation,
being about to pass into the halls of Amenti,
set down for the guidance of
those that are to come after,
these records of the mighty wisdom of Great Atlantis.

In the great city of KEOR on the island of UNDAL,
in a time far past, I began this incarnation.
Not as the little men of the present age did
the mighty ones of Atlantis live and die,
but rather from aeon to aeon did they renew
their life in the Halls of Amenti where the river of life
flows eternally onward.

A hundred times ten
have I descended the dark way that led into light,
and as many times have I ascended from the
darkness into the light my strength and power
renewed.

Now for a time I descend,
and the men of KHEM (Khem is alchemy in ancient

Egypt)
shall know me no more.

But in a time yet unborn will I rise again,
mighty and potent, requiring an accounting
of those left behind me.

Then beware, O men of KHEM,
if ye have falsely betrayed my teaching,
for I shall cast ye down from your high estate
into the darkness of the caves from whence ye came.

Betray not my secrets
to the men of the North
or the men of the South
lest my curse fall upon ye.

Remember and heed my words,
for surely will I return again
and require of thee that which ye guard.
Aye, even from beyond time and
from beyond death will I return,
rewarding or punishing
as ye have requited your trust.

Great were my people in the ancient days,
great beyond the conception of the
little people now around me;
knowing the wisdom of old,
seeking far within the heart of infinity
knowledge that belonged to Earth's youth.

Wise were we with the wisdom
of the Children of Light who dwelt among us.

Strong were we with the power drawn
from the eternal fire.

And of all these, greatest among the
children of men was my father, THOTME,
keeper of the great temple,
link between the Children of Light
who dwelt within the temple and the
races of men who inhabited the ten islands.

Mouthpiece, after the Three,
of the Dweller of UNAL,
speaking to the Kings
with the voice that must be obeyed.

Grew I there from a child into manhood,
being taught by my father the elder mysteries,
until in time there grew within the fire of wisdom,
until it burst into a consuming flame.

Naught desired I but the attainment of wisdom.
Until on a great day the command came from the
Dweller of the Temple that I be brought before him.
Few there were among the children of men
who had looked upon that mighty face and lived,
for not as the sons of men are the
Children of Light when they are not incarnate
in a physical body.

Chosen was I from the sons of men,
taught by the Dweller so that his
purposes might be fulfilled,
purposes yet unborn in the womb of time.

Long ages I dwelt in the Temple,
learning ever and yet ever more wisdom,
until I, too, approached the light emitted
from the great fire.

Taught me he, the path to Amenti,
the underworld where the great king sits
upon his throne of might.

Deep I bowed in homage before the Lords of Life
and the Lords of Death,
receiving as my gift the Key of Life.

Free was I of the Halls of Amenti,
bound not by death to the circle of life.
Far to the stars I journeyed until
space and time became as naught.

Then having drunk deep of the cup of wisdom,
I looked into the hearts of men and there found I
greater mysteries and was glad.
For only in the Search for Truth could my Soul
be stilled and the flame within be quenched.

Down through the ages I lived,
seeing those around me taste of the cup
of death and return again in the light of life.

Gradually from the Kingdoms of Atlantis passed
waves
of consciousness that had been one with me,
only to be replaced by spawn of a lower star.

In obedience to the law,
the word of the Master grew into flower.
Downward into the darkness turned the
thoughts of the Atlanteans,
Until at last in this wrath arose from his AGWANTI,
the Dweller, (this word has no English equivalent;
it means a state of detachment)
speaking The Word, calling the power.

Deep in Earth's heart, the sons of Amenti heard,
and hearing, directing the changing of the flower of
fire
that burns eternally, changing and shifting, using the
LOGOS,
until that great fire changed its direction.

Over the world then broke the great waters,
drowning and sinking,
changing Earth's balance
until only the Temple of Light was left
standing on the great mountain on UNDAL
still rising out of the water;
some there were who were living,
saved from the rush of the fountains.

Called to me then the Master, saying:
Gather ye together my people.
Take them by the arts ye have learned of far across the
waters,
until ye reach the land of the hairy barbarians,
dwelling in caves of the desert.
Follow there the plan that ye know of.

Gathered I then my people and
entered the great ship of the Master.
Upward we rose into the morning.
Dark beneath us lay the Temple.
Suddenly over it rose the waters.
Vanished from Earth,
until the time appointed,
was the great Temple.

Fast we fled toward the sun of the morning,
until beneath us lay the land of the children of
KHEM.
Raging, they came with cudgels and spears,
lifted in anger seeking to slay and utterly destroy the
Sons of Atlantis.

Then raised I my staff and directed a ray of vibration,
striking them still in their tracks as fragments
of stone of the mountain.

Then spoke I to them in words calm and peaceful,
telling them of the might of Atlantis,
saying we were children of the Sun and its
messengers.
Cowed I them by my display of magic-science,
until at my feet they groveled, when I released them.

Long dwelt we in the land of KHEM,
long and yet long again.
Until obeying the commands of the Master,
who while sleeping yet lives eternally,
I sent from me the Sons of Atlantis,
sent them in many directions,

that from the womb of time wisdom
might rise again in her children.

Long time dwelt I in the land of KHEM,
doing great works by the wisdom within me.
Upward grew into the light of knowledge
the children of KHEM,
watered by the rains of my wisdom.

Blasted I then a path to Amenti so
that I might retain my powers,
living from age to age a Sun of Atlantis,
keeping the wisdom, preserving the records.

Great grew the sons of KHEM,
conquering the people around them,
growing slowly upwards in Soul force.

Now for a time I go from among them into
the dark halls of Amenti,
deep in the halls of the Earth,
before the Lords of the powers,
face to face once again with the Dweller.

Raised I high over the entrance, a doorway, a
gateway
leading down to Amenti.

Few there would be with courage to dare it,
few pass the portal to dark Amenti.
Raised over the passage, I, a mighty pyramid,
using the power that overcomes Earth force (gravity).
Deep and yet deeper place I a force-house or
chamber;

from it carved I a circular passage
reaching almost to the great summit.

There in the apex, set I the crystal,
sending the ray into the "Time-Space,"
drawing the force from out of the ether,
concentrating upon the gateway to Amenti.

Other chambers I built and left vacant to all seeming,
yet hidden within them are the keys to Amenti.
He who in courage would dare the dark realms,
let him be purified first by long fasting.

Lie in the sarcophagus of stone in my chamber.
Then reveal I to him the great mysteries.
Soon shall he follow to where I shall meet him,
even in the darkness of Earth shall I meet him, I,
Thoth, Lord of Wisdom, meet him and hold him
and dwell with him always.

Builded I the Great Pyramid,
patterned after the pyramid of Earth force,
burning eternally so that it, too,
might remain through the ages.

In it, I builded my knowledge of "Magic-Science"
so that I might be here when again I return from
Amenti,
Aye, while I sleep in the Halls of Amenti,
my Soul roaming free will incarnate,
dwell among men in this form or another. (Hermes,
thrice-born.)

Emissary on Earth am I of the Dweller,
fulfilling his commands so many might be lifted.
Now return I to the halls of Amenti,
leaving behind me some of my wisdom.
Preserve ye and keep ye the command of the Dweller:
Lift ever upwards your eyes toward the light.

Surely in time, ye are one with the Master,
surely by right ye are one with the Master,
surely by right yet are one with the ALL.

Now, I depart from ye.
Know my commandments,
keep them and be them,
and I will be with you,
helping and guiding you into the Light.

Now before me opens the portal.
Go I down in the darkness of night.

The Halls of Amenti

Deep in Earth's heart lie the Halls of Amenti,
far 'neath the islands of sunken Atlantis,
Halls of the Dead and halls of the living,
bathed in the fire of the infinite ALL.

Far in a past time, lost in the space time,
the Children of Light looked down on the world.
Seeing the children of men in their bondage,
bound by the force that came from beyond.
Knew they that only by freedom from bondage
could man ever rise from the Earth to the Sun.

Down they descended and created bodies,
taking the semblance of men as their own.
The Masters of everything said after their forming:

"We are they who were formed from the space-dust,
partaking of life from the infinite ALL;
living in the world as children of men,
like and yet unlike the children of men."

Then for a dwelling place, far 'neath the earth crust,
blasted great spaces they by their power,
spaces apart from the children of men.
Surrounded them by forces and power,
shielded from harm they the Halls of the Dead.

Side by side then, placed they other spaces,
filled them with Life and with Light from above.
Builded they then the Halls of Amenti,
that they might dwell eternally there,
living with life to eternity's end.

Thirty and two were there of the children,
sons of Lights who had come among men,
seeking to free from the bondage of darkness
those who were bound by the force from beyond.

Deep in the Halls of Life grew a flower, flaming,
expanding, driving backward the night.

Placed in the center, a ray of great potence, Life
giving, Light giving, filling with power all who came
near it.
Placed they around it thrones, two and thirty,
places for each of the Children of Light,

placed so that they were bathed in the radiance,
filled with the Life from the eternal Light.

There time after time placed they their first created
bodies
so that they might by filled with the Spirit of Life.
One hundred years out of each thousand must the
Life-giving Light flame forth on their bodies.
Quickening, awakening the Spirit of Life.

There in the circle from aeon to aeon,
sit the Great Masters,
living a life not known among men.
There in the Halls of Life they lie sleeping;
free flows their Soul through the bodies of men.

Time after time, while their bodies lie sleeping,
incarnate they in the bodies of men.
Teaching and guiding onward and upward,
out of the darkness into the light.

There in the Hall of Life, filled with their wisdom,
known not to the races of man, living forever 'neath
the cold
fire of life, sit the Children of Light.
Times there are when they awaken,
come from the depths to be lights among men,
infinite they among finite men.

He who by progress has grown from the darkness,
lifted himself from the night into light,
free is he made of the Halls of Amenti,
free of the Flower of Light and of Life.

Guided he then, by wisdom and knowledge,
passes from men, to the Master of Life.

There he may dwell as one with the Masters,
free from the bonds of the darkness of night.
Seated within the flower of radiance sit seven
Lords from the Space-Times above us,
helping and guiding through infinite Wisdom,
the pathway through time of the children of men.

Mighty and strange, they,
veiled with their power,
silent, all-knowing,
drawing the Life force,
different yet one with the
children of men.
Aye, different, and yet One
with the Children of Light.

Custodians and watchers of the force of man's
bondage,
ready to loose when the light has been reached.
First and most mighty,
sits the Veiled Presence, Lord of Lords,
the infinite Nine,
over the other from each
the Lords of the Cycles;

Three, Four, Five, and Six, Seven, Eight,
each with his mission, each with his powers,
guiding, directing the destiny of man.
There sit they, mighty and potent,
free of all time and space.

Not of this world they,
yet akin to it,
Elder Brothers they,
of the children of men.
Judging and weighing,
they with their wisdom,
watching the progress
of Light among men.

There before them was I led by the Dweller,
watched him blend with ONE from above.

Then from HE came forth a voice saying:
"Great art thou, Thoth, among children of men.
Free henceforth of the Halls of Amenti,
Master of Life among children of men.
Taste not of death except as thou will it,
drink thou of Life to Eternity's end,
Henceforth forever is Life,
thine for the taking.
Henceforth is Death at the call of thy hand.

Dwell here or leave here when thou desireth,
free is Amenti to the son of man.
Take thou up Life in what form thou desireth,
Child of the Light that has grown among men.
Choose thou thy work, for all should must labor,
never be free from the pathway of Light.

One step thou has gained on the long pathway
upward,
infinite now is the mountain of Light.
Each step thou taketh but heightens the mountain;
all of thy progress but lengthens the goal.

Approach ye ever the infinite Wisdom,
ever before thee recedes the goal.
Free are ye made now of the Halls of Amenti
to walk hand in hand with the Lords of the world,
one in one purpose, working together,
bring of Light to the children of men."

Then from his throne came one of the Masters,
taking my hand and leading me onward,
through all the Halls of the deep hidden land.
Led he me through the Halls of Amenti,
showing the mysteries that are known not to man.

Through the dark passage, downward he led me,
into the Hall where site the dark Death.
Vast as space lay the great Hall before me,
walled by darkness but yet filled with Light.

Before me arose a great throne of darkness,
veiled on it sat a figure of night.
Darker than darkness sat the great figure,
dark with a darkness not of the night.
Before it then paused the Master, speaking

The Word that brings about Life, saying;
"Oh, master of darkness,
guide of the way from Life unto Life,
before thee I bring a Sun of the morning.
Touch him not ever with the power of night.
Call not his flame to the darkness of night.
Know him, and see him,
one of our brothers,
lifted from darkness into the Light.

Release thou his flame from its bondage,
free let it flame through the darkness of night."

Raised then the hand of the figure,
forth came a flame that grew clear and bright.
Rolled back swiftly the curtain of darkness,
unveiled the Hall from the darkness of night.

Then grew in the great space before me,
flame after flame, from the veil of the night.
Uncounted millions leaped they before me,
some flaming forth as flowers of fire.

Others there were that shed a dim radiance,
flowing but faintly from out of the night.

Some there were that faded swiftly;
others that grew from a small spark of light.
Each surrounded by its dim veil of darkness,
yet flaming with light that could never be quenched.
Coming and going like fireflies in springtime,
filled they with space with Light and with Life.

Then spoke a voice, mighty and solemn, saying:
"These are lights that are souls among men,
growing and fading, existing forever,
changing yet living, through death into life.
When they have bloomed into flower,
reached the zenith of growth in their life,
swiftly then send I my veil of darkness,
shrouding and changing to new forms of life.

Steadily upward throughout the ages, growing,
expanding into yet another flame,

lighting the darkness with yet greater power,
quenched yet unquenched by the veil of the night.

So grows the soul of man ever upward,
quenched yet unquenched by the darkness of night.

I, Death, come, and yet I remain not,
for life eternal exists in the ALL;
only an obstacle, I in the pathway,
quick to be conquered by the infinite light.

Awaken, O flame that burns ever inward,
flame forth and conquer the veil of the night."

Then in the midst of the flames
in the darkness grew there one that
drove forth the night, flaming, expanding,
ever brighter, until at last was nothing but Light.

Then spoke my guide, the voice of the master:
See your own soul as it grows in the light,
free now forever from the Lord of the night.

Forward he led me through many great spaces
filled with the mysteries of the Children of Light;
mysteries that man may never yet know of until
he, too, is a Sun of the Light.

Backward then HE led me into the Light
of the hall of the Light.
Knelt I then before the great Masters,
Lords of ALL from the cycles above.

Spoke HE then with words of great power saying:

Thou hast been made free of the Halls of Amenti.
Choose thou thy work among the children of men.

Then spoke I:
O, great master,
let me be a teacher of men,
leading then onward and upward until they,
too, are lights among men;
freed from the veil of the night that surrounds them,
flaming with light that shall shine among men.

Spoke to me then the voice:
Go, as yet will. So be it decreed.
Master are ye of your destiny,
free to take or reject at will.
Take ye the power, take ye the wisdom.
Shine as a light among the children of men.

Upward then, led me the Dweller.
Dwelt I again among children of men,
teaching and showing some of my wisdom;
Sun of the Light, a fire among men.

Now again I tread the path downward,
seeking the light in the darkness of night.
Hold ye and keep ye, preserve my record,
guide shall it be to the children of men.

The Key of Wisdom

I, Thoth, the Atlantean,
give of my wisdom,
give of my knowledge,
give of my power.

Freely I give to the children of men.
Give that they, too, might have wisdom
to shine through the world from the veil of the night.

Wisdom is power and power is wisdom,
one with each other, perfecting the whole.

Be thou not proud, O man, in thy wisdom.
Discourse with the ignorant as well as the wise.
If one comes to thee full of knowledge,
listen and heed, for wisdom is all.

Keep thou not silent when evil is spoken for Truth
like the sunlight shines above all.
He who over-steppeth the Law shall be punished,
for only through Law comes the freedom of men.
Cause thou not fear for fear is a bondage,
a fetter that binds the darkness to men.

Follow thine heart during thy lifetime.
Do thou more than is commanded of thee.
When thou hast gained riches,
follow thou thine heart,
for all these are of no avail if
thine heart be weary.
Diminish thou not the time of
following thine heart.
It is abhorred of the soul.

They that are guided go not astray,
but they that are lost cannot find a straight path.
If thou go among men, make for thyself,
Love, the beginning and end of the heart.

If one cometh unto thee for council,
let him speak freely,
that the thing for which he hath
come to thee may be done.
If he hesitates to open his heart to thee,
it is because thou, the judge, doeth the wrong.

Repeat thou not extravagant speech,
neither listen thou to it,
for it is the utterance of one
not in equilibrium.
Speak thou not of it,
so that he before thee may know wisdom.

Silence is of great profit.
An abundance of speech profiteth nothing.
Exalt not thine heart above the children of men,
lest it be brought lower than the dust.

If thou be great among men,
be honoured for knowledge and gentleness.
If thou seeketh to know the nature of a friend,
ask not his companion,
but pass a time alone with him.
Debate with him,
testing his heart by his words and his bearing.

That which goeth into the store-house must come
forth,
and the things that are thine must be shared with a
friend.

Knowledge is regarded by the fool as ignorance,
and the things that are profitable are to him hurtful.

He liveth in death.
It is therefore his food.

The wise man lets his heart overflow
but keeps silent his mouth.
O man, list to the voice of wisdom;
list to the voice of light.

Mysteries there are in the Cosmos
that unveiled fill the world with their light.
Let he who would be free from the bonds of darkness
first divine the material from the immaterial,
the fire from the earth;
for know ye that as earth descends to earth,
so also fire ascends unto
fire and becomes one with fire.
He who knows the fire that is within
himself shall ascend unto the eternal fire
and dwell in it eternally.

Fire, the inner fire,
is the most potent of all force,
for it overcometh all things and
penetrates to all things of the Earth.
Man supports himself only on that which resists.
So Earth must resist man else he existeth not.

All eyes do not see with the same vision,
for to one an object appears of
one form and color
and to a different eye of another.
So also the infinite fire,
changing from color to color,
is never the same from day to day.

Thus, speak I, THOTH, of my wisdom,
for a man is a fire burning bright
through the night;
never is quenched in the veil of the darkness,
never is quenched by the veil of the night.

Into men's hearts, I looked by my wisdom,
found them not free from the bondage of strife.
Free from the toils, thy fire, O my brother,
lest it be buried in the shadow of night!

Hark ye, O man, and list to this wisdom:
where do name and form cease?
Only in consciousness, invisible,
an infinite force of radiance bright.
The forms that ye create by brightening
they vision are truly effects that follow thy cause.

Man is a star bound to a body,
until in the end,
he is freed through his strife.
Only by struggle and toiling thy
utmost shall the star within thee
bloom out in new life.
He who knows the commencement of all things,
free is his star from the realm of night.

Remember, O man, that all which exists
is only another form of that which exists not.
Everything that has being is passing into yet other
being and thou thyself are not an exception.

Consider the Law, for all is Law.
Seek not that which is not of the Law,

for such exists only in the illusions of the senses.
Wisdom cometh to all her children
even as they cometh unto wisdom.

All through the ages,
the light has been hidden.
Awake, O man, and be wise.

Deep in the mysteries of life have I traveled,
seeking and searching for that which is hidden.

List ye, O man, and be wise.
Far 'neath the earth crust,
in the Halls of Amenti,
mysteries I saw that are hidden from men.

Oft have I journeyed the deep hidden passage,
looked on the Light that is Life among men.
There 'neath the flowers of Life ever living,
searched I the hearts and the secrets of men.
Found I that man is but living in darkness,
light of the great fire is hidden within.

Before the Lords of hidden Amenti
learned I the wisdom I give unto men.

Masters are they of the great Secret Wisdom,
brought from the future of infinity's end.
Seven are they, the Lords of Amenti,
overlords they of the Children of Morning,
Suns of the Cycles, Masters of Wisdom.

Formed are not they as the children of men?
THREE, FOUR, FIVE AND SIX, SEVEN,
EIGHT, NINE are the titles of the Masters of men.

Far from the future, formless yet forming,
came they as teachers for the children of men.
Live they forever, yet not of the living,
bound not to life and yet free from death.

Rule they forever with infinite wisdom,
bound yet not bound to the dark Halls of Death.
Life they have in them, yet life that is not life,
free from all are the Lords of the ALL.

Forth from them came forth the Logos,
instruments they of the power o'er all.
Vast is their countenance,
yet hidden in smallness,
formed by a forming, known yet unknown.

THREE holds the key of all hidden magic,
creator he of the halls of the Dead;
sending forth power, shrouding with darkness,
binding the souls of the children of men;
sending the darkness, binding the soul force;
director of negative to the children of men.

FOUR is he who looses the power.
Lord, he, of Life to the children of men.
Light is his body, flame is his countenance;
freer of souls to the children of men.

FIVE is the master, the Lord of all magic -
Key to The Word that resounds among men.

SIX is the Lord of Light, the hidden pathway,
path of the souls of the children of men.

SEVEN is he who is Lord of the vastness,
master of Space and the key of the Times.

EIGHT is he who orders the progress;
weighs and balances the journey of men.

NINE is the father, vast he of countenance,
forming and changing from out of the formless.

Meditate on the symbols I give thee.
Keys are they, though hidden from men.

Reach ever upward, O Soul of the morning.
Turn thy thoughts upward to Light and to Life.
Find in the keys of the numbers I bring thee,
light on the pathway from life unto life.

Seek ye with wisdom.
Turn thy thoughts inward.
Close not thy mind to the flower of Light.

Place in thy body a thought-formed picture.
Think of the numbers that lead thee to Life.

Clear is the pathway to he who has wisdom.
Open the door to the Kingdom of Light.

Pour forth thy flame as a Sun of the morning.
Shut out the darkness and live in the day.

Take thee, O man! As part of thy being,
the Seven who are but are not as they seem.
Opened, O man! Have I my wisdom.
Follow the path in the way I have led.

Masters of Wisdom,
SUN of the MORNING LIGHT and LIFE
to the children of men.

The Space Born

List ye, O man, to the voice of wisdom,
list to the voice of THOTH, the Atlantean.

Freely I give to thee of my wisdom,
gathered from the time and space of this cycle;
master of mysteries, SUN of the morning,
living forever, a child of the LIGHT,
shining with brightness, star of the morning,

THOTH the teacher of men, is of ALL.
Long time ago, I in my childhood,
lay 'neath the stars on long-buried ATLANTIS,
dreaming of mysteries far above men.

Then in my heart grew there a great longing to
conquer the pathway that led to the stars.
Year after year, I sought after wisdom,
seeking new knowledge, following the way,
until at last my SOUL, in great travail,
broke from its bondage and bounded away.

Free was I from the bondage of earth-men.
Free from the body, I flashed through the night.

Unlocked at last for me was the star-space.
Free was I from the bondage of night.
Now to the end of space sought I wisdom,
far beyond knowledge of finite man.

Far into space, my SOUL traveled freely
into infinity's circle of light.
Strange, beyond knowledge, were some of the
planets,
great and gigantic, beyond dreams of men.

Yet found I Law, in all of its beauty, working
through and among them as here among men.

Flashed forth my soul through infinity's beauty,
far through space
I flew with my thoughts.

Rested I there on a planet of beauty.
Strains of harmony filled all the air.

Shapes there were, moving in Order,
great and majestic as stars in the night;
mounting in harmony, ordered equilibrium,
symbols of the Cosmic, like unto Law.

Many the stars I passed in my journey,
many the races of men on their worlds;
some reaching high as stars of the morning,
some falling low in the blackness of night.

Each and all of them struggling upward,
gaining the heights and plumbing the depths,

moving at times in realms of brightness,
living through darkness, gaining the Light.

Know, O man, that Light is thine heritage.
Know that darkness is only a veil.
Sealed in thine heart is brightness eternal,
waiting the moment of freedom to conquer,
waiting to rend the veil of the night.

Some I found who had conquered the ether.
Free of space were they while yet they were men.
Using the force that is the foundation of ALL things,
far in space constructed they a planet,
drawn by the force that flows through the ALL;
condensing, coalescing the ether into forms,
that grew as they willed.

Outstripping in science, they, all of the races,
mighty in wisdom, sons of the stars.
Long time I paused, watching their wisdom.
Saw them create from out of the ether cities
gigantic of rose and gold.
Formed forth from the primal element,
base of all matter, the ether far flung.

Far in the past, they had conquered the ether,
freed themselves from the bondage of toil;
formed in their mind only a picture and swiftly
created, it grew.

Forth then, my soul sped, throughout the Cosmos,
seeing ever, new things and old;
learning that man is truly space-born,

a Sun of the Sun,
a child of the stars.

Know ye, O man, whatever from ye inhabit,
surely it is one with the stars.

Thy bodies are nothing but planets revolving
around their central suns.

When ye have gained the light of all wisdom,
free shall ye be to shine in the ether --
one of the Suns that light outer darkness --
one of the space-born grown into Light.

Just as the stars in time lose their brilliance,
light passing from them in to the great source,
so, O man, the soul passes onward,
leaving behind the darkness of night.

Formed forth ye, from the primal ether,
filled with the brilliance that
flows from the source,
bound by the ether coalesced around,
yet ever it flames until at last it is free.

Lift up your flame from out of the darkness,
fly from the night and ye shall be free.

Traveled I through the space-time,
knowing my soul at last was set free,
knowing that now might I pursue wisdom.
Until at last, I passed to a plane,
hidden from knowledge,

known not to wisdom,
extension beyond all that we know.

Now, O man, when I had this knowing,
happy my soul grew,
for now I was free.
Listen, ye space-born,
list to my wisdom:
know ye not that ye, too, will be free.

List ye again, O man, to my wisdom,
that hearing, ye too, might live and be free.
Not of the earth are ye -- earthy,
but child of the Infinite Cosmic Light.

Know ye not, O man, of your heritage?
Know ye not ye are truly the Light?
Sun of the Great Sun, when ye gain wisdom,
truly aware of your kinship with Light.

Now, to ye, I give knowledge,
freedom to walk in the path I have trod,
showing ye truly how by my striving,
I trod the path that leads to the stars.

Hark ye, O man, and know of thy bondage,
know how to free thyself from the toils.
Out of the darkness shall ye rise upward,
one with the Light and one with the stars.

Follow ye ever the path of wisdom.
Only by this can ye rise from below.
Ever man's destiny leads him onward
into the Curves of Infinity's ALL.

Know ye, O man, that all space is ordered.
Only by Order are ye One with the ALL.
Order and Balance are the Law of the Cosmos.
Follow and ye shall be One with the ALL.

He who would follow the pathway of wisdom,
open must be he to the flower of life,
extending his consciousness out of the darkness,
flowing through time and space in the ALL.

Deep in the silence,
first ye must linger until at last ye
are free from desire,
free from the longing to speak in the silence.

Conquer by silence, the bondage of words.
Abstaining from eating until we have conquered
desire for food, that is bondage of soul.

Then lie ye down in the darkness.
Close ye your eyes from the rays of the Light.
Centre thy soul-force in the place of thine
consciousness,
shaking it free from the bonds of the night.

Place in thy mind-place the image thou desireth.
Picture the place thou desireth to see.
Vibrate back and forth with thy power.
Loosen the soul from out of its night.
Fiercely must thou shake with all of thy power
until at last thy soul shall be free.

Mighty beyond words is the flame of the Cosmic,
hanging in planes, unknown to man;

mighty and balanced, moving in Order,
music of harmonies, far beyond man.

Speaking with music, singing with color,
flame from the beginning of Eternity's ALL.
Spark of the flame art thou, O my children,
burning with color and living with music.
List to the voice and thou shalt be free.

Consciousness free is fused with the Cosmic,
One with the Order and Law of the ALL.
Knew ye not man, that out of the darkness,
Light shall flame forth, a symbol of ALL.

Pray ye this prayer for attaining of wisdom.
Pray for the coming of Light to the ALL.

Mighty SPIRIT of LIGHT that shines through the
Cosmos, draw my flame closer in harmony to thee.
Lift up my fire from out of the darkness,
magnet of fire that is One with the ALL.
Lift up my soul, thou mighty and potent.
Child of the Light, turn not away.
Draw me in power to melt in thy furnace;
One with all things and all things
in One, fire of the life-strain and
One with the Brain.

When ye have freed thy soul from its bondage,
know that for ye the darkness is gone.
Ever through space ye may seek wisdom,
bound not be fetters forged in the flesh.

Onward and upward into the morning, free flash,
O Soul, to the realms of Light. Move thou in Order,
move thou in Harmony, freely shalt move
with the Children of Light.

Seek ye and know ye, my KEY of Wisdom.
Thus, O man, ye shall surely be free.

The Dweller of Unal

Oft dream I of buried Atlantis,
lost in the ages that have passed into night.
Aeon on aeon thou existed in beauty,
a light shining through the darkness of night.

Mighty in power, ruling the earth-born,
Lord of the Earth in Atlantis' day.

King of the nations, master of wisdom,
LIGHT through SUNTAL,
Keeper of the way,
dwelt in his TEMPLE,
the MASTER of UNAL,
LIGHT of the Earth in Atlantis' day.

Master, HE, from a cycle beyond us,
living in bodies as one among men.

Not as the earth-born,
HE from beyond us,
SUN of a cycle, advanced beyond men.

Know ye, O man, that HORLET the Master,
was never one with the children of men.

Far in the past time when Atlantis first grew as a
power,
appeared there one with the KEY of WISDOM,
showing the way of LIGHT to all.

Showed he to all men the path of attainment,
way of the Light that flows among men.
Mastering darkness, leading the MAN-SOUL,
upward to heights that were One with the Light.

Divided the Kingdoms, HE into sections.

Ten were they, ruled by children of men.

Upon another, built HE a TEMPLE,
built but not by the children of men.

Out of the ETHER called HE its substance,
moulded and formed by the power of YTOLAN
into the forms HE built with His mind.

Mile upon mile it covered the island,
space upon space it grew in its might.

Black, yet not black, but dark like the space-time,
deep in its heart the ESSENCE of LIGHT.

Swiftly the TEMPLE grew into being,
moulded and shaped by the WORD of the
DWELLER,
called from the formless into a form.

Builded HE then, within it, great chambers,
filled them with forms called forth from the ETHER,
filled them with wisdom called forth by His mind.

Formless was HE within his TEMPLE,
yet was HE formed in the image of men.

Dwelling among them yet not of them,
strange and far different
was HE from the children of men.

Chose HE then from among the people,
THREE who became his gateway.

Choose HE the THREE from the Highest
to become his links with Atlantis.

Messengers they, who carried his council,
to the kings of the children of men.

Brought HE forth others and taught them wisdom;
teachers, they, to the children of men.
Placed HE them on the island of UNDAL to stand as
teachers of LIGHT to men.

Each of those who were thus chosen,
taught must he be for years five and ten.

Only thus could he have understanding to bring
LIGHT to the children of men.

Thus there came into being the Temple, a dwelling
place
for the Master of men.

I, THOTH, have ever sought wisdom,
searching in darkness and searching in Light.

Long in my youth I traveled the pathway,
seeking ever new knowledge to gain.

Until after much striving, one of the THREE,
to me brought the LIGHT.

Brought HE to me the commands of the DWELLER,
called me from the darkness into the LIGHT.
Brought HE me, before the DWELLER,
deep in the Temple before the great FIRE.

There on the great throne, beheld I,
the DWELLER, clothed with the LIGHT
and flashing with fire.
Down I knelt before that great wisdom,
feeling the LIGHT flowing through me in waves.

Heard I then the voice of the DWELLER:
"O darkness, come into the Light.

Long have ye sought the pathway to LIGHT.

Each soul on earth that loosens its fetters,
shall soon be made free from the bondage of night.

Forth from the darkness have ye arisen,
closer approached the Light of your goal.

Here ye shall dwell as one of my children,
keeper of records gathered by wisdom,
instrument thou of the LIGHT from beyond.

Ready by thou made to do what is needed,
preserver of wisdom through the ages of darkness,
that shall come fast on the children of men.

Live thee here and drink of all wisdom.

Secrets and mysteries unto thee shall unveil."

Then answered I, the MASTER OF CYCLES, saying:
"O Light, that descended to men,
give thou to me of thy wisdom that
I might be a teacher of men.
Give thou of thy LIGHT that I may be free."

Spoke then to me again, the MASTER:
"Age after age shall ye live through
your wisdom, Aye, when o'er Atlantis the ocean
waves roll, holding the Light, though hidden in
darkness, ready to come when e'er thou shalt call.

Go thee now and learn greater wisdom. Grow thou
through LIGHT to Infinity's ALL."

Long then dwelt I in the Temple of the DWELLER
until at last I was One with the LIGHT.

Followed I then the path to the star planes, followed I
then the pathway to LIGHT.

Deep into Earth's heart I followed the pathway,
learning the secrets, below as above; learning the
pathway to the HALLS of AMENTI; learning the
LAW that balances the world.

To Earth's hidden chambers pierced I by my wisdom,
deep through the Earth's crust, into the pathway,
hidden for ages from the children of men.

Unveiled before me, ever more wisdom until I
reached a new knowledge: found that all is part of an
ALL, great and yet greater than all that we know.

Searched I Infinity's heart through all the ages.

Deep and yet deeper, more mysteries I found.

Now, as I look back through the ages, know I that
wisdom is boundless, ever grown greater throughout
the ages, One with Infinity's greater than all.

Light there was in ancient ATLANTIS.
Yet, darkness, too, was hidden in all.

Fell from the Light into the darkness,
some who had risen to heights among men.

Proud they became because of their knowledge,
proud were they of their place among men.
Deep delved they into the forbidden,
opened the gateway that led to below.

Sought they to gain ever more knowledge but
seeking to bring it up from below.

He who descends below must have balance,
else he is bound by lack of our Light.

Opened, they then,
by their knowledge,
pathways forbidden to man.

But, in His Temple, all-seeing, the DWELLER,
lay in his AGWANTI, while through Atlantis,
His soul roamed free.

Saw HE the Atlanteans, by their magic,
opening the gateway that would
bring to Earth a great woe.

Fast fled His soul then, back to His body.
Up HE arose from His AGWANTI.
Called HE the Three mighty messengers.
Gave the commands that shattered the world.
Deep 'neath Earth's crust to the HALLS of AMENTI,
swiftly descended the DWELLER.
Called HE then on the powers the Seven Lords
wielded;
changed the Earth's balance.

Down sank Atlantis beneath the dark waves.
Shattered the gateway that had been opened;
shattered the doorway that led down below.
All of the islands were shattered except UNAL,
and part of the island of the sons of the DWELLER.

Preserved HE them to be the teachers,
Lights on the path for those to come after,
Lights for the lesser children of men.

Called HE then, I THOTH, before him,
gave me commands for all I should do, saying;
"Take thou, O THOTH, all of your wisdom.

Take all your records, Take all your magic.
Go thou forth as a teacher of men.
Go thou forth reserving the records
until in time LIGHT grows among men.
LIGHT shalt thou be all through the ages,
hidden yet found by enlightened men.
Over all Earth, give WE ye power,
free thou to give or take it away.

Gather thou now the sons of Atlantis.
Take them and flee to the people of the rock caves.
Fly to the land of the Children of KHEM."
Then gathered I the sons of Atlantis.
Into the spaceship I brought all my records,
brought the records of sunken Atlantis.
Gathered I all of my powers,
instruments many of mighty magic.

Up then we rose on wings of the morning.
High we arose above the Temple,
leaving behind the Three and DWELLER,
deep in the HALLS 'neath the Temple,
closing the pathway to the LORDS of the Cycles.

Yet ever to him who has knowing,
open shall be the path to AMENTI.
Fast fled we then on the wings of the morning,
fled to the land of the children of KHEM.
There by my power,
I conquered and ruled them.

Raised I to LIGHT,
the children of KHEM.
Deep 'neath the rocks,
I buried my spaceship,
waiting the time when man might be free.

Over the spaceship,
erected a marker in the form
of a lion yet like unto man.
There 'neath the image rests yet my spaceship,
forth to be brought when need shall arise.

Know ye, O man, that far in the future,
invaders shall come from out of the deep.
Then awake, ye who have wisdom.
Bring forth my ship and conquer with ease.
Deep 'neath the image lies my secret.
Search and find in the pyramid I built.

Each to the other is the Keystone;
each the gateway that leads into LIFE.
Follow the KEY I leave behind me.
Seek and the doorway to LIFE shall be thine.
Seek thou in my pyramid,
deep in the passage that ends in a wall.

Use thou the KEY of the SEVEN,
and open to thee the pathway will fall.
Now unto thee I have given my wisdom.
Now unto thee I have given my way.

Follow the pathway.
Solve thou my secrets.
Unto thee I have shown the way.

The Key of Magic

Hark ye, O man, to the wisdom of magic.
Hark the knowledge of powers forgotten.
Long ago in the days of the first man,
warfare began between darkness and light.
Men then as now,
were filled with both darkness and light;
and while in some darkness held sway,
in other light filled the soul.

Aye, age old in this warfare,
the eternal struggle between darkness and light.
Fiercely is it fought all through the ages,
using strange powers hidden to man.

Adepts has there been filled with the blackness,
struggling always against the light;
but others there are who, filled with brightness,
have ever conquered the darkness of night.
Where e'er ye may be in all ages and plane,
surely, ye shall know of the battle with night.
Long ages ago,
The SUNS of the Morning
descending, found the world filled with night,
there in that past, began the struggle,
the age old Battle Darkness & Light.

Many in the time were so filled with darkness
that only feebly flamed the light from the night.

Some they were, masters of darkness, who sought
to fill all with their darkness:
Sought to draw others into their night.

Fiercely withstood they, the masters of brightness:
fiercely fought they from the darkness of night
Sought ever to tighten the fetters,
the chains that bind men to the darkness of night.
Used they always the dark magic,
brought into men by the power of darkness.
magic that enshrouded man's soul with darkness.

Banded together as in order,
BROTHERS OF DARKNESS,
they through the ages,
antagonist they to the children of men.
Walked they always secret and hidden,
found, yet not found by the children of men.

Forever, they walked and worked in darkness,
hiding from the light in the darkness of night.
Silently, secretly use they their power,
enslaving and binding the soul of men.

Unseen they come, and unseen they go.
Man, in his ignorance calls THEM from below.

Dark is the way of the DARK BROTHERS travel,
dark of the darkness not of the night,
traveling o'er Earth
they walk through man's dreams.
Power they have gained
from the darkness around them
to call other dwellers from out of their plane,
in ways that are dark and unseen by man.
Into man's mind-space reach the DARK BROTHERS.

Around it, they close the veil of their night.
There through it's lifetime
that soul dwells in bondage,
bound by the fetters of the VEIL of the night.
Mighty are they in the forbidden knowledge
forbidden because it is one with the night.

Hark ye O old man and list to my warning:
be ye free from the bondage of night.
Surrender not your soul to the BROTHERS OF
DARKNESS.
Keep thy face ever turned towards the Light.
Know ye not, O man, that your sorrow,
only has come through the Veil of the night.
Aye man, heed ye my warning:
strive ever upward,
turn your soul toward the LIGHT.
The BROTHERS OF DARKNESS seek for their
brothers
those who traveled the pathway of LIGHT.
For well know they that those who have traveled
far towards the Sun in their pathway of LIGHT
have great and yet greater power
to bind with darkness the children of LIGHT.

List ye, O man, to he who comes to you.
But weigh in the balance if his words be of LIGHT.
For many there are who walk in DARK BRIGHTNESS
and yet are not the children of LIGHT.

Easy it is to follow their pathway,
easy to follow the path that they lead.
But yet O man, heed ye my warning:

Light comes only to him who strives.
Hard is the pathway that leads to the WISDOM,
hard is the pathway that leads to the LIGHT.
Many shall ye find, the stones in your pathway:
many the mountains to climb toward the LIGHT.

Yet know ye, O man, to him that o'ercometh,
free will he be of the pathway of Light.
For ye know, O man,
in the END light must conquer
and darkness and night be banished from Light.

Listen, O man, and heed ye this wisdom;
even as darkness, so is the LIGHT.

When darkness is banished and all Veils are rended,
out there shall flash from the darkness, the LIGHT.

Even as exist among men the DARK BROTHERS,
so there exists the BROTHERS OF LIGHT.
Antagonists they of the BROTHERS OF DARKNESS,
seeking to free men from the night.
Powers have they, mighty and potent.
Knowing the LAW, the planets obey.
Work they ever in harmony and order,
freeing the man-soul from its bondage of night.

Secret and hidden, walk they also.
Known not are they to the children of men.
Ever have THEY fought the DARK BROTHERS,
conquered and conquering time without end.
Yet always LIGHT shall in the end be master,
driving away the darkness of night.

Aye, man, know ye this knowing:
always beside thee walk the Children of Light.

Masters they of the SUN power,
ever unseen yet the guardians of men.
Open to all is their pathway,
open to he who will walk in the LIGHT.
Free are THEY of DARK AMENTI,
free of the HALLS, where LIFE reigns supreme.

SUNS are they and LORDS of the morning,
Children of Light to shine among men.
Like man are they and yet are unlike,
Never divided were they in the past.

ONE have they been in ONENESS eternal,
throughout all space since the beginning of time.
Up did they come in Oneness with the ALL ONE,
up from the first-space, formed and unformed.

Given to man have they secrets
that shall guard and protect him from all harm.
He who would travel the path of the master,
free must he be from the bondage of night.
Conquer must he the formless and shapeless,
conquer must he the phantom of fear.

Knowing, must he gain of all of the secrets,
travel the pathway that leads through the darkness,
yet ever before him keep the light of his goal.
Obstacles great shall he meet in the pathway,
yet press on to the LIGHT of the SUN.

Hear ye, O Man, the SUN is the symbol
of the LIGHT that shines at the end of thy road.
Now to thee give I the secrets:
now to meet the dark power,
meet and conquer the fear from the night.
Only by knowing can ye conquer,
Only be knowing can ye have LIGHT.

Now I give unto thee the knowledge,
known to the MASTERS,
the knowing that conquers all the dark fears.
Use this, the wisdom I give thee.
MASTER thou shalt be of THE BROTHERS OF
NIGHT.

When unto thee comes a feeling,
drawing thee nearer to the darker gate,
examine thine heart and find if the feeling
thou hast has come from within.
If thou shalt find the darkness thine own thoughts,
banish them forth from the place in thy mind.

Send through thy body a wave of vibration,
irregular first and regular second,
repeating time after time until free.
Start the WAVE FORCE in thy BRAIN CENTER.
Direct it in waves from thine head to thy foot.

But if thou findest thine heart is not darkened,
be sure that a force is directed to thee.
Only by knowing can thou overcome it.
Only be wisdom can thou hope to be free.
Knowledge brings wisdom and wisdom is power.
Attain and ye shall have power o'er all.

Seek ye first a place bound by darkness.
Place ye a circle around about thee.
Stand erect in the midst of the circle.
Use thou this formula, and you shalt be free.
Raise thou thine hands to the dark space above thee
. Close thou thine eyes and draw in the LIGHT.

Call to the SPIRIT OF LIGHT through the Space-Time,
using these words and thou shalt be free:
"Fill thou my body, O SPIRIT OF LIfe,
fill thou my body with SPIRIT OF LIGHT.
Come from the FLOWER
that shines through the darkness.
Come from the HALLS where the Seven Lords rule.

Name them by name, I, the Seven:
THREE, FOUR, FIVE,
and SIX, SEVEN, EIGHT--Nine.

By their names I call them to aid me,
free me and save me from the darkness of night:
UNTANAS, QUERTAS, CHIETAL,
and GOYANA, HUERTAL, SEMVETA--ARDAL.
By their names I implore thee,
free me from darkness
and fill me with LIGHT

Know ye, O man, that when ye have done this,
ye shall be free from the fetters that bind ye,
cast off the bondage of the brothers of night.

See ye not that the names have the power
to free by vibration the fetters that bind?

Use them at need to free thou thine brother
so that he, too, may come forth from the night.

Thou, O man, art thy brother's helper.
Let him not lie in the bondage of night.

Now unto thee, give I my magic.
Take it and dwell on the pathway of LIGHT.

LIGHT unto thee, LIFE unto thee,
SUN may thou be on the cycle above.

The Seven Lords

Hark ye O man, and list to my Voice.
Open thy mind-space and drink of my wisdom.
Dark is the pathway of LIFE that ye travel.
Many the pitfalls that lie in thy way.
Seek ye ever to gain greater wisdom.
Attain and it shall be light on thy way.

Open thy SOUL, O man, to the Cosmic
and let it flow in as one with thy SOUL.
LIGHT is eternal and darkness is fleeting.
Seek ye ever, O man, for the LIGHT.
Know ye that ever as Light fills thy being,
darkness for thee shall soon disappear.

Open thy souls to the BROTHERS OF BRIGHTNESS.
Let them enter and fill thee with LIGHT.
Lift up thine eyes to the LIGHT of the Cosmos.
Keep thou ever thy face to the goal.
Only by gaining the light of all wisdom,
art thou one with the Infinite goal.

Seek ye ever the Oneness eternal.
Seek ever the Light into One.

Hear ye, O man, list to my Voice
singing the song of Light and of Life.
throughout all space, Light is prevalent,
encompassing ALL with its banners it flames.
Seek ye forever in the veil of the darkness,
somewhere ye shall surely find Light.
Hidden and buried, lost to man's knowledge,
deep in the finite the Infinite exists.
Lost, but existing,
flowing through all things,
living in ALL is the INFINITE BRAIN.

In all space, there is only ONE wisdom.
Through seeming decided, it is ONE in the ONE.
All that exists comes forth from the LIGHT,
and the LIGHT comes forth from the ALL.

Everything created is based upon ORDER:
LAW rules the space where the INFINITE dwells.
Forth from equilibrium came the great cycles,
moving in harmony toward Infinity's end.

Know ye, O man, that far in the space-time,
INFINITY itself shall pass into change.
Hear ye and list to the Voice of Wisdom:
Know that ALL is of ALL evermore.
Know that through time thou may pursue wisdom
and find ever more light on the way.
Know that through time thou may pursue wisdom
and find ever more light on the way.

Aye, thou shall find that ever receding,
thy goal shall elude thee from day unto day.

Long time ago, in the HALLS OF AMENTI,
I, Thoth, stood before the LORDS of the cycles.
Mighty, THEY in their aspects of power;
mighty, THEY in the wisdom unveiled.

Led by the Dweller, first did I see them.
But afterwards free was I of their presence,
free to enter their conclave at will.
Oft did I journey down the dark pathway
unto the HALL where the LIGHT ever glows.

Learned I of the Masters of cycles,
wisdom brought from the cycles above.
Manifest THEY in this cycle
as guides of man to the knowledge of ALL.
Seven are they, mighty in power,
speaking these words through me to men.
Time after time, stood I before them
listening to words that came not with sound.

Once said THEY unto me:
O man, wouldst thou gain wisdom?
Seek for it in the heart of the flame.
Wouldst thou gain knowledge of power?
Seek ye it in the heart of the flame.
Wouldst be one with the heart of the flame?
Seek then within thine own hidden flame.

Many the times spoke THEY to me,
teaching me wisdom not of the world;
showing me ever new paths to brightness;

teaching me wisdom brought from above.
Giving knowledge of operation,
learning of LAW, the order of ALL.

Spoke to me again, the Seven, saying:
From far beyond time are WE, come, O man,
Traveled WE from beyond SPACE-TIME,
aye, from the place of Infinity's end.
When ye and all of thy brethren were formless,
formed forth were WE from the order of ALL.
Not as men are WE,
though once WE, too, were as men.
Out of the Great Void were WE formed forth
in order by LAW.
For know ye that which is formed
truly is formless, having form only to thine eyes.

And again, unto me spoke the Seven, saying:
Child of the LIGHT, O THOTH, art thou,
free to travel the bright path upward
until at last ALL ONES become ONE

Forth were WE formed after our order:
THREE, FOUR, FIVE, SIX, SEVEN, EIGHT--NINE.
Know ye that these are the numbers of cycles
that WE descend from unto man.
Each having here a duty to fulfill;
each having here a force to control.

Yet are we ONE with the SOUL of our cycle.
Yet are WE, too, seeking a goal.
Far beyond man's conception,
Infinity extends into a greater than ALL.
There, in a time that is yet not a time,

we shall ALL become ONE
with a greater than ALL.
Time and space are moving in circles.
Know ye their law, and ye too, shall be free.
Aye, free shall ye be to move through the cycles--
pass the guardians that dwell at the door.

Then to me spoke HE of NINE saying:
Aeons and aeons have I existed,
knowing not LIFE and tasting not death.
For know ye. O man, that far in the future,
life and death shall be one with the ALL.

Each so perfected by balancing the other
that neither exists in the Oneness of ALL.
In men of this cycle, the life force is rampant,
but life in its growth becomes one with them ALL.

Here, I manifest in this your cycle,
but yet am I there in your future of time.
Yet to me, time exists not,
for in my world time exists not,
for formless are WE.
Life have WE not but yet have existence,
fuller and greater and freer than thee.

Man is a flame bound to a mountain,
but WE in our cycle shall ever be free.
Know ye, O man, that when ye have progressed
into the cycle that lengthen above,
life itself will pass to the darkness
and only the essence of Soul shall remain.

Then to me spoke the LORD of the EIGHT saying:
All that ye know is but part of little.
Not as yet have ye touched on the Great.
Far out in space where LIGHT beings supreme,
came I into the LIGHT.
Formed was I also but not as ye are.

Body of Light was my formless form formed.
Know I not LIFE and know I not DEATH,
yet master am I of all that exists.
Seek ye to find the path through the barriers.
Travel the road that leads to the LIGHT.

Spoke again to me the NINE saying:
Seek ye to find the path to beyond.
Not impossible is it to grow
to a consciousness above.
For when TWO have become ONE
and ONE has become the ALL,
know ye the barrier has lifted,
and ye are made free of the road.
Grow thou from form to the formless.
Free may thou be of the road.

Thus, through ages I listened,
learning the way to the ALL.
Now Lift I my thoughts to the ALL-THING.
List ye and hear when it calls.

O LIGHT, all prevading,
One with ALL and ALL with ONE,
flow thou to me through the channel.
Enter thou so that I may be free.
Make me One with the ALL-SOUL,

shining from the blackness of night.
Free let me be of all space-time,
free from the Veil of the night.
I, a child of LIGHT, command:
Free from the darkness to be.

Formless am I to the Light-Soul,
formless yet shining with light.
Know I the bonds of the darkness
must shatter and fall before light.

Now give I this wisdom.
Free may ye be, O man,
living in light and in brightness.
Turn not they face from the Light.
Thy soul dwells in realms of brightness.
Ye are a child of the Light.

Turn thy thoughts inward not outward.
Find thou the Light-Soul within.
Know that thou art the MASTER.
All else is brought from within.
Grow thou to realms of brightness.
Hold thou thy thought on the Light.
Know thou art one with the Cosmos,
a flame and a Child of the Light.

Now to thee gave I warning:
Let not the thought turn away.
Know that the brightness
flows through thy body for aye.
Turn not to the DARK-BROTHERS
that come from the BROTHERS OF BLACK.

But keep thine eyes ever lifted,
thy soul in tune with the Light.

Take ye this wisdom and heed it.
List to my Voice and obey.
Follow the pathway to brightness,
and thou shall be ONE with the way.

The Key of Mystery

Unto thee, O man,
have I given my knowledge.
Unto thee have I given of Light.
Hear ye now and receive my wisdom
brought from space planes above and beyond.

Not as man am I
for free have I become of dimensions and planes.
In each, take I on a new body.
In each, I change in my form.
Know I now that the formless is all there is of form.

Great is the wisdom of the Seven.
Mighty are THEY from beyond.
Manifest THEY through their power,
filled by force from beyond.

Hear ye these words of wisdom.
Hear ye and make them thine own.
Find in them the formless.
Mystery is but hidden knowledge.
Know and ye shall unveil.
Find the deep buried wisdom
and be master of darkness and Light.

Deep are the mysteries around thee,
hidden the secrets of Old.
Search through the KEYS of my WISDOM.
Surely shall ye find the way.
The gateway to power is secret,
but he who attains shall receive.
Look to the LIGHT! O my brother.
Open and ye shall receive.
Press on through the valley of darkness.
Overcome the dweller of night.
Keep ever thine eyes of the LIGHT-PLANE,
and thou shalt be One with the LIGHT.

Man is in process of changing
to forms that are not of this world.
Grows he is time to the formless,
a plane on the cycle above.
Know ye, ye must become formless before ye are with
the LIGHT,

List ye, O man, to my voice,
telling of pathways to Light,
showing the way of attainment
when ye shall be One with the Light.

Search ye the mysteries of Earth's heart.
Learn of the LAW that exists,
holding the stars in their balance
by the force of the primordial mist.
Seek ye the flame of the EARTH'S LIFE.
Bathe in the glare of its flame.
Follow the three-cornered pathway
until thou, too, art a flame.

Speak thou in words without voice
to those who dwell down below.
Enter the blue-litten temple
and bathe in the fire of all life.

Know, O man, thou art complex,
a being of earth and of fire.
Let thy flame shine out brightly.
Be thou only the fire.

Wisdom is hidden in darkness.
When lit by the flame of the Soul,
find thou the wisdom and be LIGHT-BORN,
a Sun of the Light without form.
Seek thee ever more wisdom.
Find it in the heart of the flame.
Know that only by striving
and Light pour into thy brain.
Now have I spoken with wisdom.
List to my Voice and obey.
Tear open the Veils of the darkness.
Shine a LIGHT on the WAY.

Speak I of Ancient Atlantis,
speak of the days
of the Kingdom of Shadows,
speak of the coming
of the children of shadows.
Out of the great deep were they called
by the wisdom of earth-men,
called for the purpose of gaining great power.

Far in the past before Atlantis existed,
men there were who delved into darkness,

using dark magic, calling up beings
from the great deep below us.
Forth came they into this cycle.
Formless were they of another vibration,
existing unseen by the children of earth-men.
Only through blood could they have formed being.
Only through man could they live in the world.

In ages past were they conquered by Masters,
driven below to the place whence they came.
But some there were who remained,
hidden in spaces and planes unknown to man.
Lived they in Atlantis as shadows,
but at times they appeared among men.
Aye, when the blood was offered,
for they came they to dwell among men.

In the form of man they amongst us,
but only to sight were they as are men.
Serpent-headed when the glamour was lifted
but appearing to man as men among men.
Crept they into the Councils,
taking forms that were like unto men.
Slaying by their arts
the chiefs of the kingdoms,
taking their form and ruling o'er man.
Only by magic could they be discovered.
Only by sound could their faces be seen.
Sought they from the Kingdom of shadows
to destroy man and rule in his place.

But, know ye, the Masters were mighty in magic,
able to lift the Veil from the face of the serpent,

able to send him back to his place.
Came they to man and taught him the secret,
the WORD that only a man can pronounce.
Swift then they lifted the Veil from the serpent
and cast him forth from the place among men.

Yet, beware, the serpent still liveth
in a place that is open at times to the world.
Unseen they walk among thee
in places where the rites have been said.
Again as time passes onward
shall they take the semblance of men.

Called may they be by the master
who knows the white or the black,
but only the white master may control
and bind them while in the flesh.

Seek not the kingdom of shadows,
for evil will surely appear.
For only the master of brightness
shall conquer the shadow of fear.

Know ye, O my brother,
that fear is an obstacle great.
Be master of all in the brightness,
the shadow will soon disappear.
Hear ye and heed my wisdom,
the voice of LIGHT is clear.
Seek not the valley of shadow,
and LIGHT will only appear.

List ye, O man,
to the depth of my wisdom.

Speak I of knowledge hidden from man.
Far have I been
on my journey through SPACE-TIME,
even to the end of space of this cycle.
Aye, glimpsed the HOUNDS of the Barrier,
lying in wait for he who would pass them.
In that space where time exists not,
faintly I sensed the guardians of cycles.
Move they only through angles.
Free are they not of the curved dimensions.

Strange and terrible
are the HOUNDS of the Barrier.
Follow they consciousness to the limits of space.
Think not to escape by entering your body,
for follow they fast the Soul through angles.
Only the circle will give ye protection,
save from the claws
of the DWELLERS IN ANGLES.

Once, in a time past,
I approached the great Barrier,
and saw on the shores where time exists not,
the formless forms
of the HOUNDS of the barrier.
Aye, hiding in the midst beyond time I found them;
and THEY, scenting me afar off,
raised themselves and gave the great bell cry
that could be heard from cycle to cycle
and moved through space toward my soul.

Fled I then fast before them,
back from time's unthinkable end.

But ever after me pursued they,
moving in strange angles not known to man.
Aye, on the gray shores of TIME-SPACE'S end
found I the HOUNDS of the Barrier,
ravening for the Soul
who attempts the beyond.

Fled I through circles back to my body.
Fled, and fast after me they followed.
Aye, after me the devourers followed,
seeking through angles to devour my Soul.

Aye, know ye man,
that the Soul who dares the Barrier
may be held in bondage
by the HOUNDS from beyond time,
held till this cycle is completed
and left behind
when the consciousness leaves.

Entered I my body.
Created the circles that know not angles,
created the form
that from my form was formed.
Made my body into a circle
and lost the pursuers in the circles of time.
But, even yet, when free from my body,
cautious ever must I be
not to move through angles,
else my soul may never be free.

Know ye, the HOUNDS of the Barrier
move only through angles
and never through curves of space.

Only by moving through curves
can ye escape them,
for in angles they will pursue thee.
O man, heed ye my warning;
Seek not to break open
the gate to beyond.
Few there are
who have succeeded in passing the Barrier
to the greater LIGHT that shines beyond.
For know ye, ever the dwellers,
seek such Souls to hold in their thrall.

Listen, O man, and heed ye my warning;
seek ye to move not in angles but curves,
And if while free from thy body,
though hearest the sound like the bay of a hound
ringing clear and bell-like through thy being,
flee back to thy body through circles,
penetrate not the midst mist before.

When thou hath entered the form thou hast dwelt in,
use thou the cross and the circle combined.
Open thy mouth and use thou thy Voice.
Utter the WORD and thou shalt be free.
Only the one who of LIGHT has the fullest
can hope to pass by the guards of the way.
And then must he move
through strange curves and angles
that are formed in direction not know to man.

List ye, O man, and heed ye my warning:
attempt not to pass the guards on the way.

Rather should ye seek to gain of thine own Light
and make thyself ready to pass on the way.

LIGHT is thine ultimate end, O my brother.
Seek and find ever the Light on the way.

The Key to Freedom of Space

List ye, O man, hear ye my voice,
teaching of Wisdom and Light in this cycle;
teaching ye how to banish the darkness,
teaching ye how to bring Light in thy life.

Seek ye, O man, to find the great pathway
that leads to eternal LIFE as a SUN.
Draw ye away from the veil of the darkness.
Seek to become a Light in the world.
Make of thyself a vessel for Light,
a focus for the Sun of this space.

Lift thou thine eyes to the Cosmos.
Lift thou thine eyes to the Light.
Speak in the words of the Dweller,
the chant that calls down the Light.
Sing thou the song of freedom.
Sing thou the song of the Soul.
Create the high vibration
that will make thee One with the Whole.
Blend all thyself with the Cosmos.
Grow into ONE with the Light.
Be thou a channel of order,
a pathway of LAW to the world.

Thy LIGHT, O man, is the great LIGHT,
shining through the shadow of flesh.
Free must thou rise from the darkness
before thou art One with the LIGHT.

Shadows of darkness surround thee.
Life fills thee with its flow.
But know, O man, thou must arise
and forth thy body go
far to the planes that surround thee
and yet are One with thee, too.

Look all around thee, O man.
See thine own light reflected.
Aye, even in the darkness around thee,
thine own Light pours forth through the veil.

Seek thou for wisdom always.
Let not thine body betray.
Keep in the path of the Light wave.
Shun thou the darkened way.
Know thee that wisdom is lasting.
Existing since the ALL-SOUL began,
creating harmony from by the
Law that exists in the WAY.

List ye, o man, to the teachings of wisdom.
List to the voice that speaks of the past-time.
Aye, I shall tell thee knowledge forgotten,
tell ye of wisdom hidden in past-time,
lost in the midst of darkness around me.

Know ye, man,
ye are the ultimate of all things.

Only the knowledge of this is forgotten,
lost when man was cast into bondage,
bound and fettered
by the chains of the darkness.

Long, long ago, I cast off my body.
Wandered I free
through the vastness of ether,
circled the angles
that hold man in bondage.
Know ye, O man, ye are only a spirit.
The body is nothing.
The Soul is ALL.
Let not your body be a fetter.
Cast off the darkness and travel in Light.
Cast off your body, O man, and be free,
truly a Light that is ONE with the Light.

When ye are free from the fetters of darkness
and travel in space as the SUN of the LIGHT,
then ye shall know that space in not boundless
but truly bounded by angles and curves.
Know ye, O man, that all that exists
is only an aspect of greater things yet to come.
Matter is fluid and flows like a stream,
constantly changing from one thing to another.

All through the ages has knowledge existed;
never been changed, though buried in darkness;
never been lost, though forgotten by man.

Know ye that throughout the space
that ye dwell in
are others as great as your own,

interlaced through the heart of your matter
yet separate in space of their own.

Once in a time long forgotten,
I THOTH, opened the doorway,
penetrated into other spaces
and learned of the secrets concealed.
Deep in the essence of matter
are many mysteries concealed.

Nine are the interlocked dimensions,
and Nine are the cycles of space.
Nine are the diffusions of consciousness,
and Nine are the worlds within worlds.
Aye, Nine are the Lords of the cycles
that come from above and below.

Space is filled with concealed ones,
for space is divided by time.
Seek ye the key to the time-space,
and ye shall unlock the gate.
Know ye that throughout the time-space
consciousness surely exist.
Though from our knowledge it is hidden,
yet still forever exists.

The key to worlds within thee
are found only within.
For man is the gateway of mystery
and the key that is One with the One.

Seek ye within the circle.
Use the WORD I shall give.
Open the gateway within thee,

and surely thou, too, shall live.
Man, ye think that ye liveth,
but know it is life within death.
For as sure as ye are bound to your body,
for you no life exists.
Only the Soul is space-free,
has life that is really a life.
All else is only a bondage,
a fetter from which to be free.

Think not that man is earth-born,
though come from the earth he may be.
Man is light-born spirit.
But, without knowing, he can never be free.
Darkness surrounds the light-born.
Darkness fetters the Soul.
Only the one who is seeking
may ever hope to be free.

Shadows around thee are falling
darkness fills all the space
Shine forth, O LIGHT of the man-soul.
Fill thou the darkness of space.

Ye are son of the GREAT LIGHT
Remember and ye shall be free.
Stay not thou in the shadows.
Spring forth from the darkness of night
Light, let thy Soul be, O SUN-BORN,
fill with glory of Light,
Freed from the bonds of the darkness,
a Soul that is One with the Light.

Thou art the key to all wisdom.
Within thee is all time and space.
Live not in bondage to darkness.
Free thou, thy Light-form from night.

Great Light that fills all the Cosmos,
flow thou fully to man.
Make of his body a light-torch
that shall never be quenched among men.

Long in the past, sought I wisdom,
knowledge not known to man.
Far to the past, I traveled
into the space where time began.
Sought I ever knew knowledge
to add to the wisdom I knew.
Yet only, I found, did the future
hold the key to the wisdom I thought.

Down, to the HOLES of AMENTI
I journeyed, the greater knowledge to seek.
Ask of thee, LORDS of the CYCLES,
they way to the wisdom I sought.
Asked the LORDS this question:
Where is the source of ALL?
Answered, in tones that were mighty,
the voice of the LORD of the NINE:
Free thou thy soul from thy body
and come forth with me to the LIGHT.

Forth I came from my body,
a glittering flame in the night.
Stood I before the LORD,
bathed in the fire of LIFE.

Seized was I then by a force,
great beyond knowledge of man.
Cast was I to the Abyss
through spaces unknown to man.

Saw I the moldings of Order
from the chaos and angles of night.
Saw I the LIGHT, spring from Order
and heard the voice of the Light.
Saw I the flame of the Abyss,
casting forth Order and Light.
Saw Order spring out of chaos.
Saw Light giving forth Life.

Then heard I the voice.
Hear thou and understand.
The flame is the source of all things,
containing all things in potentiality.
The Order that sent forth light
is the WORD and from the WORD,
COME LIFE and the existence of all.

And again spoke the voice saying:
THE LIFE in thee is the WORD.
Find thou the LIFE within thee
and have powers to use of the WORD.

Long I watched the Light-flame,
pouring forth from the Essence of Fire,
realizing that LIFE but Order
and that man is one with the fire.

Back I came to my body
stood again with the Nine,

listened to the voice of the Cycles,
vibrate with powers they spoke:
Know ye, O Thoth, that LIFE
is but thee WORD of the FIRE.
The LIFE forth ye seek before thee
is but the WORD in the World as a fire.
Seek ye the path to the WORD and Powers
shall surely be thine.

Then asked I of the Nine:
O Lord, show me the path.
Give the path to the wisdom.
Show me the way to the WORD.
Answered, me then,
the LORD OF THE NINE:
Through ORDER, ye shall find the way.
Saw ye that the WORD came from Chaos?
Saw ye not that LIGHT came from FIRE?

Look in thy life for this order.
Balance and order thy life.
Quell all the Chaos of the emotions
and thou shalt have order in LIFE.
ORDER brought forth from Chaos
will bring thee the WORD of the SOURCE,
will thee the power of CYCLES,
and make of thy Soul a force that
freewill extend through the ages,
a perfect SUN from the Source.

Listened I to the voice
and deep thanked the words in my heart.
Forever have I sought for order
that I might draw on the WORD.

Know ye that he who attains it
must ever in ORDER be for use
of the WORD though this order
has never and can never be.

Take ye these words, O man.
As part of thy life, let them be.
Seek thee to conquer this order
and One with the WORD thou shalt be.

Put forth thy effort in gaining LIGHT
on the pathway of Life.
Seek to be One with the SUN/state.
Seek to be solely the LIGHT.
Hold thou thy thought on the Oneness
of Light with the body of man.
Know that all is Order from Chaos
born into light.

The Key of Time

List ye, O Man. Take of my wisdom.
Learn of his deep hidden mysteries of space.
Learn of the THOUGHT that grew in the abyss,
bringing Order and Harmony in space.

Know ye, O man, that all exists
has being only because of the LAW.
Know ye the LAW and ye shall be free,
never be bound by the fetters of night.

Far, through strange spaces, have I journeyed
into the depth of the abyss of time,
until in the end all was revealed.

Know ye that mystery is only mystery
when it is knowledge unknown to man.
When ye have plumbed the heart of all mystery,
knowledge and wisdom will surely be thine.

Seek ye and learn that TIME is the secret
whereby ye may be free of this space.

Long have I, WISDOM, sought wisdom;
aye, and shall seek of eternity's end
for know that ever before me receding
shall move the goal I seek to attain.
Even the LORDS of the CYCLES
know that not yet have THEY reached the goal,
For with all of their wisdom,
they know that TRUTH ever grows.

Once, in a past time, I spoke to the Dweller.
Asked of the mystery of time and space.
Asked him the question that surged in my being,
saying: *O Master, what is time?*

Then to me spoke HE, the Master:
Know ye, O Thoth, in the beginning
there was VOID and nothingness,
a timeless, spaceless, nothingness.
And into the nothingness came a thought,
purposeful, all-pervading,
and It filled the VOID.
There existed no matter, only force,
a movement, a vortex, or vibration
of the purposeful thought
that filled the VOID.

And I questioned the Master, saying:
Was this thought eternal?
And answered me the DWELLER, Saying:
In the beginning, there was eternal thought,
and for thought to be eternal, time must exist.
So into the all-pervading thought
grew the LAW of TIME.
Aye time which exists through all space,
floating in a smooth, rhythmic movement
that is eternally in a state of fixation.

Time changes not,
but all things change in time.
For time is the force
that holds events separate,
each in its own proper place.
Time is not in motion,
but ye move through time
as your consciousness
moves from one event to another.

Aye, by time yet exist, all in all,
an eternal ONE existence.
Know ye that even though in the time ye are separate,
yet still are ONE, in all times existent.

Ceased then the voice of the DWELLER,
and departed I to ponder on time.
For knew I that in these words lay wisdom
and a way to explore the mysteries of time.

Oft did I ponder the words of the DWELLER.
Then sought I to solve the mystery of time.
Found I that time moves through strange angles.

Yet only by curves could I hope to attain the key
that would give me access to the time-space.
Found I that only by moving upward
and yet again by moving to right-ward
could I be free from the time of the movement.

Forth I came from out of my body,
moved in the movements that changed me in time.
Strange were the sights I saw in my journeys,
many the mysteries that opened to view.
Aye, saw I man's beginning,
learned from the past that nothing is new.

Seek ye, O man, to learn the pathway
that leads through the spaces
that are formed forth in time.

Forget not, O man, with all of thy seeking
that Light is the goal ye shall seek to attain.
Search ye for the Light on thy pathway
and ever for thee the goal shall endure.

Let not thine heart turn ever to darkness.
light let shine Soul be, a Sun on the way.
Know ye that eternal brightness,
ya shall ever find thy Soul hid in Light,
never fettered by bondage or darkness,
ever it shines forth a Sun of the Light.

Aye, know, though hidden in darkness,
your Soul, a spark of the true flame, exists.
Be ye One with the greatest of all Lights.
Find at the SOURCE, the END of thy goal.

Light is life, for without the great Light
nothing can ever exist.
Know ye, that in all formed matter,
the heart of Light always exists.
Aye, even though bound in the darkness,
inherent Light always exists.

Once I stood in the HALLS OF AMENTI
and heard the voice of the LORDS of AMENTI,
saying in tones that rang through the silence,
words of power, mighty and potent.
Chanted they the song of the cycles,
the words that open the path to beyond.
Aye, I saw the great path opened
and looked for the instant into the beyond.
Saw I the movements of the cycles,
vast as the thought of the SOURCE could convey.

Knew I then even Infinity
is moving on to some unthinkable end.
Saw I that the Cosmos is Order
and part of a movement that extends to all space,
a party of an Order of Orders,
constantly moving in a harmony of space.

Saw I the wheeling of cycles
like vast circles across the sky.
Knew I then that all that has being
is growing to meet yet another being
in a far-off grouping of space and of time.

Knew I then that in Words are power
to open the planes that are hidden from man.

Aye, that even in Words lies hidden the key
that will open above and below.

Hark ye, now man, this word I leave with thee.
Use it and ye shall find power in its sound.
Say ye the word:
"ZIN-URU"
and power ye shall find.
Yet must ye understand that man is of Light
and Light is of man.

List ye, O man, and hear a mystery
stranger than all that lies 'neath the Sun.
Know ye, O man, that all space
is filled by worlds within worlds;
aye, one within the other yet separate by Law.

Once in my search for deep buried wisdom,
I opened the door that bars THEM from man.
Called I from the other planes of being,
one who was fairer than the daughters of men.
Aye, I called her from out of the spaces,
to shine as a Light in the world of men.

Used I the drum of the Sertpent.
Wore I the robe of the purple and gold.
Placed on my head, I, the crown of Silver.
Around me the circle of cinnabar shone.
Raised I my arms and cried the invocation
that opens the path to the planes beyond,
cried to the LORDS of the SIGNS in their houses:
Lords of the two horizons,
watchers of the treble gates,
stand ye One at the right and One at the left

as the STAR rises to his throne
and rules over his sign.
Aye, thou dark prince of ARULU,
open the gates of the dim, hidden land
and release her whom ye keep imprisoned.

Hear ye, hear ye, hear ye,
dark Lords and Shining Ones,
and by their secret names,
names which I know and can pronounce,
hear ye and obey my will.

Lit I then with flame my circle
and called HER in the space-planes beyond.
Daughter of Light return from ARULU.

Seven times and seven times
have I passed through the fire.
Food have I not eaten.
Water have I not drunk.
I call thee from ARULU,
from the realms of EKERSHEGAL.
I summon thee, lady of Light.

Then before me rose the dark figures;
aye, the figures of the Lords of Arulu.
Parted they before me
and forth came the Lady of Light.

Free was she now from the LORDS of the night,
free to live in the Light of the earth Sun,
free to live as a child of the Light.

Hear ye and listen, O my children.
Magic is knowledge and only is Law.
Be not afraid of the power within thee
for it follows Law as the stars in the sky.

Know ye that to be without knowledge,
wisdom is magic and not of the Law.
But know ye that ever ye by your knowledge
can approach closer to a place in the Sun.

List ye, my children, follow my teaching.
Be ye ever seeker of Light.
Shine in the world of men all around thee,
a Light on the path that shall shine among men.

Follow ye and learn of my magic.
Know that all force is thine if thou wilt.
Fear not the path that leads thee to knowledge,
but rather shun ye the dark road.

Light is thine, O man, for the taking.
Cast off the fetters and thou shalt be free.
Know ye that they Soul is living in bondage
fettered by fears that hold ye in thrall.

Open thy eyes and see the great SUN-LIGHT.
Be not afraid for all is thine own.
Fear is the LORD of the dark ARULU
to he who never faced the dark fear.
Aye, know that fear has existence
created by those who are bound by their fears.

Shake off thy bondage, O children,
and walk in the Light of the glorious day.

Never turn they thoughts to the darkness
and surely ye shall be One with the Light.

Man is only what he believeth,
a brother of darkness or a child of the Light.
Come though into the Light my Children.
Walk in the pathway that leads to the Sun.

Hark ye now, and list to the wisdom.
Use thou the word I have given unto thee.
Use it and surely though shalt find power and
wisdom
and Light to walk in the way.
Seek thee and find the key I have given
and ever shalt thou be a Child of the Light.

The Key to Above and Below

Hear ye and list ye, O children of *Khem*,
to the words that I give that shall bring ye to
the *Light*.
Ye know, O men, that I knew your fathers,
aye, your fathers in a time long ago.
Deathless have I been through all the ages,
living among ye since your knowledge began.

Leading ye upward to the *Light* of the *Great Soul*
have I ever striven,
drawing ye from out of the darkness of night.

Know ye, O people amongst whom I walk,
that I, *Thoth*, have all of the knowledge
and all of the wisdom known, to man since the
ancient days.

Keeper have I been of the secrets of the great race,
holder of the key that leads into life.
Bringer up have I been to ye, O my children,
even from the darkness of the *Ancient of Days*.
List ye now to the words of my wisdom.
List ye now to the message I bring.
Hear ye now the words I give thee, and
ye shall be raised from the darkness to *Light*.

Far in the past, when first I came to thee,
found I thee in caves of rocks.
Lifted I thee by my power and wisdom
until thou didst shine as men among men.
Aye, found I thee without any knowing.
Only a little were ye raised beyond beasts.
Fanned I ever the spark of thy consciousness
until at last ye flamed as men.

Now shall I speak to thee knowledge ancient
beyond the thought of thy race.
Know ye that we of the *Great Race*
had and have knowledge that is more than man's.
Wisdom we gained from the star-born races,
wisdom and knowledge far beyond man.
Down to us had descended the masters of wisdom
as far beyond us as I am from thee.
List ye now while I give ye wisdom.
Use it and free thou shalt be.

Know ye that in the pyramid I builded are the *Keys*
that shall show ye the *Way* into life.
Aye, draw ye a line from the great image I builded,
to the apex of the pyramid, built as a gateway.

Draw ye another opposite in the same angle and
direction.
Dig ye and find that which I have hidden.
There shall ye find the underground entrance to
the secrets hidden before ye were men.

Tell ye I now of the mystery of cycles
that move in movements that are strange to the finite,
for infinite are they beyond knowledge of man.
Know ye that there are nine of the cycles;
aye, nine above and fourteen below,
moving in harmony to the place of joining
that shall exist in the future of time.
Know ye that the *Lords of the Cycles*
are units of consciousness sent from the others to
unify
This with the *All*.
Highest are *They* of the consciousness
of all the *Cycles*, working in harmony with the *Law*.
Know They that in time all will be perfected,
having none above and none below, but all *One*
in a perfected *Infinity*, a harmony of all in the *Oneness*
of All.

Deep neath the Earth surface in the *Halls of Amenti*
sit the *Seven, the Lords of the Cycles,*
aye, and another, the *Lord* from below.
Yet know thee that in *Infinity* there is
neither above nor below.
But ever there is and ever shall be
Oneness of All when all is complete.
Oft have I stood before the *Lords of the All*.

Oft at the fount of their wisdom have drunken and
filled both my body and *Soul* with their *Light*.

Spake they to me and told me of cycles
and the *Law* that gives them the means to exist.
Aye, spake to me the *Lord of the Nine* saying:
O, Thoth, great are ye among Earth children,
but mysteries exist of which ye know not.
Ye know that ye came from a space-time below
this and know ye shall travel to a space-time beyond.
But little ye know of the mysteries within them,
little ye know of the wisdom beyond. Know ye that
ye as a whole in this consciousness
are only a cell in the process of growth.

The consciousness below thee is ever-expanding
in different ways from those known to thee.
Aye, it, though in space-time below thee,
is ever growing in ways that are different from
those that were part of the ways of thine own.
For know that it grows as a result of thy growth
but not in the same way that thou didst grow.
The growth that thou had and have in the present
have brought into being a cause and effect.
No consciousness follows the path of those before it,
else all would be repetition and vain.
Each consciousness in the cycle it exists in
follows its own path to the ultimate goal.
Each plays its part in the Plan of the Cosmos.
Each plays its part in the ultimate end.
The farther the cycle, the greater its
knowledge and ability to blend the Law of the whole.

Know ye, that ye in the cycles below us
are working the minor parts of the Law,
while we of the cycle that extends to Infinity
take of the striving and build greater Law.

Each has his own part to play in the cycles.
Each has his work to complete in his way.
The cycle below thee is yet not below thee
but only formed for a need that exists.
For know ye that the fountain of wisdom
that sends forth the cycles is eternally
seeking new powers to gain.
Ye know that knowledge is gained only by practice,
and wisdom comes forth only from knowledge,
and thus are the cycles created by Law.
Means are they for the gaining of knowledge
for the Plane of Law that is the Source of the All.

The cycle below is not truly below but only
different in space and in time.
The consciousness there is working and
testing lesser things than those ye are.
And know, just as ye are working on greater,
so above ye are those who are also working
as ye are on yet other laws.
The difference that exists between the cycles
is only in ability to work with the Law.
We, who have being in cycles beyond thee,
are those who first came forth from the
Source and have in the passage through
time-space gained ability to use
Laws of the Greater that are far beyond
the conception of man.

Nothing there is that is really below thee
but only a different operation of Law.

Look thee above or look thee below,
the same shall ye find.
For all is but part of the Oneness
that is at the Source of the Law.
The consciousness below thee is
part thine own as we are a part of thine.

Ye, as a child had not the knowledge
that came to ye when ye became a man.
Compare ye the cycles to man in his journey
from birth unto death,
and see in the cycle below thee the child
with the knowledge he has;
and see ye yourself as the child grown older,
advancing in knowledge as time passes on.
See ye, We, also, the child grown to manhood
with the knowledge and wisdom that came
with the years.
So also, O Thoth, are the cycles of consciousness,
children in different stages of growth,
yet all from the one Source, the Wisdom,
and all to the Wisdom returning again.

Ceased then *He* from speaking and sat
in the silence that comes to the *Lords*.
Then again spake *He* unto me, saying:
Oh Thoth, long have We sat in Amenti,
guarding the flame of life in the Halls.
Yet know, we are still part of our
Cycles with our Vision reaching unto them and beyond.
Aye, know we that of all,

nothing else matters excepting the growth
we can gain with our Soul.
Know we the flesh is fleeting.
The things men count great are nothing to us.
The things we seek are not of the body
but are only the perfected state of the Soul.
When ye as men can learn that nothing but
progress of Soul can count in the end,
then truly ye are free from all bondage,
free to work in a harmony of Law.

Know, O man, ye should aim at perfection,
for only thus can ye attain to the goal.
Though ye should know that nothing is perfect,
yet it should be thy aim and thy goal.
Ceased again the voice of the *Nine*,
and into my consciousness the words had sunk.
Now, seek I ever more wisdom
that I may be perfect in *Law* with the *All*.

Soon go I down to the *Halls of Amenti*
to live beneath the cold flower of life.
Ye whom I have taught shall nevermore see me.
Yet live I forever in the wisdom I taught.

All that man is is because of his wisdom.
All that he shall be is the result of his cause.

List ye, now to my voice and become
greater than common man.
Lift thine eyes upward,
let *Light* fill thy being,
be thou ever *Children of Light*.
Only by effort shall ye grow upward to

the plane where *Light* is the *All* of the *All*.
Be ye the master of all that surrounds thee.
Never be mastered by the effects of thy life.
Create then ever more perfect causes
and in time shalt thou be a *Sun of the Light*

Free, let thine soul soar ever upward,
free from the bondage and fetters of night.
Lift thine eyes to the *Sun* in the sky-space.
For thee, let it be a symbol of life.
Know that thou art the *Greater Light*,
perfect in thine own sphere,
when thou art free.
Look not ever into the blackness.
Lift up thine eyes to the space above.
Free let thine *Light* flame upward
and shalt thou be a *Child of the Light*.

The Law of Cause and Effect, The Key of Prophecy

Hear ye and list ye, O children of *Khem*,
to the words that I give that shall bring ye to
the *Light*.
Ye know, O men, that I knew your fathers,
aye, your fathers in a time long ago.
Deathless have I been through all the ages,
living among ye since your knowledge began.

Leading ye upward to the *Light* of the *Great Soul*
have I ever striven,
drawing ye from out of the darkness of night.

Know ye, O people amongst whom I walk,
that I, *Thoth*, have all of the knowledge

and all of the wisdom known, to man since the
ancient days.
Keeper have I been of the secrets of the great race,
holder of the key that leads into life.
Bringer up have I been to ye, O my children,
even from the darkness of the *Ancient of Days*.
List ye now to the words of my wisdom.
List ye now to the message I bring.
Hear ye now the words I give thee, and
ye shall be raised from the darkness to *Light*.

Far in the past, when first I came to thee,
found I thee in caves of rocks.
Lifted I thee by my power and wisdom
until thou didst shine as men among men.
Aye, found I thee without any knowing.
Only a little were ye raised beyond beasts.
Fanned I ever the spark of thy consciousness
until at last ye flamed as men.

Now shall I speak to thee knowledge ancient
beyond the thought of thy race.
Know ye that we of the *Great Race*
had and have knowledge that is more than man's.
Wisdom we gained from the star-born races,
wisdom and knowledge far beyond man.
Down to us had descended the masters of wisdom
as far beyond us as I am from thee.
List ye now while I give ye wisdom.
Use it and free thou shalt be.

Know ye that in the pyramid I builded are the *Keys*
that shall show ye the *Way* into life.

Aye, draw ye a line from the great image I builded,
to the apex of the pyramid, built as a gateway.
Draw ye another opposite in the same angle and
direction.
Dig ye and find that which I have hidden.
There shall ye find the underground entrance to
the secrets hidden before ye were men.

Tell ye I now of the mystery of cycles
that move in movements that are strange to the finite,
for infinite are they beyond knowledge of man.
Know ye that there are nine of the cycles;
aye, nine above and fourteen below,
moving in harmony to the place of joining
that shall exist in the future of time.
Know ye that the *Lords of the Cycles*
are units of consciousness sent from the others to
unify
This with the *All.*
Highest are *They* of the consciousness
of all the *Cycles,* working in harmony with the *Law.*
Know They that in time all will be perfected,
having none above and none below, but all *One*
in a perfected *Infinity,* a harmony of all in the *Oneness*
of All.

Deep neath the Earth surface in the *Halls of Amenti*
sit the *Seven, the Lords of the Cycles,*
aye, and another, the *Lord* from below.
Yet know thee that in *Infinity* there is
neither above nor below.
But ever there is and ever shall be
Oneness of All when all is complete.

Oft have I stood before the *Lords of the All*.
Oft at the fount of their wisdom have drunken and
filled both my body and *Soul* with their *Light*.

Spake they to me and told me of cycles
and the *Law* that gives them the means to exist.
Aye, spake to me the *Lord of the Nine* saying:
O, Thoth, great are ye among Earth children,
but mysteries exist of which ye know not.
Ye know that ye came from a space-time below
this and know ye shall travel to a space-time beyond.
But little ye know of the mysteries within them,
little ye know of the wisdom beyond. Know ye that
ye as a whole in this consciousness
are only a cell in the process of growth.

The consciousness below thee is ever-expanding
in different ways from those known to thee.
Aye, it, though in space-time below thee,
is ever growing in ways that are different from
those that were part of the ways of thine own.
For know that it grows as a result of thy growth
but not in the same way that thou didst grow.
The growth that thou had and have in the present
have brought into being a cause and effect.
No consciousness follows the path of those before it,
else all would be repetition and vain.
Each consciousness in the cycle it exists in
follows its own path to the ultimate goal.
Each plays its part in the Plan of the Cosmos.
Each plays its part in the ultimate end.
The farther the cycle, the greater its
knowledge and ability to blend the Law of the whole.

Know ye, that ye in the cycles below us
are working the minor parts of the Law,
while we of the cycle that extends to Infinity
take of the striving and build greater Law.

Each has his own part to play in the cycles.
Each has his work to complete in his way.
The cycle below thee is yet not below thee
but only formed for a need that exists.
For know ye that the fountain of wisdom
that sends forth the cycles is eternally
seeking new powers to gain.
Ye know that knowledge is gained only by practice,
and wisdom comes forth only from knowledge,
and thus are the cycles created by Law.
Means are they for the gaining of knowledge
for the Plane of Law that is the Source of the All.

The cycle below is not truly below but only
different in space and in time.
The consciousness there is working and
testing lesser things than those ye are.
And know, just as ye are working on greater,
so above ye are those who are also working
as ye are on yet other laws.
The difference that exists between the cycles
is only in ability to work with the Law.
We, who have being in cycles beyond thee,
are those who first came forth from the
Source and have in the passage through
time-space gained ability to use
Laws of the Greater that are far beyond
the conception of man.

Nothing there is that is really below thee
but only a different operation of Law.

Look thee above or look thee below,
the same shall ye find.
For all is but part of the Oneness
that is at the Source of the Law.
The consciousness below thee is
part thine own as we are a part of thine.

Ye, as a child had not the knowledge
that came to ye when ye became a man.
Compare ye the cycles to man in his journey
from birth unto death,
and see in the cycle below thee the child
with the knowledge he has;
and see ye yourself as the child grown older,
advancing in knowledge as time passes on.
See ye, We, also, the child grown to manhood
with the knowledge and wisdom that came
with the years.
So also, O Thoth, are the cycles of consciousness,
children in different stages of growth,
yet all from the one Source, the Wisdom,
and all to the Wisdom returning again.

Ceased then *He* from speaking and sat
in the silence that comes to the *Lords.*
Then again spake *He* unto me, saying:
Oh Thoth, long have We sat in Amenti,
guarding the flame of life in the Halls.
Yet know, we are still part of our
Cycles with our Vision reaching unto them and beyond.
Aye, know we that of all,

nothing else matters excepting the growth
we can gain with our Soul.
Know we the flesh is fleeting.
The things men count great are nothing to us.
The things we seek are not of the body
but are only the perfected state of the Soul.
When ye as men can learn that nothing but
progress of Soul can count in the end,
then truly ye are free from all bondage,
free to work in a harmony of Law.

Know, O man, ye should aim at perfection,
for only thus can ye attain to the goal.
Though ye should know that nothing is perfect,
yet it should be thy aim and thy goal.
Ceased again the voice of the *Nine*,
and into my consciousness the words had sunk.
Now, seek I ever more wisdom
that I may be perfect in *Law* with the *All*.

Soon go I down to the *Halls of Amenti*
to live beneath the cold flower of life.
Ye whom I have taught shall nevermore see me.
Yet live I forever in the wisdom I taught.

All that man is is because of his wisdom.
All that he shall be is the result of his cause.

List ye, now to my voice and become
greater than common man.
Lift thine eyes upward,
let *Light* fill thy being,
be thou ever *Children of Light*.
Only by effort shall ye grow upward to

the plane where *Light* is the *All* of the *All*.
Be ye the master of all that surrounds thee.
Never be mastered by the effects of thy life.
Create then ever more perfect causes
and in time shalt thou be a *Sun of the Light*

Free, let thine soul soar ever upward,
free from the bondage and fetters of night.
Lift thine eyes to the *Sun* in the sky-space.
For thee, let it be a symbol of life.
Know that thou art the *Greater Light,*
perfect in thine own sphere,
when thou art free.
Look not ever into the blackness.
Lift up thine eyes to the space above.
Free let thine *Light* flame upward
and shalt thou be a *Child of the Light*.

The Keys of Life and Death

List ye, O man, hear ye the wisdom.
Hear ye the *Word* that shall fill thee with *Life*.
Hear ye the *Word* that shall banish the darkness.
Hear ye the voice that shall banish the night.

Mystery and wisdom have I brought to my children;
knowledge and power descended from old.
Know ye not that all shall be opened
when ye shall find the oneness of all?

One shall ye be with the *Masters of Mystery,*
Conquerors of Death and Masters of Life.
Aye, ye shall learn of the flower of *Amenti*
the blossom of life that shines in the *Halls*.

In *Spirit* shall ye reach that *Halls of Amenti*
and bring back the wisdom that liveth in *Light*.
Know ye the gateway to power is secret.
Know ye the gateway to life is through death.
Aye, through death but not as ye know death,
but a death that is life and is fire and is *Light*.

Desireth thou to know the deep, hidden secret?
Look in thy *heart* where the knowledge is bound.
Know that in thee the secret is hidden,
the source of all life and the source of all death.

List ye, O man, while I tell the secret,
reveal unto thee the secret of old.

Deep in *Earth's* heart lies the flower,
the source of the *Spirit*
that binds all in its form.
or know ye that the *Earth* is living in body
as thou art alive in thine own formed form.
The *Flower of Life* is as thine own place of *Spirit*
and streams through the *Earth*
as thine flows through thy form;
giving of life to the *Earth* and its children,
renewing the *Spirit* from form unto form.
This is the *Spirit* that is form of thy body,
shaping and moulding into its form.

Know ye, O man, that thy form is dual,
balanced in polarity while formed in its form.
Know that when fast on thee *Death* approaches,
it is only because thy balance is shaken.
It is only because one pole has been lost.

Know that the secret of life in *Amenti*
is the secret of restoring the balance of poles.
All that exists has form and is living
because of the *Spirit* of life in its poles.

See ye not that in *Earth's heart*
is the balance of all things that exist
and have being on its face?
The source of thy *Spirit* is drawn from *Earth's heart*,
for in thy form thou are one with the *Earth*

When thou hast learned to hold thine own balance,
then shalt thou draw on the balance of *Earth*.
Exist then shalt thou while *Earth* is existing,
changing in form, only when *Earth*, too, shalt change:
Tasting not of death, but one with this planet,
holding thy form till all pass away.

List ye, O man, whilst I give the secret so that
ye, too, shalt taste not of change.
One hour each day shalt thou lie
with thine head pointed to the
place of the positive pole (north).
One hour each day shalt thy head be
pointed to the place of the negative pole (south).
Whilst thy head is placed to the northward,
hold thou thy consciousness from the chest to the
head.

And when thy head is placed southward,
hold thou thy thought from chest to the feet.
Hold thou in balance once in each seven,
and thy balance will retain the whole of its strength.
Aye, if thou be old, thy body will freshen

and thy strength will become as a youth's.
This is the secret known to the Masters
by which they hold off the fingers of Death.
Neglect not to follow the path I have shown,
for when thou hast passed beyond years
to a hundred to neglect
it will mean the coming of *Death.*

Hear ye, my words, and follow the pathway.
Keep thou thy balance and live on in life.

Hear ye, O man, and list to my voice.
List to the wisdom that gives thee of *Death.*
When at the end of thy work appointed,
thou may desire to pass from this life,
pass to the plane where the *Suns of the Morning*
live and have being as *Children of Light.*
Pass without pain and pass without sorrow
into the plane where is eternal *Light.*

First lie at rest with thine head to the eastward.
Fold thou thy hands at the Source of thy life (solar plexus).

Place thou thy consciousness in the life seat.
Whirl it and divide to north and to south.

Send thou the one out toward the northward.
Send thou the other out to the south.
Relax thou their hold upon thy being.
Forth from thy form will thy silver spark fly,
upward and onward to the Sun of the morning,
blending with Light, at one with its source.

There it shall flame till desire shall be created.
Then shall return to a place in a form.

Know ye, O men, that thus pass the great Souls,
changing at will from life unto life.
Thus ever passes the Avatar,
willing his Death as he wills his own life.

List ye, O man, drink of my wisdom.
Learn ye the secret that is Master of Time.
Learn ye how those ye call Masters are
able to remember the lives of the past.

Great is the secret yet easy to master,
giving to thee the mastery of time.
When upon thee death fast approaches,
fear not but know ye are master of Death.

Relax thy body, resist not with tension.
Place in thy heart the flame of thy Soul.
Swiftly then sweep it to the seat of the triangle.

Hold for a moment, then move to the goal.
This, thy goal, is the place between thine eyebrows,
the place where the memory of life must hold sway.
Hold thou thy flame here in thy brain-seat
until the fingers of Death grasp thy Soul.
Then as thou pass through the state of transition,
surely the memories of life shall pass, too.

Then shalt the past be as one with the present.
Then shall the memory of all be retained.
Free shalt thou be from all retrogression.
The things of the past shall live in today.

Supplementary

List ye, O Man, to the deep hidden wisdom,
lost to the world since the time of the *Dwellers*,
lost and forgotten by men of this age.

Know ye this Earth is but a portal,
guarded by powers unknown to man.
Yet, the *Dark Lords* hide the entrance
that leads to the *Heaven-born* land.
Know ye, the way to the sphere of *Arulu*
is guarded by barriers opened only to *Light-born* man.

Upon Earth, I am the holder of the keys
to the gates of the *Sacred Land*.
Command I, by the powers beyond me,
to leave the keys to the world of man.

Before I depart, I give ye the Secrets of how
ye may rise from the bondage of darkness,
cast off the fetters of flesh that have bound ye,
rise from the darkness into the *Light*.

Know ye, the soul must be cleansed of its darkness,
ere ye may enter the portals of Light.
Thus, I established among ye the *Mysteries*
so that the *Secrets* may always be found.

Aye, though man may fall into darkness,
always the *Light* will shine as a guide.
Hidden in darkness, veiled in symbols,
always the way to the portal will be found.
Man in the future will deny the mysteries
but always the way the seeker will find.

Now I command ye to maintain my secrets,
giving only to those ye have tested,
so that the pure may not be corrupted,
so that the power of *Truth* may prevail.

List ye now to the unveiling of Mystery.
List to the symbols of Mystery I give.
Make of it a religion for only thus will its essence remain.

Regions there are two between
this life and the Great One,
traveled by the Souls
who depart from this Earth;
Duat, the home of the powers of illusion;
Sekhet Hetspet, the House of the Gods.
Osiris, the symbol of the guard of the portal,
who turns back the souls of unworthy men.

Beyond lies the sphere of the heaven-born powers,
Arulu, the land where the Great Ones have passed.
There, when my work among men has been finished,
will I join the Great Ones of my Ancient home.

Seven are the mansions of the house of the Mighty;
Three guards the portal of each house from the darkness;
Fifteen the ways that lead to Duat.
Twelve are the houses of the Lords of Illusion,
facing four ways, each of them different.

Forty and Two are the great powers,
judging the Dead who seek for the portal.
Four are the Sons of Horus,
Two are the Guards of East and West of Isis,
the mother who pleads for her children, Queen of the

Moon,
reflecting the Sun.

Ba is the Essence, living forever.
Ka is the Shadow that man knows as life.
Ba cometh not until Ka is incarnate.
These are mysteries to preserve through the ages.

Keys are they of life and of Death.
Hear ye now the mystery of mysteries:
learn of the circle beginningless and endless,
the form of He who is One and in all.
Listen and hear it, go forth and apply it,
thus will ye travel the way that I go.

Mystery in Mystery,
yet clear to the Light-born,
the Secret of all I now will reveal.
I will declare a secret to the initiated,
but let the door be wholly shut against the profane.

Three is the mystery, come from the great one.
Hear, and *Light* on thee will dawn.

In the primeval, dwell three unities.
Other than these, none can exist.
These are the equilibrium, source of creation:
one God, one Truth, one point of freedom.

Three come forth from the three of the balance:
all life, all good, all power.

Three are the qualities of *God* in his *Light*-home:
Infinite power, Infinite Wisdom, Infinite Love.

Three are the powers given to the *Masters*:
To transmute evil, assist good, use discrimination.

Three are the things inevitable for *God* to perform:
Manifest power, wisdom and love.

Three are the powers creating all things:
Divine Love possessed of perfect knowledge,
Divine Wisdom knowing all possible means,
Divine Power possessed by the joint will of
Divine Love and Wisdom.

Three are the circles (states) of existence:
The circle of Light where dwells nothing but God,
and only God can traverse it;
the circle of Chaos where all things
by nature arise from death;
the Circle of awareness where
all things spring from life.

All things animate are of three states of existence:
chaos or death, liberty in humanity and felicity of Heaven.

Three necessities control all things:
beginning in the Great Deep, the circle of chaos, plenitude
in Heaven.

Three are the paths of the *Soul*:
Man, Liberty, Light.

Three are the hindrances:
lack of endeavor to obtain knowledge;
non-attachment to god; attachment to evil.
In man, the three are manifest.

Three are the *Kings* of power within.
Three are the chambers of the mysteries,
found yet not found in the body of man.

Hear ye now of he who is liberated,
freed from the bondage of life into *Light*.
Knowing the source of all worlds shall be open.
Aye, even the *Gates of Arulu* shall not be barred.
Yet heed, O man, who would'st enter heaven.
If ye be not worthy,
better it be to fall into the fire.
Know ye the celestials pass through the pure flame.
At every revolution of the heavens,
they bathe in the fountains of *Light*.

List ye, O man, to this mystery:
Long in the past before ye were man-born,
I dwelled in Ancient <u>Atlantis.</u>
There in the *Temple*,
I drank of the *Wisdom*,
poured as a fountain of *Light*
from the *Dweller*.

Give the key to ascend to the
Presence of *Light* in the Great world.
Stood I before the *Holy One*
enthroned in the Flower of Fire.
Veiled was he by the lightnings of darkness,
else my *Soul* by the *Glory* have been shattered.

Forth from the feet of his *Throne* like the diamond,
rolled forth four rivers of flame from his footstool,
rolled through the channels of clouds to the Man-
world.

Filled was the hall with *Spirits of Heaven.*
Wonder of wonders was the Starry palace.

Above the sky, like a rainbow of *Fire* and *Sunlight,*
were Formed the Spirits.
Sang they the glories of the *Holy One.*
Then from the midst of the *Fire* came a voice:
Behold the Glory of the first Cause.
I beheld that *Light,* high above all darkness,
reflected in my own being.
I attained, as it were, to the *God of all Gods,*
the Spirit-Sun, the Sovereign of the Sun spheres.

There is One, Even the First,
who hath no beginning,
who hath no end;
who hath made all things,
who govern all,
who is good,
who is just,
who illumines,
who sustains.

Then from the throne, there poured a great radiance,
surrounding and lifting my soul by its power.
Swiftly I moved through the spaces of *Heaven,*
shown was I the mystery of mysteries,
shown the *Secret* heart of the cosmos.

Carried was I to the land of *Arulu,*
stood before the *Lords* in their *Houses.*

Opened they the *Doorway* so I might
glimpse the primeval chaos.

Shuddered my soul to the vision of horror,
shrank back my soul from the ocean of darkness.
Then saw I the need for the barriers,
saw the need for the *Lords of Arulu*..

Only they with their Infinite balance could
stand in the way of the inpouring chaos.
Only they could guard *God's* creation.

Then did I pass around the circle of eight.
Saw all the souls who had conquered the darkness.
Saw the splendor of *Light* where they dwelled.

Longed I to take my place in their circle,
but longed I also for the way I had chosen,
when I stood in the *Halls of Amenti*
and made my choice to the work I would do.

Passed I from the *Halls of Arulu*
down to the earth space where my body lay.
Arose I from the earth where I rested.
Stood I before the *Dweller*.

Gave my pledge to renounce my Great
right until my work on *Earth* was completed,
until the *Age* of darkness be past.

List ye, O man, to the words I shall give ye.
In them shall ye find the *Essence* of Life.
Before I return to the *Halls of Amenti*,
taught shall ye be the *Secrets of Secrets*,
how ye, too, may arise to the *Light*.

Preserve them and guard them,
hide them in symbols,
so the profane will laugh and renounce.
In every land, form ye the mysteries.
Make the way hard for the seeker to tread.

Thus will the weak and the wavering be rejected.
Thus will the secrets be hidden and guarded,
held till the time when the wheel shall be turned.

Through the dark ages, waiting and watching,
my *Spirit* shall remain in the deep hidden land.
When one has passed all the trials of the outer,
summon ye me by the *Key* that ye hold.

Then will I, the *Initiator*, answer,
come from the *Halls of the Gods in Amenti.*
Then will I receive the initiate, give him the words of
power.

Hark ye, remember, these words of warning:
bring not to me one lacking in wisdom,
impure in heart or weak in his purpose.
Else I will withdraw from ye your power
to summon me from the place of my sleeping.

Now go ye forth and summon thy brothers
so that I may impart the wisdom to light thy
path when my presence is gone.
Come to the chamber beneath my temple.
Eat not food until three days are past.

There will I give thee the essence of wisdom
so that with power ye may shine amongst men.

There will I give unto thee the secrets so that
ye, to, may rise to the
Heavens, God-men in Truth
as in essence ye be.
Depart now and leave me while I summon
those ye know of but as yet know not.

Secret of Secrets

Now ye assemble, my children,
waiting to hear the *Secret of Secrets*
which shall give ye power to unfold the God-man,
give ye the way to Eternal life.

Plainly shall I speak of the *Unveiled Mysteries*.
No dark sayings shall I give unto thee.
Open thine ears now, my children.
Hear and obey the words that I give.

First I shall speak of the fetters of darkness
which bind ye in chains to the sphere of the Earth.

Darkness and light are both of one nature,
different only in seeming,
for each arose from the source of all.
Darkness is disorder.
Light is Order.
Darkness transmuted is light of the Light.
This, my children, your purpose in being;
transmutation of darkness to light.

Hear ye now of the mystery of nature,
the relations of life to the Earth where it dwells.

Know ye, ye are threefold in nature,
physical, astral and mental in one.

Three are the qualities of each of the natures;
nine in all, as above, so below.

In the physical are these channels,
the blood which moves in vortical motion,
reacting on the heart to continue its beating.
Magnetism which moves through the nerve paths,
carrier of energies to all cells and tissues.
Akasa which flows through channels,
subtle yet physical, completing the channels.

Each of the three attuned with each other,
each affecting the life of the body.
Form they the skeletal framework through
which the subtle ether flows.
In their mastery lies the *Secret of Life* in the body.
Relinquished only by will of the adept,
when his purpose in living is done.

Three are the natures of the *Astral*,
mediator is between above and below;
not of the physical, not of the Spiritual,
but able to move above and below.

Three are the natures of *Mind*,
carrier it of the *Will* of the *Great One*.
Arbitrator of *Cause and Effect* in thy life.
Thus is formed the threefold being,
directed from above by the power of four.

Above and beyond man's threefold nature
lies the realm of the *Spiritual Self.*

Four is it in qualities,
shining in each of the planes of existence,
but thirteen in one,
the mystical number.
Based on the qualities of man are the *Brothers*:
each shall direct the unfoldment of being,
each shall channels be of the *Great One.*

On Earth, man is in bondage,
bound by space and time to the earth plane.
Encircling each planet, a wave of vibration,
binds him to his plane of unfoldment.
Yet within man is the *Key* to releasement,
within man may freedom be found.

When ye have released the self from the body,
rise to the outermost bounds of your earth-plane.
Speak ye the word Dor-E-Lil-La.

Then for a time your Light will be lifted,
free may ye pass the barriers of space.
For a time of half of the sun (six hours),
free may ye pass the barriers of earth-plane,
see and know those who are beyond thee.

Yea, to the highest worlds may ye pass.
See your own possible heights of unfoldment,
know all earthly futures of Soul.

Bound are ye in your body,
but by the power ye may be free.

This is the *Secret* whereby bondage
shall be replaced by freedom for thee.

Calm let thy mind be.
At rest be thy body:
Conscious only of freedom from flesh.
Center thy being on the goal of thy longing.
Think over and over that thou wouldst be free.
Think of this word La-Um-I-L-Ganoover
and over in thy mind let it sound.
Drift with the sound to the place of thy longing.
Free from the bondage of flesh by thy will.

Hear ye while I give the greatest of secrets:
how ye may enter the *Halls of Amenti*,
enter the place of the immortals as I did,
stand before the *Lords* in their places.

Lie ye down in rest of thy body.
Calm thy mind so no thought disturbs thee.
Pure must ye be in mind and in purpose,
else only failure will come unto thee.

Vision Amenti as I have told in my Tablets.
Long with fullness of heart to be there.
Stand before the Lords in thy mind's eye.

Pronounce the words of power I give (mentally);
Mekut-El-Shab-El Hale-Sur-Ben-El-Zabrut Zin-Efrim-
Quar-El.
Relax thy mind and thy body.
Then be sure your soul will be called.

Now give I the *Key to Shambbalah*,
the place where my *Brothers* live in the darkness:
Darkness but filled with *Light of the Sun*
Darkness of Earth, but *Light of the Spirit*,
guides for ye when my day is done.

Leave thou thy body as I have taught thee.
Pass to the barriers of the deep, hidden place.
Stand before the gates and their guardians.
Command thy entrance by these words:

I am the Light. In me is no darkness.
Free am I of the bondage of night.
Open thou the way of the Twelve and the One,
so I may pass to the realm of wisdom.

When they refuse thee, as surely they will,
command them to open by these words of power:
I am the Light. For me are no barriers.
Open, I command, by the Secret of Secrets
Edom-El-Ahim-Sabbert-Zur Adom.

Then if thy words have been *Truth* of the highest,
open for thee the barriers will fall.

Now, I leave thee, my children.
Down, yet up, to the *Halls* shall I go.
Win ye the way to me, my children.
Truly my brothers shall ye become.

Thus finish I my writings.
Keys let them be to those who come after.
But only to those who seek my wisdom,
for only for these am *I the Key and the Way.*"

*The Emerald Tablets of Thoth the Atlantean, Dr.
Doreal, Great White Lodge, 1930*

CHAPTER FIVE
The Glory of the World, the Table of Paradise or the Science of the Philosophers Stone

"THE GLORY OF THE WORLD;

OR,

TABLE OF PARADISE;

THAT IS TO SAY,

*A TRUE ACCOUNT OF THE ANCIENT SCIENCE
WHICH ADAM LEARNED
FROM GOD HIMSELF; WHICH NOAH, ABRAHAM,
AND SOLOMON
HELD AS ONE OF THE GREATEST GIFTS OF GOD;
WHICH
ALSO ALL SAGES, AT ALL TIMES, PREFERRED TO
THE
WEALTH OF THE WHOLE WORLD, REGARDED
AS
THE CHIEF TREASURE OF THE WHOLE
WORLD, AND BEQUEATHED ONLY TO
GOOD MEN;*

NAMELY,

THE SCIENCE OF THE PHILOSOPHER'S STONE.

---

2 PET. iii., 5:

*"For this they willingly, through their
wickedness, are ignorant of, that through
the Word at God the heavens were of old,
and the earth standing out of the water, and
in the water."*

THE GLORY OF THE WORLD,

OR,

TABLE OF PARADISE:

A most precious book, containing art, the like of
which is not to be found upon earth; shewing the
truth concerning the true Philosophy, and the most
noble medicine, and priceless Tincture, together with
divers other valuable Arts, and the Instruments
required for them.

NOW, in the name of God, the Almighty Creator and Preserver of this World, I venture to shew forth the hidden mysteries of Nature, which God has planted there, and deigns to reveal to men, that they may see how marvellously things are created, and how wonderfully all classes of natural objects are brought forth: for a testimony to all believing Christian men, and for a comfort to all afflicted and troubled hearts — seeing that all things created perish and are decomposed only to be renewed again, to be multiplied, animated, and perfected after their kind. For nothing that is created, or born, is at rest, but daily undergoes increase or multiplication on the part of Nature, until it becomes that which is created and ordained to be the treasure of all mankind.

Therefore, beseech God to give you such wisdom and understanding as will enable you to understand this Art, and to bring it, by His blessing, to a good issue for His own glory, and the good of your neighbour.

If then you would obtain this knowledge at the hand of God, you must confess yourself a miserable sinner, and implore His blessing, which alone can enable you to receive His Gift unworthily, and to bear in mind that He has bestowed it upon you out of pure mercy, and that any pride or presumptuous insolence on your part will most certainly entail its loss, in addition to His wrath, and eternal condemnation. You must resolve to begin this blessed and divine work in the name of God, for the service of all good Christians, and the building up of our faith; to be a good athlete in the war against unbelievers; to shun the company of wicked men; never to open your mouth against the righteous; but to bestow your bounty upon the needy in order that after this life you may receive the crown of eternal joy and beatitude. For this treasure, which is above all other earthly treasures, is granted to him alone who approves himself humble, honest, gentle, and faithful, as far as the weakness of human nature allows, and keeps the laws of God through God's bounty and blessing, and who is not likely to mistake the true nature of the gift, or to abuse it against his own eternal welfare. It is the gift of the Holy Spirit, the loving bounty of the great God, which comes down from the Father of light. He who masters this Art, must have asked and obtained wisdom of God, since he has not only gold, silver, and all the riches of this world, but also perfect health, length of days, and, what is better still, the comfort to he derived from a reassuring type of the bitter passion and death of our Lord and Saviour Jesus Christ, His descent into hell, His glorious and most holy Resurrection on the third day, and His victory and triumph over sin, death, Devil, and hell — a victory that must carry joy and comfort to all that have the breath of life.

Let me now shew you how wonderfully the human and divine natures of Jesus Christ were united and joined together in one Person. The soul and body of Christ and His divine nature were so inseparably joined together that they cannot be severed throughout all eternity. Nevertheless Christ had to die, and His soul had to be separated from His body, and once more joined to it on the third day, that His body might be glorified, and rendered as subtle as His soul and spirit. For He had received His body of the substance of the most Blessed Virgin Mary, and therefore it had to be perfected by temporary separation from His soul and spirit. Nevertheless, His divinity remained united in one essence with the body and soul of

Christ—it was with the body in the tomb, and with His soul in Paradise.

The body of Christ had to be separated from its soul in order that it might receive the same power and glory. But now, Christ having been dead, and His soul having afterwards been reunited to His body, they are henceforth inseparably conjoined into one subtle essence. His divine omnipotence which He received from His Father, which governs all things in heaven and earth, and is equally perfect from all eternity, is now one Person with the Christ Jesus, who suffered, died, rose again, and ascended into heaven, in endless power, glory, majesty, might, and honour.

Therefore, O sinful man, render thanks to Almighty God for the grace and fatherly loving kindness shewn to you; and rest assured that you may obtain the glorification which was given to Christ. For Christ rose first that he might open up for you a way unto His heavenly Father. Like Him, you too must be crucified to this world by many hardships, tribulations, and anxieties. But that you may understand the glorification of the body, and its renewal to eternal life, you should diligently consider God's fatherly love and mercy towards fallen man. Bear in mind that all things that come down from Him are good and perfect gifts. Take care, therefore, lest you foully abuse the gifts bestowed upon you freely, without any merit of your own, to the destruction of your soul; rather let all your actions shew that you love and fear God, and then every labour to which you set your hand will prosper, and from beginning to end you will pursue the work successfully and joyously. Commit your care to God, trust His word, and keep His holy commandments: then God will be with you in all things, will bless your toil, and in His fatherly love forefend all loss and harm. Your art will then afford you true comfort, yield you all you need, refresh you amid all your hardships, supply you with the means of relieving the necessities of others, and constantly keep before your eyes a living type of your own glorious resurrection, and of that of all Christian believers—whereby we must exchange this earthly and mortal life for endless joy and the glory of eternal and incorruptible beatitude.

Let me then tell you, who would be a true lover of this Art, that it was first delivered by God to Adam in Paradise. For it is a true revelation of many secrets and mysteries. It shews you the vanity of your body and of your life in this world; but it also solaces you with the hope of eternal salvation. It suggests to you the reflection that if God has infused such wonderful virtues into mere inanimate natural objects, surely we, who are so much better than they, must be reserved for some high and glorious destiny. I beseech you, therefore, to acquit yourself wisely in all that you do—not to be in haste,—but to reveal this mystery to no mortal man, unless he be a lover of this Art and of a godly, sincere, and merciful temper. Such was the practice of the ancient Sages to whom this wisdom was revealed by the inspiration of the Holy Spirit. You must also confess that this Art is real, for the sake of those who will not believe that Jesus Christ proceeded from His Almighty Heavenly Father, and was also born of a pure virgin. Moreover, you must ask God to enlighten you by the gift of His Holy Spirit, to sharpen your understanding, to open your eyes, and to grant you a profound insight into that unfathomable wisdom which lies hid in our Art, and which no Sage has ever been able to express in his writings. For there are many secrets in Nature which it is impossible for our unaided human reason to apprehend. If you follow my directions and suffer yourself to be guided by the grace of God, then the work which you undertake for the glory of God, and for the good of your neighbour, will have a joyful issue. Feed the hungry; give drink to the thirsty; clothe the naked; comfort the afflicted; visit the sick and the prisoners: and you shall have what you desire.

ROBERT VALENS RUGL.

"A spirit is within, which by deliberate skill you must separate from the body. Simply disjoin the material part from the vapour. You should then add the cold water of the spring. With this you should unweariedly sprinkle both. You will then have the true Elixir of all this Art."

Exhortation and Information

to all the lovers of this Art, in which they can see, as in a mirror, all the fundamental and essential requirements thereof; whether it is possible or not to arrive at the true Art, and concerning the same.

I would warn all and sundry, but especially you, my beloved disciples, in clear and impressive language, to be on your guard against all fantastical teaching, and to listen to the truthful information which I shall now proceed to give you.

In the first place, you must give a wide berth to the false Alchemy of the vulgar herd. I have experienced this so much that I am loath to recommend any to undertake the work, since this Art is so well hidden that no mortal on earth can discover it unless Sol and Luna meet. If you give diligent heed to my warning you may attain to a knowledge thereof, but if you do not, you will never approach any nearer to it. Know also that there is only *one*thing in the whole world that enters into the composition of the Stone, and that, therefore, all coagulation, and admixture, of different ingredients, would shew you to be on a wrong scent altogether. If you could perform all the different operations of our art, yet all your dissolving, coagulating, decomposing, distilling, augmenting, albefying, &c., would be useless, without a true knowledge of our Matter. For our Art is good and precious, nor can any one become a partaker of it, unless it be revealed to him by God, or unless he be taught by a skilled Master. It is a treasure such as the whole world cannot buy. Do not, therefore, my sons, spend your toil until you know what that is on which you are to operate. For even if you knew the right Matter, your information would be useless to you without a knowledge of the method of preparing it. The Stone in its final and effective form is not to be found anywhere in the whole world, either in the heavens above, or in the earth beneath; nor in any metal, nor in anything that grows, nor yet even in gold or silver. It must he prepared, *i.e.*, developed, into its final form; yet for all that, it cannot, strictly speaking, be made better than God created it, nor can the Tincture be prepared out of it: the 'Tincture' must be added to it, and therefore has nothing to dowith our main object, since it is a different thing altogether. If it were in. any metal, we should surely have to look for it in the Sun or Moon; yet the Moon cannot contain it, or it would long since have become the Sun. Neither is it in mercury, or in any sulphur, or salt, or in herbs, or anything of that nature, as you shall see hereafter. Now we will conclude our exhortation, and proceed to describe the Art itself.

There follow some Methods of Recognising our Stone.

I.

Know that our Stone is one, and that it is justly called a Stone. For it *is* a Stone, and could bear no name so characteristic, as that of the Stone of the Sages. Yet it is not any one of our existing stones, but only derives its appellation from its similarity to them. For our Stone is so prepared as to be composed of the four elements. On this account it has been called by different names, and assumes different forms, although it is *one* thing, and its like is not found upon earth. It is a Stone, and not a stone in the sense of having the nature of any one stone; it is fire, yet it has not the appearance, or properties, of fire; it is air, yet neither has it the appearance, or properties, of air; it is water, but has no resemblance, or affinity, to the nature of water. It is earth, though it has not the nature, or appearance, of earth, seeing that it is a thing by itself.

Another way of Knowing our Precious Stone.

II.

An ancient philosopher says: Our Stone is called the sacred rock, and is divided, or signified, in four ways. Firstly, into earth; secondly, into its accretion; thirdly, into fire; and fourthly, into the flame of fire. If any one knows the method of dissolving it, of extracting its salt, and of perfectly coagulating it, he is initiated in the mysteries of the Sages. Therefore if the salt turn white, and assume an oily appearance, then it tinges. There are three stages in our Art. Firstly, the transmutation of the whole thing into one salt;

secondly, the rendering of three subtle bodies intangible; thirdly, the repetition of the whole solution of the whole thing. If you understand this, set your hand to the work. For the Matter is only one thing, and would remain one thing, though a hundred thousand books had been written about it, because this Art is so great a treasure that the whole world would not be a sufficient compensation for it. It is described in obscure terms, yet openly named by all, and known to all. But if all knew its secret, no one would work, and it would lose its value. On this account it would he impious to describe it in universally intelligible language. He to whom God will reveal it, may understand these dark expressions. But because most men do not understand them, they are inclined to regard our Art as impossible, and the Sages are branded as wicked men and swindlers. Learned doctors, who thus speak of us, have it before their eyes every day, but they do not understand it, because they never attend to it And then, forsooth, they deny the possibility of finding the Stone; nor will any one ever be able to convince them of the reality of our Art, so long as they blindly follow their own bent and inclination In short, they are too wise to discern it, since it transcends the range of the human intellect, and must be humbly received at the hand of God.

Yet Another Way of Knowing our Blessed Stone.

The philosopher, Morienus, calls our Stone, water: and he had good reasons for the name. O water of bitter taste, that preservest the elements! O glorious nature, that overcomest Nature herself! O thou that resemblest Nature, which dissolvest her tractable nature, that exaltest Nature—that art crowned with light, and preservest in thyself the four elements, out of which the quintessence is made! Thou art for the simple, seeing that thou art most simple in thy operation. Having conceived by a natural process, thou bringest forth vapour, and art a good mother. Thou needest no outward help; nature preserves nature, and is not separated from nature by the operation of nature. The thing is easy to find, the knowledge is easy, altogether familiar, yet it is as a miracle to many. Thy solution is great glory, and all thy lovers are named above. Thou art a great arcanum and to the many thou appearest impossible!

Explanation.

Know, my son, that our Stone is such that it cannot adequately be described in writing. For it is a stone, and becomes water through evaporation; yet it is no stone, and it by a chemical process it receives. a watery form it is at first like any other liquid water, being a thin fluid; yet its nature is not like that of any other water upon earth. There is only one spring in all the world from which this water may be obtained. That spring is in Judæa, and is called, the Spring of the Saviour, or of beatitude. By the grace of God its situation was revealed to the Sages. It issues in a secret place, and its waters flow over all the world. It is familiar to all, yet none knows the principle, reason, or way to find the spring, or discover the way to Judæa. But whoever does not know the right spring will never attain to a knowledge of our Art. For this reason, that Sage might well exclaim, "O water of a harsh and bitter taste!" For, in truth, the spring is difficult to find; but he who knows it may reach it easily, without any expense, labour, or trouble. The water is, of its own nature, harsh and bitter, so that no one can partake of it; and, because it is of little use to the majority of mankind, the Sage doth also exclaim, "O water, that art lightly esteemed by the vulgar, who do not perceive thy great virtues, in thee lie, as it were, hid the four elements. Thou hast power to dissolve, and conserve, and join nature, such as is possessed by no other thing upon earth." If you would know the properties and appearance of this Stone, know that its appearance is aqueous, and that the water is first changed into a stone, then the stone into water, and the water at length into the Medicine. If you know the Stone without the method of its preparation, your knowledge can be of no more use to you than if you knew the right method without being acquainted with the true Matter. Therefore our hearts are filled with gratitude to God for both kinds of knowledge.

Concerning the Treasure in the Tincture.

For let me tell you that when you have the red [tincture] you have something that all the treasures of the world will not buy. For it transmutes all metals into true gold, and is therefore much better than the preparation of the Sun. As a medicine it excels all other gold; all diseases may be cured by drinking one drop of the tincture in a glass of wine; and it has power to work many other marvels which we cannot here mention at length. If you wish to prepare the tincture for the Moon, take five half-ounces of the red tincture, and mix it well with five hundred half-ounces of the Moon, which have. been subjected to the action of fire, then melt it, and the whole will be changed into the Tincture and the Medicine. Of this take half an ounce, and inject it into five hundred half-ounces of Venus or any other metal, and it will be transmuted into pure silver. Of the red tincture, which you have diligently prepared, take one part to a thousand parts of gold, and the whole will be changed into the red tincture. Of this, again, you may take one part to a thousand parts of Venus, or any other metal, and it will be changed into pure gold. For this purpose you need not buy any gold or silver. The first injection you can make with about a drachm of both; and then you can transmute with the tincture more ands more.

You should also know that in our Art we distinguish two things — the body and the spirit: the former being constant, or fixed, while the other is volatile. These two must be changed, the one into the other: the body must become water, and the water body. Then again the body becomes water by its own internal operation, and the two, *i.e.*, the dry and the liquid, must once more be joined together in an inseparable union. This conjunction could not take place if the two had not been obtained from *one* thing; for an abiding union is possible only between things of the same nature. Of this kind is the union which takes place in our Art; for the constituent parts of the Matter are joined together by the operation of nature, and not by any human hand. The substance is divided into two parts, as we shall explain further on. For instance, the Eagle is a "water," which being extracted is then a body dead and lifeless: if it is to be restored to life, the spirit must once more be joined to it, and that in a unique fashion, as we see that it devours gradually again the one eagle after the other. Then the body loses all its grossness, and becomes new and pure; nor can this body and soul ever die, seeing that they have entered into an eternal union, such as the union of our bodies and souls shall be at the last day.

Another Description of our Stone.

The Enigma of the wise (the Stone) is the Salt and Root of the whole Art, and, as it were, its Key, without which no one is able either to lock or unlock its secret entrance. No man can understand this Art who does not know the Salt and its preparation, which takes place in a convenient spot that is both moist and warm; there the dissolution of its liquid must be accomplished, while its substance remains unimpaired. These are the words of Geber.

Explanation.

Know that the Salt of which Geber speaks has none of the specific properties of salt, and yet is called a Salt, and is a Salt. It is black and fetid, and when chemically prepared, assumes the appearance of blood, and is at length rendered white, pure, and clear. It is a good and precious Salt which, by its own operation, is first impure and then pure. It dissolves and coagulates itself, or, as the Sage says, it locks and unlocks itself. No Salt has this property but the Salt of the Sages. Its chemical development it may undergo in a moist and convenient place, where its moisture (as the Sage says) may be dissolved in the Bath of Mary. He means that it must be warm enough for its water to be distilled, yet not warmer than the excrement of horses, which is not fresh.

Another Description of our Stone.

Alexander the Great, King of Macedonia, in his "Philosophy" has the following words: Know that the Salt is fire and dryness. Fire coagulates, and its nature is hot, dry, and penetrating, even unto the inmost part. Its property is to become white even as the Sun and the Moon with the variations in the extremes of fire, to wit, of the natural fire, while the Sun restores redness and the Moon whiteness, and brings bodies to their spiritual condition at the same time that it removes their blackness and bad sulphur. With it bodies are calcined: it is the secret of the red and white tincture, the foundation and root of all things, and the best of all created things after the rational soul of man. For no Stone in the whole world has a greater efficacy, nor can any child of this earth find the Art without this Stone. Blessed be

God in heaven, who hath created this Art in Salt for the transmutation of all things, seeing that it is the quintessence which is above all things, and in all things. God Most High has not only from Heaven blessed creatures in this fashion, but praise, excellence, power, and wisdom are to be recognised as existing in this Salt. He who can dissolve and coagulate it, is well acquainted with the arcana of this Art. Our Salt is found in a certain precious Salt, and in all things. On this account the ancient Sages called it the "common moon," because all men need it. If you would become rich, prepare this Salt till it is rendered sweet. No other salt is so permanent, or has such power to fix the "soul," and to resist fire. The Salt of the earth is the soul; it coagulates all things, is in the midst of the earth when the earth is destroyed; nor is there anything on the earth like its tincture. It is called Rebis (Two-thing), is a Stone, Salt, *one* body, and, to the majority of mankind, a vile and a despised thing. Yet it purifies and restores bodies, represents the Key of our whole Art, and all things are summed up in it. Only its entering in is so subtle that few perceive it: yet if it enter a body, it tinges it and brings it to perfection. What then should you desire of God but this Salt and the ingression thereof?

If a man lived a hundred thousand years, he could never sufficiently marvel at the wonderful manner in which this noble treasure is obtained from ashes, and again reduced to ashes. In the ashes is Salt, and the more the ashes are burnt, the more ashes it affords; notice also, that that proceeds from fire, and returns to fire, which proceeds from [the] earth. All must confess that in the Salt there are two salts that kill mercury. This is a most profound saying. For sulphur, and the radical liquid, are generated in earth of a most subtle nature, and thus is prepared the Philosopher's Stone, which causes all things, even as the philosophers set forth, to arise out of *one* thing, and one nature, without the addition of any foreign substance. Our Matter is one of the commonest things upon earth, and contains within itself the four elements. It is, indeed, nothing short of marvellous that so many seek so ordinary a thing, and yet are unable to find it. We might put down many other characteristics of this Salt, but I prefer to leave the further elaboration of this subject to the reader, and to confine myself to a more detailed account of its fruits, entrance, and life, of the mode of opening the garden, and catching a glimpse of the glorious roses, of the way in which they multiply, and bear fruit a thousand-fold; also how you may cause the dead body to re-appear, and to be raised again to immortal life, by the power of which it may be able to enter imperfect bodies, purify them, and bring them to perfection, and to a state of immutable permanence.

I now propose to speak of the Stone under three aspects, viz., as the vegetable, the animal, and the mineral Stone; and among these again, of the one which contains those four elements that impart life to all. Place this one substance in an air-tight alembic, and treat it according to the precepts of our Art, which we shall set forth further on. Then the sowing in the field can take place, and you obtain the Mineral Stone, and the Green Lion that imbibes so much of its own spirit. Then life returns to its spirit through the alembic, and the dead body lies at the bottom of the vessel. In the latter there are still two elements which the fire cannot sever — for sooner [than that] the ashes are burned in the fire itself, and the Salt thereby becomes stronger. The earth must be calcined until it turns white; then the earth is severed of its own accord, and is united .to its own earth. For every thing strives to be joined to its like. Give it the cold and humid element to drink, and leave it standing eight days, that the two may be well mixed. You must see yourself what is best to be done after this: for I cannot give you any further information at present. Sun and Moon must have intercourse, like that of a man and woman: otherwise the object of our Art cannot be attained. All other teaching is false and erroneous. Think upon this Salt as the true foundation of our Art; for its worth outweighs all the treasures of this world. Itself is not developed into the tincture, but the tincture must be added to it. Nor is the substance of our Art found in any metal.

Another Description of the Matter and the Method.

By Senior.

Natural things, according to this Sage, are those which have been generated and produced out of a natural substance by a natural method. Now in its first, or lunar, stage, our Stone is produced from a coagulated white earth, as the Sage says: Behold our Sun in our white earth, and that by which the union in our Art is effected; which is twice transmuted into water, and whose volatile exhalation, representing that which is most precious in our Substance, is the highest consolation of the human body. With this water the inward mercury of the metals must be extracted. Hence it follows that our Stone is obtained from the elements of two luminaries (gold and silver), being called our quicksilver and incombustible oil, the soul and light of bodies—which alone can afford to dead and imperfect bodies eternal light and life. Therefore I pray and beseech you, my son, to crush quicksilver from our Substance with intelligence and great activity.

The Purging the "Earth" of Its Superfluous Earth.

The aforesaid earth, or Matter, you must purify, or calcine, so as to extract its water and spirit. The latter you must enclose in a phial, and pour common aqua vitæ upon it till the substance is covered to the height of three or four fingers; then subject it to the action of fire for an hour, and diligently distil it by the bath. What remains you must again calcine, and extract with its water till you find nothing more in the "earth." The earth keep for the second stage of the process. The water you have extracted distil over a gentle fire. Then you will find at the bottom of the distilling vessel a certain beautiful substance, resembling a crystal stone, which is purged of all earthly grossness, and is called "our earth." This substance you must place in a glass (pumpkin-shaped) distilling vessel, and calcine until it becomes dry and white, and yet liquid withal. Then you have obtained the treasure of this world, which has virtue to purify and perfect all earthly things: it enters into all, it nourishes the fixed salt in all things by means of Mercury or the body.

Another Description of our Stone.

Know, my sons, that the Stone out of which our Art is elaborated, never touches the earth after its generation. If it touch the earth, it is of no use for our purpose, although at its first birth it is generated by the Sun and Moon, and embodies certain earthy elements. It is generated in the earth, then broken, destroyed, and mortified. Out of it arises a vapour which is carried with the wind into the sea, and thence brought back again to the land, where it almost immediately disappears. It must be caught in the air, before it touches the ground; otherwise it evaporates. As soon as it is borne from the sea to the land, you must promptly seize it, and enclose it in your phial, then manipulate it in the manner described. You may know its coming by the wind, rain, and thunder, which accompany it; therefore it should not escape you. Though it is born anew every day, yet it existed from the beginning of the world. But as soon as it falls to the ground, it becomes useless for the purposes of our Art.

> "From our earth wells forth a fertilizing fountain, whence flow two precious stones. The first straightway hastens to the rising of the Sun; the other makes its way to the setting thereof. From them fly forth two Eagles, plunge into the flames, and fall once more to the earth. Both are furnished with feathers, and Sun and Moon, being placed under their wings, are perfected."

Know also that two waters flow forth from this fountain; the one (which is the *spirit*) towards the rising Sun, and the other, *the body*, towards the setting Sun. The two are really only *one* very limpid water, which is so bitter as to be quite undrinkable. The quantity of this water is so great that it flows over the whole earth, yet leads to nothing but the knowledge of this Art. The same also is misused too often by those who desire it. Take also the "fire," and in it you will find the Stone, and nowhere else in the whole world. It is familiar to all men, both young and old, is found in the country, in the village, in the town, in all things created by God; yet it is despised by all. Rich and poor handle it every day. It is cast into the street by servant maids. Children play with it. Yet no one prizes it, though, next to the human soul, it is the most beautiful and the most precious thing upon earth, and has power to pull down kings and princes. Nevertheless, it is esteemed the vilest and meanest of earthly things. It is cast away and rejected by all. Indeed it is the Stone which the builders of Solomon disallowed. But if it be prepared in the right way, it is a pearl without price, and, indeed, the earthly antitype of Christ, the heavenly Corner Stone. As Christ was despised and rejected in this world by the people of the Jews, and nevertheless was more precious than heaven and earth; so it is with our Stone among earthly things: for the spring where it is found is called the fount of nature. For even as through Nature all growing things are generated by the heat of the Sun, so also through Nature is our Stone born after that it has been generated.

When you have found the water which contains our Stone, you must take nothing away from it, nor add anything to it: for it must be entirely prepared by means of that which it contains within itself. Then extract the water in an alembic, and separate the liquid from the dry. The body will then remain alone on the glass, while the water runs down into the lower part. Thereupon unite the water once more to the body in the manner described above, and your task will be accomplished. Know also that the water in which is our Stone, is composed in well-balanced proportions of the four elements. In the chemical process you will learn to distinguish earth, oil, and water, or body, spirit, and soul: the earth is at the bottom of the glass vessel, the oil, or soul, is with the earth, and the water is the spirit which is distilled from it. In the same way you will come upon two colours, namely, white and red, representing the Moon and the Sun. The oil is the fire, or the Sun, the water is air, or the Moon; and Sun and Moon are silver and gold which must enter into union. But enough, what I have said in this Epistle ought to enable you to find the Stone, and if herein you fail to discover it, rest assured that it will never become known to you. Be thou, therefore, a lover of the Art, and commended unto God the Almighty even unto all eternity. Written in the year 1526 after the birth of our Lord.

Thus do the Sages write concerning the two waters which yet are only *one* water—and in this alone the Stone is to be found. Know also that by so much as the earthly part is wanting, by also so much does the heavenly part abound more fully. Now this Stone renders all dry and arid bodies humid, all cold bodies warm, all impure bodies clear and pure. It contains within itself all healing and transmuting virtue, breathed

p. 182

into it by the art of the Master and the quickening spirit of fire. Thanks be unto God therefore in all time.

The Sun is its Father, the Moon its Mother.

If you have those two spirits, they bring forth the Stone, which is prepared out of one part of Sulphur, or Sun, and four parts of Mercury, or Moon. The Sulphur is warm and dry, the Mercury cold and moist. That must again be dissolved into water, which before was water, and the body, which before was mercury, must again become mercury.

Concerning the First Matter, or Seed of the Metals, including that of the Husband, and that of the Spouse.

Metals have their own seed, like all other created things. Generation and parturition take place in them as in everything else that grows. If this were not the case, we should never have had any metals. Now, the seed is a metallic Matter which is liquefied from earth. The seed must be cast into its earth, and there grow, like that of every other created thing. Therefore, we must prepare the earth, or our first Matter, and cast into it the seed, whereupon it will bring forth fruit after its kind. This motion is required for the generation out of *one* thing, viz., that first Matter; the body must become [a] spirit, and the spirit body: thence arises the medicine which is transmuted from one colour to another. Now, that which is sought in the white produces white, and the red, in like manner, gives red. The first Matter is *one* thing, and fashioned into its present shape by the hand of God, and not of man—joined together, and transmuted into its [being] essence by Nature alone. This we take, dissolve, and again conjoin, and wash with its own water, until it becomes white, and then again red. Thus our earth, in which we now may easily see our Sun and Moon, is purified. For the Sun is the Father of metals, and the Moon is their Mother: and if generation is to take place, they must be brought together as husband and wife. By itself neither can produce anything, and therefore the red and the white must be brought together. And though a thousand books have been written about it, yet for all that, the first substance is riot more than one. It is the earth into which we cast our grain, that is to say, our Sun and Moon, which then

p. 183

bear fruit after their kind. If itself be cast into metals, it is changed into that which is best, viz., Sun and Moon. This is most true. Thanks be unto God.

A Simple Account of the True Art.

According to the Sages, no body is dissolved without the coagulation of the spirit. For as soon as the spirit is transmuted into the body, [the Stone] receives its power. So long as the spirit is volatile, and liable to evaporate, it cannot produce any effect: when it is fixed, it immediately begins to operate. You must therefore prepare it as the baker prepares the bread. Take a little of the spirit, and add it to the body, as the baker adds leaven to the meal, till the whole substance is leavened. It is the same with our spirit, or leaven. The Substance must be continuously penetrated with the leaven, until it is wholly leavened. Thus the spirit purges and spiritualizes the body, till they are both transmuted into one. Then they transmute all things, into which they are injected, into their own nature. The two must be united by a gentle and continuous fire, affording the same degree of warmth as that with which a hen hatches her eggs. It must then be placed in a St. Mary's Bath, which is neither too warm nor too cold. The humid must be separated from the dry, and again joined to it. When united, they change mercury into pure gold and silver. Thenceforward you will be safe from the pangs of poverty. But take heed that you render thanks unto God for His gracious gift which is hidden from many. He has revealed the secret to you that you may praise His holy name, and succour your needy neighbour. Therefore, take diligent heed, lest you hide the talent committed to your care. Rather put it out at interest for the glory of God, and the good of your neighbour. For every man is bound to help his fellowman, and to be an instrument in the hand of God for relieving his necessities. Of this rule Holy Scripture affords an illustration in the example of Joseph, Habakkuk, Susanna, and others.

Here follows my TESTAMENT *which I have drawn up in your favour, my beloved Sons, with all my Heart.*

For your sakes, beloved students of this Art, and dear Sons, I have committed to writing this my testament, for the purpose

p. 184

of instructing, admonishing, warning, and informing you as to the substance, the method, the pitfalls to be avoided, and the only way of understanding the writings of the Sages. For as Almighty God has created all things out of the dry and the humid elements, our Art, by divine grace, may be said to pursue a precisely similar course. If therefore any man know the principle and method of creative nature, he should have a good understanding of our Art. If anyone be unacquainted with Natures methods, he will find our Art difficult, although in reality it is as easy as to crush malt, and brew beer. In the beginning when, according to the testimony of Scripture, God made heaven and earth, there was only *one* Matter, neither wet nor dry, neither earth, nor air, nor fire, nor light, nor darkness, but one single substance, resembling vapour or mist, invisible and impalpable. It was called Hyle, or the first Matter. If a thing is once more to be made out of nothing, that "nothing" must be united, and become *one*thing; out of this *one* thing must arise a palpable substance, out of the palpable substance *one* body, to which a living soul must be given—whence through the grace of God, it obtains its specific form. When God made the substance, it was dry, but held together by moisture. If anything was to grow from that moisture, it had to be separated from that which was dry, so as to get the fire by itself, and the earth by itself. Then the earth had to be sprinkled with water, if anything moist was to grow out of it, for without moisture nothing can grow. In the same way, nothing grows in water, except it have earth wherein to strike root. It then the water is to bedew the earth, there must be something to bring the water into contact with the earth; for example, the wind prevents all ordinary water from flowing to the sea, and remaining there. Thus one element without the aid of another can bear no fruit; if there was nothing to set the wind in motion it would never blow — therefore the fire has received the office of impelling and obliging it to do its work. This you may see when you boil water over the fire; for then there arises a steam which is really *air*, *water* being nothing but coagulated air, and air being generated from water by the heat of the Sun. For the Sun shines upon the water, and heats it until steam is seen to issue forth. This vapour becomes wind, and, on account of the large quantity of [the] air, we get moisture and rain: so air is once more changed or coagulated into water, or rain, and causes all things upon earth to grow, and fills the rivers and the seas.

It is the same with our Stone, which is daily generated from [the] air by the Sun and Moon, in the form of a certain vapour, yea, even through the Red Sea; it flows in Judea in the channel of Nature whither it behoves us to bring it. If we catch it, we lop off its hands and feet, tear off its head, and try to bring it to the red [colour]. If we find anything black in it, we throw it away with the entrails and the filth. When it has been purified, we take its limbs, join them together again, whereupon our King revives, never to die again, and is so pure and subtle as to pervade all hard bodies, and render them even more subtle than itself. Know also that when God, the Almighty, had set Adam in Paradise, He shewed him these two things in the following words: "Behold, Adam, here are two things, one fixed and permanent, the other volatile: their secret virtue thou must not make known to *all* thy sons."

Earth, my brother, is constant, and water volatile, as you may see when anything is burnt. For then that which is constant remains, while that which is volatile evaporates. That which remains resembles ashes, and if you pour water on it, it becomes an alkali, the efficacy of the ashes passing into the water. If you clarify the lye, put it into an iron vessel, and let the moisture evaporate over a fire, you will find at the bottom the substance which before was in the lye, that is to say, the salt of the matter from which the ashes were obtained. This salt might very well be called the Philosopher's Stone, from being obtained by a process exactly similar to that which is employed in preparing the *real* Stone, though at the same time it profits nothing in our work. For the substance which contains our Stone is a lye, not indeed prepared by the hand of man from ashes and water, but joined together by Nature, according to the creation and ordination of God, commingled of the four elements, possessed of all that is required for its perfect chemical development. If you take the substance, which contains our Stone, subject it to a S. Mary's Bath in an alembic, and distil it, the water will run down into the antisternium, and the salt, or earth, remain at the bottom, and is so dry as to be without any water, seeing that you have separated the moist from the dry. Pound the body small, put it into the S. Mary's Bath, and expose it to heat till it is quite decomposed. Then give it its water to drink, slowly, and at long intervals, till it is clarified. For it coagulates, dissolves, and purifies itself. The distilled water is the spirit which imparts life to its body, and is the alone soul thereof. Water is wind (air), and wind is life, and the life is [in the] soul. In the chemical process, you find water and oil—but the oil always remains with the body, and is, as it were, burnt blood. Then it is purified with the body by long-continued gentle heat. But you should be careful not to set about this Art before you understand my instructions, which at the end of this first part are bequeathed to you in the form of a Testament. For the Stone is prepared out of nothing in the whole world, except this substance, which is essentially one. He who is unacquainted therewith can never attain the Art. It is that one thing which is not dug up from mines, or from the caverns of the earth, like gold, silver, sulphur, salt, &c., but is found in the form which God originally imparted to it. It is formed and manifested by an excessive thickening of air; as soon as it leaves its body, it is clearly seen, but it vanishes without a trace as soon as it touches the earth, and, as it is never seen again, it must therefore be caught while it is still in the air—as I told you once before. I have called it by various names, but the simplest is perhaps that of "Hyle," or first principle of all things. It is also denominated the One Stone of the Philosophers, composed of hostile elements, the Stone of the Sun, the Stone of the Metals, the runaway slave, the aëriform Stone, the Thirnian Stone, Magnesia, the corporeal Stone, the Stone of the jewel, the Stone of the free, the golden Stone, the fountain of earthly things, Xelis, or Silex (flint), Xidar, or Radix (root), Atrop, or Porta (gate). By these and many other names it is called, yet it is only *one*. If you would be a true Alchemist, give a wide berth to all other substances, turn a deaf ear to all other advisers, and strive to obtain a good knowledge of our Stone, its preparation, and its virtue.

My Son, esteem this my Testament very highly: for in it I have, out of love and compassion towards you, given the reins to the warm-hearted impulse which constrains me to reveal more than I ought to reveal. But I beseech you, by the Passion of our Lord and Saviour Jesus Christ, not to communicate my Testament to ignorant, unworthy, or wicked men, lest God's righteous vengeance light upon you, and hurl you into the yawning gulf of everlasting punishment, from which also may the same merciful God most mercifully preserve us.

It is by no means a light thing to shew the nature of the aforesaid Hyle. Hyle is the first Matter, the Salt of the Sages, Azoth, the seed of all metals, which is extracted from the body of "Magnesia" and the Moon.

Hyle is the first principle of all things—the Matter that was from the beginning. It was neither moist, nor dry, nor earth, nor water, nor light, nor darkness, but a mixture of all these things, and this mixture is HYLE.

HERE FOLLOWS THE SECOND PART OF THIS BOOK.

In the beginning, when God Almighty had created our first parent Adam, together with all other earthly and heavenly bodies, He set him in Paradise, and forbade him, under penalty of eternal death, to eat of the fruit of the tree of the knowledge of good and evil. So long as Adam obeyed the Divine precept he had immortality, and possessed all that he needed for perfect happiness. But when he had partaken of the forbidden fruit, he was, by the command of God, driven forth into this world, where he and his descendants have since that time suffered nothing but poverty, disease, anxiety, bitter sorrow, and death. If he had been obedient to the Divine injunction, he would have lived a thousand years in Paradise in perfect happiness, and would then have been translated to heaven; and a like happy destiny would have awaited all his descendants. For his disobedience God visited him with all manner of sufferings and diseases; but in His mercy also shewed him a medicine whereby the different defects brought in by sin might be remedied, and the pangs of hunger and disease resisted, as we are, for instance, preserved and strengthened by bodily meat and drink.

It was on account of this original sin that Adam, in spite of his great wisdom and the many arts that God had taught him, could not accomplish his full thousand years. But if he had not known the virtues of herbs, and the Medicine, he would certainly not have lived as long as he did. When, however, at length his Medicine would no longer avail to sustain life, he sent his son Seth to Paradise to fetch the tree of life. This he obtained after a spiritual manner. But Seth did seek also and was given some olives of the Tree of the Oil of Mercy, which he planted on the grave of his father. From them sprang up the blessed Tree of the Holy Cross, which through the atoning death of our Redeemer became to us wretched, sinful men, a most potent tree of life, in gracious fulfilment of the request of our first parent Adam. On the other hand, the suffering, disease, and imperfection brought not only upon men, but also upon plants and animals, by the fall of Adam, found a remedy in that precious gift of Almighty God, which is called the Elixir, and Tincture, and has power to purge away the imperfections not only of human, but even of metallic bodies; which excels all other medicines, as the brightness of the sun shames the moon and the stars. By means of this most noble Medicine many men, from the death of Adam to the fourth monarchy, procured for themselves perfect health and great length of days. Hence those who had a good knowledge of the Medicine, attained to three hundred years, others to four hundred, some to five hundred, like Adam; others again to nine hundred, like Methusalem and Noah; and some of their children to a longer period still, like Bacham, Ilrehur, Kalix, Hermes, Geber, Albanus, Ortulanus, Morienus, Alexander of Macedonia, Anaxagoras, Pythagoras, and many others who possessed the Medicine of the Blessed Stone in silence, and neither used it for evil purposes, nor made it known to the wicked; just as God Himself has in all times hidden this knowledge from the proud, the impure, and the froward. But cease to wonder that God has put such excellent virtue into the Stone, and has imparted to it the power of restoring animal bodies, and of perfecting metals: for I hope to explain to you the whole matter in the three parts of my Book, which I have entitled GLORY of the WORLD. If you will accept my teaching, and follow my directions, you will be able to prove the truth of my assertions by your own happy experience. Now when you have attained this great result, take care that you do not hide your talent. Use it for the solace of the suffering, the building of Christian schools and churches, and the glory of the Holy Trinity. Otherwise God will call you to an eternal account for your criminal neglect of His gift. May God deign to keep us from such a sin, and to establish us in His Holy Word!

To the Reader.

If it should seem unto you a tedious matter, my friendly reader, to read through and digest my book, I advise you to cheer yourself on by bearing in mind the great object you have in view. If you do so you will find the book very pleasant reading, and a joy indeed. Since God — praised in all times be his Holy and Venerable Name! — in His unspeakable mercy has made known to me the magistery of this most true and noble Art, I am moved and constrained by brotherly love to shew you the manner of producing this treasure, in order that you may be able to avoid the ruinous trouble and expense to which I was put in the course of a long and fruitless search. I will endeavour to be as clear and outspoken as possible, in order to vindicate myself from the possible charge of imposture, malice, and avarice. I am most anxious that the gift which God has committed to my trust shall not rust, or rot, or be useless in my hands. For this most precious Medicine is so full of glorious potency as to be most justly styled the Oil of Mercy, for reasons which your own understanding will suggest to you. It is therefore unnecessary for me to go into this preliminary question at any great length. I may at once proceed to give you an account of the Art itself, and to put you on your guard against all seducing deceivers, — in short, to open up to you a true, unerring, and joyful road to the knowledge and possession of the Stone, and to the operations of this Art.

Therefore, I — who possess the Stone, and communicate to you this Book — would faithfully admonish and beseech you to keep this my TABLE of PARADISE and GLORY of the WORLD, from all proud and unjust oppressors of the poor; from all presumptuous, shallow, scornful, calumnious, and wicked persons, so as not to put it into their hands, on pain of God's everlasting punishment. I beseech you to take this warning to heart; but, on the other hand, to communicate and impart this my Table to all true, poor, pious, honest, and benevolent persons, who will gratefully reverence and rightly use the merciful gift of God, and conceal it from the unworthy. Nevertheless, even if my book should find its way into the hands of wicked men, God will so smite them with blindness as to prevent them from apprehending too much of my meaning, and frustrate all their attempts to carry out my directions. For God knows how to confound the wicked, and bring their presumption to nought; as we are also told by David in his psalms: "Thine enemies shalt thou hold in thine hand, and shalt restrain them in the snares of their mind." I beseech you, therefore, my sons, to give diligent heed to my teaching; then you will spend this life in health and happiness, and at length inherit everlasting joy. I pray that God the Father, the Son, and the Holy Ghost, may grant this my petition.

An Account of the True Art.

I make known to all ingenuous students of this Art that the Sages are in the habit of using words which may convey either a true or a false impression; the former to their own disciples and children, the latter to the ignorant, the foolish, and the unworthy. Bear in mind that the philosophers themselves never make a false assertion. The mistake (if any) lies not with them, but with those whose dulness makes them slow to apprehend the meaning. Hence it comes that, instead of the waters of the Sages, these inexperienced persons take pyrites, salts, metals, and divers other substances which, though very expensive, are of no use whatever for our purpose. For no one would dream of buying the true Matter at the apothecary's; nay, that tradesman daily casts it into the street as worthless refuse. Yet the matter of our Stone is found in all those things which are used by ignorant charlatans: for it is our Stone, our Salt, our Mercury, our verdigris, halonitre, salmiac, Mars, sulphur, &c. It is not dug out with pick-axes from ordinary mountains, seeing that our Stone is found in our mountains and springs; our Salt is found in our salt-spring, our metal in our earth, and from the same place we dig up our mercury and sulphur. But what we mean by our mines and springs these charlatans cannot understand. For God has blinded their minds and made gross their senses, and left them to carry on their experiments with all manner of false substances. Nor do they seem able to perceive their error, or to be roused from their idle imaginations by persistent failure. Where they should have distilled with gentle heat they sublime over a fierce fire, and reduce their substance to ashes, instead of developing its inherent principles by vitalizing warmth. Again, when they should have dissolved, they coagulated instead, and so on. By these false methods they could, of course, obtain no good result; but instead of blaming their own ignorance they lay the fault on their teacher, and even deny the genuineness of our Art. As a matter of fact, all their mistakes arise from their misinterpreting the meaning of words which should have put them on the right scent. For instance, when the Sages speak of calcining, these persons understand that word to mean "burning," and consequently render their substance useless by burning it to ashes. When the Sages "dissolve," or transmute into "water," these shallow persons corrode with aqua fortis. They do not understand that the dissolution must be effected with something that is contained within our substance, and not by means of any foreign appliance. These foolish devices bear the same relation to our Art that a dark hole bears to a transparent crystal. It is their own ignorance that prevents them from attaining to a true knowledge; but they put the blame on our writings, and call us charlatans and impostors. They argue that if the Stone could be found at all, they must have discovered it long ago, their eyes being as keen and their minds as acute as they are. "Behold," say they, "how we have toiled day and night, how many books we have read, how many years we have spent in our laboratories: surely if there were anything in this Art, it could not have escaped us." By speaking thus, they only exhibit their own presumption and folly. They themselves have no eyes, and they make that an argument for blaspheming our high and holy Art. Therefore, you should first strive to make yourself acquainted with the secrets of Nature's working, and with the elementary principles of the world, before you set your hand to this task. After acquiring this knowledge, carefully peruse this book from beginning to end; you will then be in a position to judge whether our Art is true or false. You will also know what substance you must take, how you must prepare it, and how your eager search may be brought to a successful issue. Let me enjoin you, therefore, to preserve strict silence, to let nobody know what you are doing, and to keep a good heart: then God will grant you the fulfilment of all your wishes.

Here follows my own Opinion and Philosophical Dictum.

I now propose to put down a brief statement of the view which I take of this matter. He who understands my meaning, may at once pass on to the opinions of the various Sages, which I have placed at the end of my book. He who does not apprehend my meaning, will find it explained in the following treatise.

Since I know the blessed and true Art, with the nature and the matter of the Stone, I have thought it my duty freely to communicate it to you—not in a lawyer's style, nor in pompous language, but in few and simple words. Whoever peruses this book carefully, and with an elementary knowledge of natural relations, cannot miss the secret which I intend to convey. I am afraid that I shall be overwhelmed with reproaches for speaking out with so much plainness, seeing that this Art has never, from the beginning of the world, been so clearly explained as I mean to explain it in this Book. Nevertheless, I am well aware that I am now declaring a secret which must for ever remain hidden from the wise of this world, and from those who are established in their own conceits. But I must now proceed to give you the result of my experience.

My beloved sons and disciples, and all ye that are students of this Art; I herewith, in the fulness of Christian faith and charity, do make known to you that the Philosopher's Stone grows not *only* on "*our*" tree, but is found, as far as its effect and operation are concerned, in the fruit of all other trees, in all created things, in animals, and vegetables, in things that grow, and in things that do not grow. For when it rises, being stirred and distilled by the Sun and the Moon, it imparts their own peculiar form and properties to all living creatures by a divine grace; it gives to flowers their special form and colour, whether it be black, red, yellow, green, or white; in the same way all metals and minerals derive their peculiar qualities from the operation of this Stone. All things, I say, are endowed with their characteristic qualities by the operation of this Stone, *i.e.*, the conjunction of the Sun and Moon. For the Sun is the Father, and the Moon the Mother of this Stone, and the Stone unites in itself the virtues of both its parents. Such are the peculiar properties of our Stone, by which it may be known. If you understand the operation, the form, and the qualities, of this Stone, you will be able to prepare it; but if you do not, I faithfully counsel you to give up all thought of ever accomplishing this task.

Observe, furthermore, how the seeds of all things that grow, as, for instance, grains of wheat or barley, spring forth from the ground, by the operation of the Stone, and the developing influences of Sun and Moon; how they grow up into the air, are gradually matured, and bring forth fruit, which again must be sown in its own proper soil. The field is prepared for the grain, being well ploughed up, and manured with well rotted dung; for the earth consumes and assimilates the manure, as the body assimilates its food, and separates the subtle from the gross Therewith it calls forth the life of the seed, and nourishes it with its own proper milk, as a mother nourishes her infant, and causes it to increase in size, and to grow upward. The earth separates, I say, the good from the bad, and imparts it as nutriment to all growing things; for the destruction of one thing is the generation of another. It is the same in our Art, where the liquid receives its proper nutriment from the earth. Hence the earth is the Mother of all things that grow; and it must be manured, ploughed, harrowed, and well prepared, in order that the corn may grow, and triumph over the tares, and not be choked by them. A grain of wheat is raised from the ground through the distillation of the moisture of the Sun and Moon, if it has been sown in its own proper earth. The Sun and Moon must also impel it to bring forth fruit, if it is to bring forth fruit at all. For the Sun is the Father, and the Moon the Mother, of all things that grow.

In the same way, in our soil, and out of our seed, our Stone grows through the distilling of the Sun and Moon; and as it grows it rises upwards, as it were, into the air, while its root remains in the ground. That which is above is even as that which is below; the same law prevails; there is no error or mistake. Again, as herbs grow upward, put forth glorious flowers and blossoms, and bear fruit, so our grain blossoms, matures its fruit, is threshed, sifted, purged of its chaff, and again put in the earth, which, however, must previously have been well manured, harrowed, and otherwise prepared. When it has been placed in its natural soil, and watered with rain and dew, the moisture of heaven, and roused into life by the warmth of the Sun and Moon, it produces fruit after its own kind. These two sowings are peculiar characteristics of our Art. For the Sun and Moon are our grain, which we put into our soil, as soul and spirit—and such as are the father and the mother will be the children that they generate. Thus, my sons, you know our Stone, our earth, our grain, our meal, our ferment, our manure, our verdigris, our Sun and Moon. You understand our whole magistery, and may joyfully congratulate yourselves that you have at length risen above the level of those blind charlatans of whom I spoke. For this, His unspeakable mercy, let us render thanks and praise to the Creator of all things, through Jesus Christ our Lord. Amen.

Concerning the Origin of Metals.

My son, I will now proceed to explain to you more in detail the generation of the metals, and the way in which they receive their growth and development, with their special form and quality. You will thereby be enabled to understand, even from the very foundation, with marvellous accuracy and clearness, the principle that underlies our whole Art. Permit me, therefore, to inform you that all animals, trees, herbs, stones, metals, and minerals, grow and attain to perfection, without being necessarily touched by any human hand: for the seed is raised up from the ground, puts forth flowers, and bears fruit, simply through the agency of natural influences. As it is with plants, so it is with metals.

While they lie in the heart of the earth, in their natural ore, they grow, and are developed, day by day, through the influence of the four elements: their fire is the splendour of the Sun and Moon; the earth conceives in her womb the splendour of the Sun, and by it the seeds of the metals are well and equally warmed, just like the grain in the fields. Through this warmth there is produced in the earth a vapour or spirit, which rises upward and carries with it the most subtle elements. It might well be called a fifth element: for it is a quintessence, and contains the most volatile parts of all the elements. This vapour strives to float upward through the summit of the mountains, but, being covered with great rocks, they prevent it from doing so: for when it strikes against them, it is compelled to descend again. It is drawn up by the Sun, it is forced down again by the rocks, and as it falls the vapour is transmuted into a liquid, *i.e.,* sulphur and mercury. Of each of these a part is left behind — but that which is volatile rises and descends again, more and more of it remaining behind, and becoming fixed after each descent. This "fixed" substance is the metals, which cleave so firmly to the earth and the stones that they must be smelted out in a red-hot furnace. The grosser the stones and the earth of the mountains are, the less pure will the metal be; the more subtle the soil and the stones are, the more subtle will be the vapour, and the sulphur and mercury formed by its condensation — and the purer these latter are, the purer, of course, will the metals themselves be. When the earth and the stones of the mountain are gross, the sulphur and mercury must partake of this grossness, and cannot attain to their proper development. Hence arise the different metals, each after its own kind. For as each tree of the field has its own peculiar shape, appearance, and fruit, so each mountain bears its own particular ore; those stones and that earth being the soil in which the metals grow. The quality of this soil is to a great extent dependent upon planetary influences. The nearer the mountains lie to the planets, the more do metals grow in them; for the qualities of metals are determined by planetary influences. Mountains that are turned towards the sun have subtle stones and earth, and produce nothing but gold. If they are more conveniently situated for being influenced by the moon, their metallic substance is turned into silver. For all metals, when perfectly developed, must ultimately become Moon and Sun, though some need to be operated on by the Sun and Moon longer than others: for the Sun is the Father, and the Moon the Mother, of all things that grow. Thus you see that gold glitters like the Sun, and silver like the Moon. Now, children always resemble their parents; and all metallic bodies contain within themselves the properties of the Sun: to change the baser metals into gold and silver, there is positively nothing wanting but gentle solar warmth. In this respect there exists a close analogy between animal and vegetable growth. When the Sun retires in the winter, the flowers droop and die, the trees shed their leaves, and all vegetable development is temporarily suspended. In the summer again, when the heat of the Sun is too great, not being sufficiently tempered by the cooling influences of the Moon, all vegetation is withered and burnt up. If there is to be perfect growth, the Sun and Moon must work together, the one heating and the other cooling. If the influence of the Moon prevails unduly, it must be corrected by the warmth of the Sun; the excessive heat of the Sun must be tempered by the coldness of the Moon. All development is sustained by solar fire. Imperfect metals are what they are, simply because they have not yet been duly developed by solar influences.

Now, by the special grace of God, it is possible to bring this natural fire to bear on imperfect metals by means of our Art, and to supply the conditions of metallic growth without any of the hindrances which in a natural state prevent perfection. Thus by applying our natural fire, we can do more towards "fixing" imperfect bodies and metals in a moment, than the Sun in a thousand years. For this reason our Stone has also power to cure all things that grow, acting on each one according to its kind. For our Matter represents a perfect and inseparable union of the four elements, which indeed is the sum of our Art, and is consequently able to reconcile and heal all discord in all manner of metals and in all things that grow, and to put to flight all diseases, For disease is discord of the elements, (one unduly lording it over the rest) in animal as well as in metallic bodies. Now as soon as our blessed Medicine is applied, the elements are straightway purified, and joined together in amity; thus metallic bodies are fixed, animal bodies are made whole of all their diseases, gems and precious stones attain to their own proper perfection.

You should also know that all stones are generated by the Sun and Moon out of the sulphur and volatile mercury; if they do not become metals, that is entirely due to their own grossness. In the same way, all plants are generated from sulphur and mercury, and that by the heat of the Sun and Moon. For the Sun and Moon are the mercury in our Matter. The Sun is warm and dry, the Moon warm and moist; for in [the] earth is hid a warm and dry fire, and in that fire dwells warm and moist air—and from these is generated mercury which is both warm and moist. Hence there may be distinguished two chief constituent principles, to wit, moist and dry, that is, earth, wind, and water, unto which mercury is conjoined, and the same is warm and moist. Mercury and sulphur, in our substance, and in all things, spring from the moist and dry, the moist and dry being stirred by the warmth of the Sun, and distilled and sublimed,—in each thing according to its specific nature. Thus our Stone is that mercury which is mixed of the dry and the moist. But the common mercury is useless for our purpose—for it is volatile, while our mercury is fixed and constant. Therefore have nothing to do with the common mercury, but take our mercury which is the principle of growth in all bodies, whether human, vegetable, or metallic; which imparts to all flowers their fragrance and colour. This mercury represents an harmonious mixture of the four elements, hot and dry, Sun and Moon. It is generated in the form of a vapour in the fields and on the mountains, by the warmth of the Sun: that vapour is condensed into a moisture, from which arise sulphur and mercury, and from them again metals The same process takes place in our Art, which represents the union of the warm and moist, by means of warmth. For our substance is generated in the form of a vapour out of warmth and moisture, and changed into sulphur. In this fire and water, and nowhere else, is our Stone to be found. For the vapour carries upward with it most subtle earth, most subtle fire, most subtle water, and most subtle air, and thus presents a close union of the most subtle elements. This is the first Matter, and may be divided into water and earth, which two are again joined together by gentle heat, even as in the woods and mountains mercury is joined with a quick earth and rare water by means of a temperate warmth, and in the long process of time is converted into metal. So is it ordained in our Art, and not otherwise does the process take place. When you, therefore, see that our substance, having been first generated in the form of a vapour, permits itself to be separated into water and earth, you may know that the Stone is composed of the four elements. Know also that the vapour in the mountains is true mercury (which cannot be said of the ordinary mercury); for wherever there is vapour in the mountains, there is true mercury, which by ascending and descending, in the manner described above, becomes fixed, and inseparable from its earth, so that where the one is, there the other must abide.

Thus I have told you plainly enough how the metals are generated, what mercury is, and how it is transmuted into metals. I will therefore conclude this part of my treatise, and tell you in the following section how you may actually perform the chemical process. You see that it is not so incredible, after all, that all metals should be transmuted into gold and silver, and all animal bodies delivered from every kind of disease; and I hope and trust that God will permit you practically to experience the truth of this assertion.

Now I will tell you how you must produce the Fire and Water, in which is prepared the Mercury required for the red and white Tincture,

Take fire, or the quicklime of the Sages, which is the vital fire of all trees, and therein doth God Himself burn by divine love. In it purify Mercury, and mortify it for the purposes of our Art; understand, with vulgar Mercury, which you wish to fix in water or fire. But the Mercury which lies hidden in this water, or fire, is therein fixed of itself. The Mercury which is in the fire must be decomposed, clarified, coagulated, and fixed with indelible, living, or Divine fire, of that kind which God has placed in the Sun; and wherein God Himself burns as with Divine love for the consolation of all mankind. Without this fire our Art can not be brought to a successful issue. This is the fire of the Sages which they describe in such obscure terms, as to have been the indirect cause of beguiling many innocent persons to their ruin; so even that they have perished in poverty because they knew not this fire of the Philosophers. It is the most precious fire that God has created in the earth, and has a thousand virtues—nay, it is so precious that men have averred that the Divine Power itself works effectually in it. It has the purifying virtue of Purgatory, and everything is rendered better by it. It is not wonderful, therefore, that a fire should be able to fix and clarify Mercury, and to cleanse it from all grossness and impurity. The Sages call it the living fire, because God has endowed it with His own Divine, and vitalising power.

In the writings of the Sages, this fire goes by different names. Some call it "burnt" wine, others assign to it three names from the analogy of the Three Persons of the Holy Trinity, God the Father, God the Son, and God the Holy Ghost; Body, Soul, and Fire, or Spirit.

The Sages further say: The fire is fire, and also water, containing within itself both cold and heat, moisture, and dryness, nor can anything extinguish it but itself. Hence others say that it is an inextinguishable fire, which is continually burning, purifying, and tinging all metals, consuming all their impurities, and combining Mercury with the Sun in so close an union that they become one and inseparable.

Therefore our great Teachers say that as God the Father, the Son, and the Holy Ghost, are three Persons, and yet but one God; so this fire unites these three things, namely, the Body, Spirit, and Soul, or Sun, Mercury, and Soul. The fire nourishes the Soul which binds together the Body and the Spirit, and thus all three become one, and remain united for ever. Again, as an ordinary fire, on being supplied with fuel, may spread and fill the whole world, so this Tincture may be multiplied, and so this fire may enter into all metals; and one part of it has power to change two, three, or five hundred parts of other metals into gold.

Again, the Sages call this fire the fire of the Holy Spirit, because as the Divinity of Christ took upon itself true flesh and blood without forfeiting anything of its Divine Nature, so the Sun, the Moon, and Mercury, are transmuted into the true Tincture, which remains unaffected by all outward influences, and endures, and will endure, for ever. Once more, as God feeds many wicked sinners with his blood, so this Tincture tinges all gross and impure metals, without being injured by contact with them. So also, therefore, may it be compared with the sacro-saintly Sacrament of the Most Holy Eucharist, from which no sinner is excluded, how impure soever he may have been. You have thus been made acquainted with the all but miraculous virtue of this fire: remember that no student of this Art can possibly do without it. For another Sage says: "In this invisible fire you have the whole mystery of this Art, as the three Persons of the Holy Trinity are truly concluded in one substance." In this fire the true Art is summed up in three palpable things, which yet are invisible and incomprehensible, like the Holy Spirit. Without those three things our Art can never be brought to perfection. One of them is fire; the second, water; the third, earth; and all those three are invisibly present in one essence, and are the instrumental cause of all perfection in Nature.

Now will I also describe the operation of those Three Things in our Art, and will at once begin with all Three.

Our wise Teacher Plato says: "Every husbandman who sows good seed, first chooses a fertile field, ploughs and manures it well, and weeds it of all tares; he also takes care that his own grain is free from every foreign admixture. When he has committed the seed to the ground, he needs moisture, or rain, to decompose the grain, and to raise it to new life. He also requires fire, that is, the warmth of the Sun, to bring it to maturity." The needs of our Art are of an analogous nature. First, you must prepare your seed, *i.e.*, cleanse your Matter from all impurity, by a method which you will find set forth at length in the Dicta of the Sages which I subjoin to this Treatise. Then you must have good soil in which to sow your Mercury and Sun; this earth must first be weeded of all foreign elements if it is to yield a good crop. Hence the Sage enjoins us to "sow the seed in a fruitful field, which has been prepared with living fire, and it will produce much fruit."

What is the Urine of Children?

I will now truly inform you concerning the Urine of Children, and of the Sages. The spirit which is extracted from the metals is the urine of children: for it is the seed and the first principle of metals. Without this seed there is no consummation of our Art, and no Tincture, either red or white. For the sulphur and mercury of gold are the red, the sulphur and mercury of silver are the white Tincture: the Mercury of the

Sun and Moon fixes all Mercury in imperfect metals, and imparts excellence and durability even to common Mercury. Dioscorides has written an elegant treatise concerning this Urine of Children, which he calls the first Matter of metals.

What is the Mercury of the Sages?

Mercury is nothing but water and salt, which have been subjected for a long space of time to natural heat so as to be united into one. This is Mercury, or dry water, which is not moist, and does not moisten anything; of course, I do not speak of crude common mercury, but of the Mercury of the Sages. The Sages call it the fifth element. It is the vital principle which brings all plants to maturity and perfection. The other quintessence, which is in the earth, and partly material, contains within itself its own seed which grows out of its soil. The heavenly quintessence comes to the aid of the earthly, removes the grossness of its earth, and brings the aforesaid seed to maturity. For Mercury, and the Celestial Quintessence, drain off all harmful moisture from the quintessence of the earth. This Mercury is also called sulphur of the air, sulphur being a hardening of mercury; or we may describe them as husband and wife, from whom issue many children in the earth. You must not think that I desire to hide from you my true meaning: nay, I will further endeavour to illustrate it in the following way. Common sulphur, as you know, coagulates common mercury; for sulphur is poisonous, and mercury deadly. How then can you obtain from either of them anything suitable for perfecting the other, seeing that both require to be assisted by some external agent? On the other hand, I tell you that if, after the conjunction of our fixed sulphur with our sublimed mercury, you sprinkle a mere particle of it upon crude mercury, the latter is at once brought to perfection. Again, you may clearly perceive that the quintessence of the earth has its operation in the winter when the earth is closed up with frost; while the Quintessence of the Stars operates in the summer time, when it removes all that is injurious in the inferior quintessence, and thus quickens everything into vigorous growth. The two quintessences may also be driven off into water, and there conserved. An earthly manifestation you may behold in the colours of the rainbow, when the rays of the Sun shine through the rain. But, indeed, there is not a stone, an animal, or a plant, that does not contain both quintessences. In short, they embody the secret of our whole Magistery, and out of them our Stone is prepared. Hermes, in his Emerald Table, expresses himself as follows: "Our Blessed Stone, which is of good substance, and has a soul, ascends from earth to heaven, and again descends from heaven to earth. Its effectual working is in the air; it is joined to Mercury; hence the Sun is its Father, the Moon its Mother; the wind has borne it in her womb, the earth is its nursing mother, and at length that which is above is also that which is below. The whole represents a natural mixture: for it is a Stone and not a Stone, fixed and volatile, body and soul, husband and wife, King and Queen." Let what I have said suffice, instead of many other words and parables.

Composition.

Albertus expresses himself thus concerning the conjunction of the Stone: "The elements are so subtle that no ordinary method of mingling will avail. They must first be dissolved into water, then mixed, and placed in a warm spot, where they are united after a time by natural warmth. For the Elixir and the two solutions must be conjoined in the proportion of three parts of the Elixir and one part of the crushed body. This must again be coagulated and dissolved, and so also again until the whole has become *one*, without any transmutation. All this is accomplished by the virtue of our mercurial water; for with it the body is dissolved. It is that which purifies, conjoins, dissolves, and makes red and white." Aristotle says of it as follows: This water is the earth in which Hermes bids us sow the seed; the Sun or Moon, as Senior hath it, for extraction of the Divine water of sulphur and mercury, which is fire, warming and fructifying by the igneous virtue thereof. This is the Mercury and that is the water which wets not the hand. It is the Mercury which all Sages have loved and used, and of which they have acknowledged the virtue so long as they lived.

THE THIRD PART OF THIS TREATISE, CONTAINING
THE DICTA OF THE SAGES.

i. I will now proceed to quote the very words of the various Sages in regard to this point, in order that you may the more easily understand our meaning. Know then that Almighty God first delivered this Art to our Father, Adam, in Paradise. For as soon as He had created him, and set him in the Garden of Eden, He imparted it to him in the following words: "Adam, here are two things: that which is above is volatile, that which is below is fixed. These two things contain the whole mystery. Observe it well, and make not the virtue that slumbers therein known to thy children; for these two things shall serve thee, together with all other created things under heaven, and I will lay at thy feet all the excellence and power of this world, seeing that thou thyself art a small world."

ii. ABEL, the son of Adam, wrote thus in his Principles: After God had created our Father, Adam, and set him in Paradise, He subjected to his rule all animals, plants, minerals, and metals. For man is the mountain of mountains, the Stone of all stones, the tree of trees, the root of roots, the earth of earths. All these things he includes within himself, and God has given to him to be the preserver of all things.

iii. SETH, the son of Adam, describes it thus: Know, my children, that in proportion as the acid is subjected to coction, by means of our Art, and is reduced into ashes, the more of the substance is extracted, and becomes a white body. If you cook this well, and free it from all blackness, it is changed into a stone, which is called a white stone until it is crushed. Dissolve it in water of the mouth, which has been well tempered, and its whiteness will soon change to redness. The whole process is performed by means of this sharp acid and the power of God.

iv. ISINDRUS: Our great and precious Matter is air, for air ameliorates the Matter, whether the air be gross or tenuous, warm or moist. For the grossness of the air arises from the setting, the approach, and the rising of the Sun. Thus the air may be hot or cold, or dry and rarefied, and the degrees of this distinguish summer and winter.

v. ANAXAGORAS says: God and His goodness are the first principle of all things. Therefore, the mildness of God reigns even beneath the earth, being the substance of all things, and thus also the substance beneath the earth. For the mildness of God mirrors itself in creating, and His integrity in the solidity that is beneath the earth. Now we cannot see His goodness, except in bodily form.

vi. SENIOR, or PANDOLPHUS, says: I make known to posterity that the thinness, or softness, of air is in water, and is not severed from the other elements. If the earth had not its vital juice, no moisture would remain in it.

vii. ARISTEUS delivers himself thus briefly: Know that the earth is round, and not flat. For if it were perfectly flat, the Sun would shine everywhere at the same moment.

viii. PYTHAGORAS: That which is touched and not seen, also that which is known but not looked upon, these are only heaven and earth; again, that which is not known is in the world and is perceived by sight, hearing, smell, taste, or touch. Sight shews the difference between black and white; hearing, between good and evil; taste, between sweet and bitter; touch, between subtle and gross; smell, between fragrant and fetid.

ix. ARISTEUS, in his Second Table, says: Beat the body which I have made known to you into thin plates; pour thereon our salt water, *i.e.,* water of life, and heat it with a gentle fire until its blackness disappears, and it becomes first white, and then red.

x. PARMENIDES: The Sages have written about many waters, stones, and metals, for the purpose of deceiving you. You that desire a knowledge of our Art, relinquish Sun, Moon, Saturn, and Venus, for our ore, and our earth, and why so? Every thing is of the nature of no thing.

xi. LUCAS: Take the living water of the Moon, and coagulate it, according to our custom. By those last words I mean that it is already coagulated. Take the living water of the Moon, and put it on our earth, till it becomes white: here, then, is our magnesia, and the natures of natures rejoice.

xii. ETHEL: Subject our Stone to coction till it becomes as bright as white marble. Then it is made a great and effectual Stone, sulphur having been added to sulphur, and preserving its property.

xiii. PYTHAGORAS: We exhibit unto you the regimen concerning these things. The substance must drink its water, like the fire of the Moon, which you have prepared. It must continue drinking its own water and moisture, till it turns white.

xiv. PHILETUS: Know, ye sons of philosophy, that the substance, the search after which reduces so many to beggary, is not more than one thing of most effectual properties. It is looked down upon by the ignorant, but held in great esteem by the Sages. Oh, how great is the folly, and how great also is the presumptuous ignorance of the vulgar herd! If you knew the virtue of this substance, kings, princes, and nobles would envy you. We Sages call it the most sharp acid, and without this acid nothing can be obtained, neither blackness, whiteness, nor the Tincture.

xv. METHUSALEM: With air, vapour, and spirit we shall have vulgar mercury changed into as good a silver as the nature of minerals will allow in the absence of heat.

xvi. SIXION: Ye sons of philosophy, if you would make our substance red, you must first make it white. Its three natures are summed up in whiteness and redness. Take, therefore, our Saturn, subject it to coction in aqua vitæ until it turns white, becomes thick, and is coagulated, and then again till it becomes red. Then it is *red lead*, and without this lead of the Sages nothing can be effected.

xvii. MUNDINUS: Learn, O imitators of this Art, that the philosophers have written variously of many gums in their books, but the substance they refer to is nothing but fixed and living water, out of which alone our noble Stone can be prepared. Many seek what they call the essential "gum," and cannot find it. I reveal unto you the knowledge of this gum and the mystery which abides therein. Know that our gum is better than Sun and Moon. Therefore it is highly esteemed by the Sages, though it is very cheap; and they say: Take care that you do not waste any of our "gum." But in their books they do not call it by its common name, and that is the reason why it is hidden from the many, according to the command which God gave to Adam.

xviii. DARDANIUS: Know, my sons, that the Sages take a living and indestructible water. Do not, then, set your hands to this task until you know the power and efficacy of this water. For nothing can be done in our Art without this indestructible water. For the Sages have described its power and efficacy as being that of spiritual blood. Transmute this water into body and spirit, and then, by the grace of God, you will have the spirit firmly fixed in the body.

xix. PYTHAGORAS, in his Second Book, delivers himself as follows: The Sages have used different names for the substance, and have told us to make the indestructible water white and red. They have also apparently indicated various methods, but they really agree with each other in regard to all essentials, and it is only their mystic language that causes a semblance of disagreement. Our Stone is a stone, and not a stone. It has neither the appearance nor the properties of stone, and yet it is a stone. Many have called it after the place where it is found; others after its colour.

xx. NEOPHIDES: I bid you take that mystic substance, white magnesia. And have a care that the Stone be pure and bright. Then place it in its aqueous, vessel, and subject it to gentle heat, until it first becomes black, then again white, and then red. The whole process should be accomplished in forty days. When you have done this, God shows you the first substance of the Stone, which is an eagle-stone, and known to all men.

xxi. THEOPHILUS: Take white Magnesia, i.e., quicksilver, mingled with the Moon. Pound it till it becomes thin water; subject it to coction for forty days; then the flower of the Sun will open with great splendour. Close well the mouth of the phial, and subject it to coction during forty days, when you will obtain a beautiful water, which you must treat in the same way for another forty days, until it is thoroughly purged of its blackness, and becomes white and fragrant.

xxii. BÆLUS says: I bid you take Mercury, which is the Magnesia of the Moon, and subject it and its body to coction till it becomes soft, thin, and like flowing water. Heat it again till all its moisture is coagulated, and it becomes a Stone.

xxiii. BASAN says: Put the yellow Matter into the bath, together with its spouse, and let not the bath be too hot, lest both be deprived of consciousness. Let a gentle temperature be kept up till the husband and the wife become one; sprinkle it with its sweat, and set it in a quiet place. Take care you do not drive off its virtue by too great heat. Honour then the King and his Queen, and do not burn them. If you subject them to gentle heat, they will become, first black, then white, and then red. If you understand this, blessed are ye. But if you do not, blame not Philosophy, but your own gross ignorance.

xxiv. ARISTOTLE: Know, my disciples, the Sages call our Stone sometimes earth, and sometimes water. Be directed in the regulation of your fire by the guidance of Nature. In the liquid there is first water, then a stone, then the earth of philosophers in which they sow their grain, which springs up, and bears fruit after its kind.

xxv. AGODIAS: Subject our earth to coction, till it becomes the first substance. Pound it to an impalpable dust, and again enclose it in its vessel. Sprinkle it with its own moisture till an union is effected. Then look at it carefully, and if the water presents the appearance of) (, continue to pound and heat. For, if you cannot reduce it to water, the water cannot be found. In order to reduce it to water, you must stir up the body with fire. The water I speak of is not rain water, but indestructible water which cannot exist without its body, which, in its turn, cannot exist, or operate, without its own indestructible water.

xxvi. SIRETUS: What is required in our Art is our water and our earth, which must become black, white, and red, with many intermediate colours which shew themselves successively. Everything is generated through our living and indestructible water. True Sages use nothing but this living water which supersedes all other substances and processes. Coction, califaction, distillation, sublimation, desiccation, humectation, albefaction, and rubrefaction, are all included in the natural development of this one substance.

xxvii. MOSINUS: The Sages have described our substance, and the method of its preparation, under many names, and thus have led many astray who did not understand our writing. It is composed of red and white sulphur, and of fixed or indestructible water, called permanent water.

xxviii. PLATO: Let it suffice you to dissolve bodies with this water, lest they be burned. Let the substance be washed with living water till all its blackness disappears, and it becomes a white Tincture.

xxix. ORFULUS: First, subject the Matter to gentle coction, of a temperature such as that with which a hen hatches her eggs, lest the moisture be burnt up, and the spirit of our earth destroyed. Let the phial be tightly closed that the earth may crush our substance, and enable its spirit to be extracted. The Sages say that quicksilver is extracted from the flower of our earth, and the water of our fire extracted from two things, and transmuted into our acid. But though they speak of many things, they mean only *one* thing, namely, that indestructible water which *is*our substance, and our acid.

xxx. BATHON: If you know the Matter of our Stone, and the mode of regulating its coction, and the chromatic changes which it undergoes—as though it wished to warn you that its names are as numerous as the colours which it displays—then you may perform the putrefaction, or first coction, which turns our Stone quite black. By this sign you may know that you have the key to our Art, and you will be able to transmute it into the mystic white and red. The Sages say that the Stone dissolves itself, coagulates itself, mortifies itself, and is quickened by its own inherent power, and that it changes itself to black, white, and red, in Christian charity and fundamental truth.

xxxi. BLODIUS. Take the Stone which is found everywhere, and is called Rebis (Two-thing), and grows in two mountains. Take it while it is still fresh, with its own proper blood. Its growth is in its skin, also in its flesh, and its food is in its blood, its habitation in the air. Take of it as much as you like, and plunge it into the Bath.

xxxii. LEAH, the prophetess, writes briefly thus: Know, Nathan, that the flower of gold is the Stone; therefore subject it to heat during a certain number of days, till it assumes the dazzling appearance of white marble.

xxxiii. ALKIUS: You daily behold the mountains which contain the husband and wife. Hie you therefore to their caves, and dig up their earth, before it perishes.

xxxiv. BONELLUS: All ye lovers of this Art, I say unto you, in faith and love: Relinquish the multiplicity of your methods and substances, for our substance is one thing, and is called living and indestructible water. He that is led astray by many words, will know the persons against whom he should be on his guard.

xxxv. HIERONYMUS: Malignant men have darkened our Art, perverting it with many words; they have called our earth, and our Sun, or gold, by many misleading names. Their salting, dissolving, subliming, growing, pounding, reducing to an acid, and white sulphur, their coction of the fiery vapour, its coagulation, and transmutation into red sulphur, are nothing but different aspects of one and the same thing, which, in its first stage, we may describe as incombustible and indestructible sulphur.

xxxvi. HERMES: Except ye convert the earth of our Matter into fire, our acid will not ascend.

xxxvii. PYTHAGORAS, in his Fourth Table, says: How wonderful is the agreement of Sages in the midst of difference! They all say that they have prepared the Stone out of a substance which by the vulgar is looked upon as the vilest thing on earth. Indeed, if we were to tell the vulgar herd the ordinary name of our substance, they would look upon our assertion as a daring falsehood. But if they were acquainted with its virtue and efficacy, they would not despise that which is, in reality, the most precious thing in the world. God has concealed this mystery from the foolish, the ignorant, the wicked, and the scornful, in order that they may not use it for evil purposes.

xxxviii. HAGIENUS: Our Stone is found in all mountains, all trees, all herbs, and animals, and with all men. It wears many different colours, contains the four elements, and has been designated a microcosm. Can you not see, you ignorant seekers after the Stone, who try, and vainly try, such a multiplicity of substances and methods, that our Stone is one earth, and one sulphur, and that it grows in abundance before your very eyes? I will tell you where you may find it. The first spot is on the summit of two mountains; the second, in all mountains; the third, among the refuse in the street; the fourth, in the trees and metals, the liquid of which is the Sun and Moon, Mercury, Saturn, and Jupiter. There is but one vessel, one method, and one consummation.

xxxix. MORIENUS: Know that our Matter is not in greater agreement with human nature than with anything else, for it is developed by putrefaction and transmutation. If it were not decomposed, nothing could be generated out of it. The goal of our Art is not reached until Sun and Moon are conjoined, and become, as it were, one body.

xl. THE EMERALD TABLE: It is true, without any error, and it is the sum of truth; that which is above is also that which is below, for the performance of the wonders of a certain one thing, and as all things arise from one Stone, so also they were generated from one common Substance, which includes the four elements created by God. And among other miracles the said Stone is born of the First Matter. The Sun is its Father, the Moon its Mother, the wind bears it in its womb, and it is nursed by the earth. Itself is the Father of the whole earth, and the whole potency thereof. If it be transmuted into earth, then the earth separates from the fire that which is most subtle from that which is hard, operating gently and with great artifice. Then the Stone ascends from earth to heaven, and again descends from heaven to earth, and receives the choicest influences of both heaven and earth. If you can perform this you have the glory of the world, and are able to put to flight all diseases, and to transmute all metals. It overcomes Mercury, which is subtle, and penetrates all hard and solid bodies. Hence it is compared with the world. Hence I am called Hermes, having the three parts of the whole world of philosophy.

xli. LEPRINUS says: The Stone must be extracted from a two-fold substance, before you can obtain the Elixir which is fixed in one essence, and derived from the one indispensable Matter, which God has created, and without which no one can attain the Art. Both these parts must be purified before they are joined together afresh. The body must become different, and so must the volatile spirit. Then you have the Medicine, which restores health, and imparts perfection to all things. The fixed and the volatile principle must be joined in an inseparable union, which defies even the destructive force of fire.

xlii. LAMECH: In the Stone of the Philosophers are the first elements, and the final colours of minerals, or Soul, Spirit, and Body, joined unto one. The Stone which contains all these things is called Zibeth, and the working of Nature has left it imperfect.

xliii. SOCRATES: Our Mystery is the life of all things, or the water. For water dissolves the body into spirit, and summons the living spirit from among the dead. My son, despise not my Practical Injunction. For it gives you, in a brief form, everything that you really need.

xliv. ALEXANDER: The good need not remain concealed on account of the bad men that might abuse it. For God rules over all, according to His Divine Will. Observe, therefore, that the salt of the Stone is derived from mercury, and is that Matter, most excellent of all things, of which we are in search. The same also contains in itself all secrets. Mercury is our Stone, which is composed of the dry and the moist elements, which have been joined together by gentle heat in an inseparable union.

xlv. SENIOR teaches us to make the Salt out of ashes, and then, by various processes, to change it into the Mercury of the Sages, because our Magistery is dependent on our water alone, and needs nothing else.

xlvi. ROSARIUS: It is a stone, and not a stone, viz., the eagle-stone. The substance has in its womb a stone, and when it is dissolved, the water that was coagulated in it bursts forth. Thus the Stone is the extracted spirit of our indestructible body. It contains mercury, or liquid water, in its body, or fixed earth, which retains its nature. This explanation is sufficiently plain.

xlvii. PAMPHILUS: The Salt of the Gem is that which is in its own bowels; it ascends with the water to the top of the alembic, and, after separation, is once more united and made one body with it by means of natural warmth. Or we may, with King Alexander, liken the union to that of a soul with its body.

xlviii. DEMOCRITUS: Our Substance is the conjunction of the dry and the moist elements, which are separated by a vapour or heat, and then transmuted into a liquid like water, in which our Stone is found. For the vapour unites to the most subtle earth the most subtle air, and contains all the most subtle elements. This first substance may be separated into water and earth, the latter being perceptible to the eye. The earth of the vapour is volatile when it ascends, but it is found fixed when the separation takes place, and when the elements are joined together again it becomes fixed mercury. For the enjoyment of this, His precious gift, we Sages ceaselessly praise and bless God's Holy Name.

xlix. SIROS: The body of the Sages, being calcined, is called everlasting water, which permanently coagulates our Mercury. And if the Body has been purified and dissolved, the union is so close as to resist all efforts at separation.

l. NOAH, the man of God, writes thus in his Table: My children and brethren, know that no other stone is found in the world that has more virtue than this Stone. No mortal man can find the true Art without this Stone. Blessed be the God of Heaven who has created this property in the Salt, even in the Salt of the Gem!

li. MENALDES: The fire of the Sages may be extracted from all natural things, and is called the quintessence. It is of earth, water, air, and fire. It has no cause of corruption or other contrary quality.

lii. HERMES, in his second Table, writes thus: Dissolve the ashes in the second element, and coagulate this substance into a Stone. Let this be done seven times. For as Naaman the Syrian was purged of his leprosy by washing himself seven times in Jordan, so our substance must undergo a seven-fold cleansing, by calcining and dissolving, and exhibiting a variety of ever deepening colours. In our water are hidden the four elements, and this earth, which swallows its water, is the dragon that swallows its tail, *i.e.*, its strength.

liii. NUNDINUS: The fire which includes all our chemical processes, is three-fold: the fiery element of the air, of water, and of the earth. This is all that our Magistery requires.

liv. ANANIAS: Know, ye Scrutators of Nature, that fire is the soul of everything, and that God Himself is fire and soul. And the body cannot live without fire. For without fire the other elements have no efficacy. It is, therefore, a most holy, awful, and divine fire which abides with God Himself in the Most Holy Trinity, for which also we give eternal thanks to God.

lv. BONIDUS: In the fountain of Nature our Substance is found, and nowhere else upon earth; and our Stone is fire, and has been generated in fire, without, however, being consumed by fire.

lvi. ROSINUS: Two things are hidden in two things, and indicate our Stone: in earth is fire, and air in water, yet there are only two outward things, viz., earth and water. For Mercury is our Stone, consisting as it does both of moist and dry elements. Mercury is dry and moist in its very nature, and all things have their growth from the dry and moist elements.

lvii. GEBER: We cannot find anything permanent, or fixed, in fire, but only a viscous natural moisture which is the root of all metals. For our venerable Stone nothing is required but mercurial substances, if they have been well purified by our Art, and are able to resist the fierce heat of fire. This Substance penetrates to the very roots of metals, overcomes their imperfect nature, and transmutes them, according to the virtue of the Elixir, or Medicine.

lviii. AROS: Our Medicine consists of two things, and one essence. There is one Mercury, of a fixed and a volatile substance, composed of body and spirit, cold and moist, warm and dry.

lix. ARNOLDUS: Let your only care be to regulate the coction of the Mercurial substance. In proportion as it is itself dignified shall it dignify bodies.

lx. ALPHIDIUS: Transmute the nature, and you will find what you want. For in our Magistery we obtain first from the gross the subtle, or the spirit; then from the moist the dry, *i.e.*, earth from water. Thus we transmute the corporeal into the spiritual, and the spiritual into the corporeal, the lowest into the highest, and the highest into the lowest.

lxi. BERNARDUS: The middle substance is nothing but coagulated mercury; and the first Matter is nothing but twofold mercury. For our Medicine is composed of two things, the fixed and the volatile, the corporeal and the spiritual, the cold and the warm, the moist and the dry. Mercury must be subjected to coction in a vessel with three divisions, that the dryness of the active fire may be changed into vaporous moisture of the oil that surrounds the substance. Ordinary fire does not digest our substance, but its heat converted into dryness is the true fire.

lxii. STEPHANUS: Metals are earthly bodies, and are generated in water. The water extracts a vapour from the Stone, and out of the moisture of [the] earth, by the operation of the Sun, God lets gold grow and accumulate. Thus earth and water are united into a metallic body.

lxiii. GUIDO BONATUS writes briefly concerning the quintessence, as being purer than all elements. The quintessence contains the four elements, that is, the first Matter, out of which God has created, and still creates, all things. It is Hyle, containing in a confused mixture the properties of every creature.

lxiv. ALRIDOS: The virtue and efficacy of everything is to be found in its quintessence, whether its nature be warm, cold, moist, or dry. This quintessence gives out the sweetest fragrance that can be imagined. Therefore the highest perfection is needed.

lxv. LONGINUS describes the process in the following terms: Let your vessel be tightly closed and exposed to an even warmth. This water is prepared in dry ashes, and is subjected to coction till the two become one. When one is joined to the other, the body is brought back to its spirit. Then the fire must be strengthened till the fixed body retains that which is not fixed by its own heat. With this you can tinge ten thousand times ten thousand of other substances.

lxvi. HERMES, in his Mysteries, says: Know that our Stone is lightly esteemed by the thankless multitude; but it is very precious to the Sages. If princes knew how much gold can be made out of a particle of Sun, and of our Stone, they would never suffer it to be taken out of their dominions.

> "The Sages rejoice when the bodies are dissolved; for our Stone is prepared with two waters. It drives away all

sickness from the diseased body, whether it be human or metallic."

By means of our Art, we do in one month what Nature cannot accomplish in a thousand years: for we purify the parts, and then join them together in an inseparable and indissoluble union.

lxvii. NERO: Know that our Mercury is dry and moist, and conjoined with the Sun and Moon. Sun and Moon in nature are cold and moist mercury and hot and dry sulphur, and both have their natural propagation by being joined in one thing.

Here follows a True Explanation of some of the Foregoing Philosophical Dicta, the meaning, word for word and point for point, being clearly set forth.

I now propose to say something about the meaning of the obscure and allegorical expressions used by some of the Sages whom I have quoted. Be sure that they all were true Sages, and really possessed our Stone. It may have been possessed by more persons since the time of Adam, but the above list includes all of whom I have heard. I need not here review all their sayings; for the words of the least of them are sufficient for imparting to you a knowledge of this Art; and my ambition goes no higher than that. If I have enumerated so large a number of authorities, I have only done so in order that you might the better understand both the theory and practice of this Art, and that you might be saved all unnecessary expense. For this reason I have declared this true philosophy with all the skill that God has given me. I hope the initiated will overlook any verbal inaccuracy into which I have fallen, and that they will be induced by my example to abstain from wilfully misleading anxious enquirers. I may have fallen into some errors of detail, but as to the gist of my work, I know what I have written, and that it is God's own truth.

Explanation of the Saying of Adam.

When God had created our first parent Adam, and set him in Paradise, He shewed him two things, namely, earth and water. Earth is fixed and indestructible, water is volatile and vaporous. These two contain the elements of all created things: water contains air, and earth fire — and of these four things the whole of creation is composed. In earth are enclosed fire, stones, minerals, salt, mercury, and all manner of metals; in water, and in air, all manner of living and organic substances, such as beasts, birds, fishes, flesh, blood, bones, wood, trees, flowers, and leaves. To all these things God imparted their efficacy and virtue, and subjected them to the mastery and use of Adam. Hence you may see how all these things are adapted to the human body, and are such as to meet the requirements of his nature. He may incorporate the virtue of outward substances by assimilating them in the form of food. In the same way, his mind is suitably constructed for the purpose of gaining a rational knowledge of the physical world. That this is the case, you may see from the first chapter of Genesis.

On the sixth day of the first year of the world, that is to say, on the 15th day of March, God created the first man, Adam, of red earth, in a field near Damascus, with a beautiful body, and after His own image. When Adam was created, he stood naked before the Lord, and with outstretched hands rendered thanks to Him, saying: O Lord, Thy hands have shaped me: now remember, I pray Thee, the work of Thy hands, which Thou hast clothed with flesh, and strengthened with bones, and grant me life and loving-kindness.

So the Lord endowed Adam with great wisdom, and such marvellous insight that he immediately, without the help of any teacher — simply by virtue of his original righteousness — had a perfect 'knowledge of the seven liberal arts, and of all animals, plants, stones, metals, and minerals. Nay, what is more, he had perfect understanding of the Holy Trinity, and of the coming of Christ in the flesh. Moreover, Adam was the Lord, King, and Ruler of all other creatures which, at the Divine bidding, were brought to him by the angel to receive their names. Thus all creatures acknowledged Adam as their Lord, seeing that it was he to whom the properties and virtues of all things were to be made known. Now the wisdom, and knowledge of all things, which Adam had received, enabled him to observe the properties, the origin, and the end of all things. He noted the division and destruction, the birth and decay of physical substances. He saw that they derive their origin from the dry and the moist elements, and that they are again transmuted into the dry and the moist. Of all these things Adam took notice, and especially of that which is called the first Matter. For he who knows how all things are transmuted into their first Matter, has no need to ask any questions. It was that which existed in the beginning before God created heaven and earth; and out of it may be made one new thing which did not exist before, a new earth, fire, water, air, Sun, Moon, Stars, in short, a new world.

As in the beginning all things were created new, so there is a kind of new creation out of the first substance in our Art. Now although God warned Adam generally not to reveal this first substance — viz., the moist and the dry elements — yet He permitted him to impart the knowledge to his son Seth. Abel discovered the Art for himself, by the wisdom which God had given him, and inscribed an account of it on beechen tablets. He was also the first to discover the art of writing; further, he foretold the destruction of the world by the Flood, and wrote all these things on wooden tablets, and hid them in a pillar of stone, which was found, long afterwards, by the children of Israel Thus you see that our Art was a secret from the beginning, and a secret it will remain to the end of the world. For this reason it is necessary carefully to consider all that is said about it, and especially the words of the Lord to Adam: for they exhibit in a succinct form the secret of the whole Art.

Explanation of the Saying of Abel.

This saying partly explains itself, and is partly explained by what we said about God's words to Adam. Yet I will add a few remarks concerning it.

Man hath within him the virtue and efficiency of all things, whence he is called a small world, and is compared to the large world, because the bones which are beneath his skin, and support his body, may be likened to the mountains and stones, his flesh to the earth, his veins to the rivers, and his small veins to the brooks which are discharged into them. The heart is the sea into which the great and small rivers flow; his hair resembles the growing herbs — and so with all other parts of his body. Again, his inward parts, such as the heart, lungs, and liver, are comparable to the metals. The hairs have their head in the earth (*i.e.*, the flesh) and their roots in the air, as the Sages say, that the root of their minerals is in the air, and their head in the earth. That which ascends by distillation is volatile, and is in the air; that which remains at the bottom, and is fixed, is the head, which is in the earth. Therefore, the one must always exist in conjunction with the other if it is to be effectual. Hence man may be compared to an inverted tree: for he has his roots, or his hair, in the air, while other trees have their hairs. or their roots, in the earth.

And of our Stone, too, the Sages have justly said that it has its head in the earth, and its root in the air. This similitude has a two-fold interpretation. First, with regard to the place in which our Matter is found; secondly, with regard to the dissolution and second conjunction of the Stone. For when our Stone rises upward in the alembic, it has its root in the air; but if it would regain its virtue and strength, it must once more return to its earth, and then it has its head and perfect potency in the earth. Hence our Stone, too, is not inaptly denominated a small world; it is called the mountain of mountains, from which our ore is derived, since it is evolved from the first substance in a way analogous to that in which the great world was created. Know that if you bury anything in [the] earth, and it rots, as food is digested in the human body, and the gross is separated from the subtle, and that which is fetid from that which is pure, then that which is pure is the first Matter which has been set free by decay. If you understand this, you know the true Art. But keep it to yourself, and cast not pearls before swine; for the vulgar regard our Art with ignorant contempt.

Explanation of the Saying of Seth, Son of Adam.

By "acid which is to be subjected to coction, and transmuted into ashes," the Sage Seth means distilled water, which we call seed. If this, by diligent coction, is condensed into a body — which he calls ashes — the body loses its blackness by being washed till it becomes white; for, by constant

p. 219

coction, all blackness and gross impurity are removed. If it were not for this earth, the spirit would never be coagulated; for it would have no body into which it could enter — seeing that it cannot be coagulated and fixed anywhere but in its own body. On the other hand, the spirit purifies its body, as Seth says, and makes it white. He says further: "If you diligently heat it, and free it from its blackness, it is changed into a Stone, which is called the white coin of the Stone." That is to say, if it is slowly heated with a gentle fire, it is by degrees changed into a body which resists fire, and is named a Stone. It is fixed, and it has a brilliantly white appearance. A coin it is called, because, as he who has a coin may purchase with it bread or whatever else he needs, so he who has this Stone may purchase for himself health, wisdom, longevity, gold, silver, gems, etc. Hence it is justly called the Coin, since it can buy what all the riches in the world cannot procure. It is struck by the Sages, who, instead of the image of a prince, impress upon it their own image. Therefore it is denominated the COIN of the SAGES, because it is their own money, struck in their own mint.

Again, when the Sage says, "Heat the Stone till it breaks [itself], and dissolve it in the well-tempered water of the Moon," he means that the Stone must be heated by that which is in itself, until it is changed into water, or dissolved. All this is done by its own agency; for the body is called Moon, when it has been changed into water; and the extracted spirit, or distilled water, is called Sun. For the element of [the] air is concealed in it; but the body must be broken in its own water, or dissolved by itself. The "well-tempered water of the Moon" is the gentle inward heat which changes it into water, and yields two waters, viz., the distilled spirit, and the dissolved body. These two waters are again united by slow and gentle coction, the distilled spirit becoming coagulated into a body, the dissolved body becoming a spirit. The fixed becomes volatile, and the volatile fixed, by dissolution and coagulation, and both assume, first a white, and then a red colour. The change to white and red is produced by the same water, and the white is always followed by the red, just as the black is followed by the white. When the Sage says, in conclusion, "that the whole can be accomplished only with the best acid, through the power of God alone," he means that the one thing from which alone our Stone can be procured may be compared to the sharpest acid, and that, by means of our Art, this acid is changed into the best of earthly things, which all the treasures of all kings and princes are not sufficient to buy.

Explanation of the Saying of Isindrus.

Good Heavens! How skilfully the Sages have contrived to conceal this matter. It would surely have been far better if they had abstained from writing altogether. For the extreme obscurity of their style has overwhelmed thousands in ruin, and plunged them into the deepest poverty, especially those who set about this task without even the slightest knowledge of Nature, or of the requirements of our Art. What the Sages write is strictly true; but you cannot understand it unless you are already initiated in the secrets of this Art. Yea, even if you were a Doctor of the Doctors, and a Light of the World, you would be able to see no meaning in their words without this knowledge. They have written, but you are none the wiser. They half wished to communicate the secret to their posterity; but a jealous feeling prevented them from doing so in plain language. To the uninitiated reader these words of Isindrus must appear nothing short of nonsense:

"Great is the air, because the air corrects the thing, if it is thin or thick, hot or cold." But the Sage means that when it ascends with the water, it is hot air, for fire and air bear our Stone like secret fire concealed therein, and the water which ascends from the earth, by that ascension becomes air, and thin; and when it descends, it descends into water which contains fire; thus the earth is purified, seeing that the water takes [the] fire with it into the earth. For the fire is the Soul, and the Moon the Spirit. Therefore, the air is great, because it bears with it water and fire, and imparts them to all things, though thereby (by this loss of water) itself becomes cold. Then the air becomes thick, when with its fire it is transmuted into the body, and thus the air corrects the thing by its thickness. For it bears out our Stone as it carries it in, and purifies it both in its ascent and in its descent. In the same way air purifies all things that grow (*i.e.*, plants), gives them their food (*i.e.*, water), and imparts to them its fire, by which they are sustained. Of this you may convince yourself by ocular demonstration. For the air bears the clouds, and sheds them upon earth in the form of rain; which rain contains secret fire derived from the earth, and the rays of the Sun by which it was drawn upward—and this fire it gives to all things as food. And although the rays of the Sun and Moon are immeasurably subtle, swift, and intangible; yet the rays of our Sun and Moon are much swifter and more subtle than those which are received by the plants in their growth. For the earth digests the rays of the Sun and Moon, and they sustain in the most wonderful manner things of vegetable growth; and all the living rays of the Sun and Moon nourish all created things. For by this digestion they obtain their life. For this reason the air may be called great, because through the grace of God it accomplishes great things.

Again, when the Sage says, "If the air becomes thick," *i.e.*, when the Sun turns aside, or is changed, "there is a thickness, till it rises," he means that if the distilled water which is taken for the Sun, or fire, approaches its body, and is changed into it, then the Sun stoops down to the earth. Thereby the air becomes thick, being joined to the earth, and if the Sun is once more elevated the air becomes thin; that is to say, when the water is extracted from the earth by means of the alembic, the fire rises upward, *i.e.*, the Sun is exalted, and the air becomes thin. Again, when he says, "This also is hot and cold, and thickness, and thinness, or softness," the Sage means that the Sun is hot, and the Moon cold; for the earth, when dissolved, is the Moon, and water, in which is fire, is the Sun: these two must be conjoined in an inseparable union. This union enables them to reduce the elements of all metallic and animal bodies, into which they are injected, to perfect purity and health. When the Sage adds that thickness and thinness denote summer and winter, he means that our Art is mingled of thickness and thinness, or two elements which must be united by gentle warmth, like that of winter and summer combined. This temperate warmth, which resembles that of a bath, brings the Sun and Moon together. Thus I have, by the grace of God, interpreted to you the parabolic saying of Isindrus.

Explanation of the Saying of Anaxagoras.

From the beginning of all things God is. He is likened to light and fire, and He may be likened to the latter in His essence, because fire is the first principle of all things that are seen and grow. In the same way, the first principle of our Art is fire. Heat impels Nature to work, and in its working are manifested Body, Spirit, and Soul; that is, earth and water. Earth is the Body, oil the Soul, and water the Spirit; and all this is accomplished through the Divine goodness and lenity, without which Nature can do nothing; or, as the Sage says: "God's lenity rules all things; and beneath the thickness of the earth, after creation, are revealed lenity and integrity." That is to say: If the earth is separated from the water, and itself dissolved into oil and water, the oil is integrity, and the water lenity; for the water imparts the soul to the oil and to the body, and [the body] receives nothing but what is imparted to it by heaven, that is, by the water — and the water is revealed under the oil, the oil under the earth. For the fire is subtle, and floats upward from the earth with subtle waters, and is concealed in the earth. Now oil and air and earth are purified by their own spirit. Therefore the oil is integrity in the body, and the spirit lenity. And the spirit in the first operation descends to the body and restores life to the body; although the oil is pure and remains with the body, yet it cannot succour the body without the help of the spirit; for the body suffers violence and anguish while it is dissolved and purified. Then, again, the "thickness of the earth" is transmuted into a thin substance such as water or oil, and thus the "lenity" is seen in the body. For the body is so mild or soft as to be changed into water, or oil, although before it was quite dry. Therefore oil is seen in the earth, which is the fatness or life of the water, &e., an union of fire, air, and water. Now give the water to the body to drink, and it will be restored to life. And though those three elements have ascended from the earth, yet the virtue remains with the body, as you may see by dissolving it into oil and water. But the oil cannot operate without the spirit, nor can the spirit bear fruit without the oil and the body. Therefore they must be united; and all "lenity" and "integrity" are seen in the body when it is transmuted to white and red.

Explication of the Opinion of Pythagoras.

This Sage asks what that is which is touched, and yet not seen. He means that the substance which is prepared by our Art is one thing, which is tangible and invisible. That is to say, it is felt, but not seen, nor is the mode of its operation known. He who knows it, but knows not its operation, as yet knows nothing as he ought. This one thing, which alone is profitable for the purposes of our Art, proceeds from a certain dark place, where it is not seen, nor are its operation or its virtue known to any but the initiated. A great mystery is also concealed in the Matter itself, namely, air and fire, or the Sun, the Moon, and the Stars. This is concealed in it, and yet is invisible, as the Sage says: What is not seen, or known, is only heaven. That which is felt, and not seen, is earth. Earth, says the Sage, is thickness, or body, which is found at the bottom of the Matter, has accumulated in the Matter, and can be felt and known. By the words, "that is between heaven and earth, which is not known," (*i.e.*, in the world), the Sage means that the Matter of our Stone is found in the small world; not in rocks and mountains, or in the earth, but between heaven and earth, *i.e.*, in the air. Again, when he says that "in it are senses, and entirety, as smell, taste, hearing, touch," he would teach us that in human nature there is entirety of mind and perception; for man can know, feel, and understand. He would also teach us how our Stone is to be found, namely, by sight, hearing, smell, taste, and touch. By sight, because the Matter of the Stone is thick, or thin and clear, and turns black, white, and red. By smell, because, when its impurity is purged away, it emits a most sweet fragrance. By taste, because it is first bitter and disagreeable, but afterwards becomes most pleasant. By touch, because that sense enables us to distinguish between the hard and the soft, the gross and the subtle, between water and earth, and between the different stages of distillation, putrefaction, dissolution, coagulation, fermentation, and injection, which the substance goes through. The different processes of the task are perceived with the senses, and it should be accomplished within forty-six days.

Loosening of the Knot of Aristeus.

"Take the body which I have shewn you, and beat it into thin leaves," *i.e.*, take the earth which cleaves to our substance, and, by having become dry, becomes visible and knowable; for now it is water and earth. The earth is thus shewn, and divided into two parts, earth and water. Let that earth be taken, placed in a phial, and put in a warm bath, by the warmth of which it is dissolved, through its own internal coction, into water; this the Sage calls beating into thin leaves. The body which is thus obtained is variously described as the Philosopher's Stone, or the Stone of leaves. "Add some of our salt water, and this is the water of life." That means: After its dissolution into water, it must receive our salt water to drink — for this water has been previously distilled from it, and is the water of life; for the soul and spirit of the body are hidden in it, and it is called our sea water; the same also is its natural name, because it is obtained from the invisible hidden sea of the Sages, the sea of the smaller world. For our Art is called the smaller world, and thus it is the water of our sea. If this water is added to the body, and heated and purified with it, the body is purged by long coction, and its colour changes from black to a brilliant white, while the water is coagulated, and forms, by indissoluble union with the body, the imperishable Philosopher's Stone, which you must use to the glory of God, and the good of your neighbour.

Exposition of the Saying of Parmenides.

Jealous Sages have named many waters and metals and stones, simply for the purpose of deceiving you; herein the philosophers would warn us that they have used secrecy, lest the whole mystery should be manifested before all the world. Those who follow the letter of their directions are sure to be led astray, and to miss entirely the true foundation of our Art. The fault, however, lies not with the Sages so much with the ignorance of their readers. The Sages name it a *stone*; and so it *is* a stone, which is dug up from our mine. They speak of metals; and there are such things as metals liquefied from our ore. They speak of water; but our water we obtain from our own spring. The red and white sulphur they refer to are obtained from our air. Their salt is obtained from our salt mines. *It* is our Sun, our verdigris, halonitre, alkali, orpiment, arsenic, our poison, our medicine, etc. By whatever name they call it they cannot make it more than one thing. It is rightly described by all the Sages, but not plainly enough for the uninitiated enquirer. For such an one knows neither the substance nor its operation. The Sage says: "Relinquish Sun, Moon, and Venus for our ore," *i.e.*, it is not to be found in any earthly metals, but only in *our* ore. Whoever rightly understands the concluding words of the Sage has received a great blessing at the hand of God.

Explanation of the Saying of Lucas.

By the living water of the Moon this Sage means our water, which is twofold. The distilled water is the Moon; the Sun, or fire, is hidden in it, and is the Father of all things. Hence it is compared to a man, because the Sun is in the water. It is also called living water; for the life of the dead body is hidden in the water. It is the water of the Moon, because the Sun is the Father and the Moon the Mother. Hence, also, they are regarded as husband and wife. The Body is the Moon, or Mother, and the distilled water, or male principle, rises upward from the earth; and for that reason is sometimes called Moon. For it is the water of the Moon, or Body. It has left the Body, and must enter it again before our Art can be perfected. Hence the Body, or Moon, has well been designated the female principle, and the water, or Sun, the male principle, for reasons which have been set forth at length in this book.

Again, when the Sage says, "Coagulate it after our fashion," those last three words mean that the body must receive its spirit to drink gradually, and little by little, until it recovers its life, and health, and strength, which takes place by means of the same gentle heat which digests food in the stomach, and matures fruit in its place. For it is our custom to eat, drink, and live in gentle warmth. By this regimen our body is preserved, and all that is foul and unprofitable is driven out from our body. According to the same fashion of gentle coction, all that is fetid and black is gradually purged out of our Stone. For when the Sage says "after *our* fashion," he wishes to teach you that the preparation of the Stone bears a strict analogy to the processes of the human body. That the chemical development of our substance is internal, and caused by the operation of Nature and of its four elements, the Sage indicates by the words, "Everything is already coagulated." The substance contains all that is needed; there is nothing to be added or taken away, seeing that it is dissolved and again conjoined by its own inherent properties. When the Sage continues, "I bid you take water of life, which descends from the Moon, and pour it upon our earth till it turns white," he means that if water and earth are separated from each other, then the dry body is our earth, and the extracted water is the water of the Moon, or water of life. This process of adfusion, desiccation, attrition, coagulation, etc., is repeated till the body turns white; and then takes place our conglutination, which is indissoluble. "Then," as the Sage says, "we have our Magnesia, and the Nature of natures rejoices." Its spirit and body become one thing: they were one thing, and after separation have once more become one thing; therefore, one nature rejoices in the restoration of the other.

Exposition of the Saying of Ethelius.

He says: "Heat our Stone until it shines like dazzling marble; then it becomes great, and a mystic Stone; for sulphur added to sulphur preserves it on account of its fitness." That is to say: When the moist and the dry have been separated, the dry which lies at the bottom, and is called our Stone, is as black as a raven. It must be subjected to the coction of our water (separated from it), until it loses its blackness, and becomes as white as dazzling marble. Then it is the mystic Stone which by coction has been transmuted into fixed mercury with the blessing of God. The Stone is mystic, or secret, because it is found in a secret place, in an universally despised substance where no one looks for the greatest treasure of the world. Hence it may well be called The HIDDEN STONE. By the joining of two sulphurs and their mutual preservation, he means that though, after the separation of spirit and body, there seem to be two substances, yet, in reality, there is only one substance;

so the body which is below is "sulphur," and the spirit
which is above is also "sulphur." Now, when the spirit
returns to the body, one sulphur is added to another;
and they are bound together by a mutual fitness, since
the body cannot be without the spirit, nor the spirit
without the body. Hence there are these two sulphurs
in the body, the red and the white, and the white
sulphur is in the black body, while the red is hid
beneath it. If the spirit is gradually added to the body,
it is entirely coagulated into the body, sulphur is
added to sulphur, and perfection is attained through
the fitness which exists between them. The body
receives nothing but its own spirit; for it has retained
its soul, and what has been extracted from a body can
be joined to nothing but that same body. The spirit
delights in nothing so much as in its own soul, and its
own body. Hence the Sage says: "When the spirit has
been restored to the body, the sulphur to the sulphur,
and the water to the earth, and all has become white,
then the body retains the spirit, and there can be no
further separation." Thus you have the well purged
earth of the Sages, in which we sow our grain, unto
infinity, that it may bring forth much fruit.

Explanation of the Saying of Pythagoras.

You have good cause to wonder at the great variety of
ways in which the Sages have expressed the same
thing. Nevertheless, their descriptions apply only to
one Matter, and their sayings refer only to a single
substance. For when our Sage says, "We give you
directions concerning these things: We tell you that it
is dry water, like the water of the Moon, which you

have prepared," he means that we Sages must give directions, according to the best of our ability. If those directions, rightly understood, do not answer the purpose, you may justly charge us with fraud and imposture. But if you fail through not taking our meaning, you must blame your own unspeakable stupidity, which follows the letter, but not the spirit of our directions. When the Sage further says that it must drink its own water, he would teach you that after the separation of the dry from the moist, the water extracted from the body is the right water, and the water of the Moon, prepared by putrefaction and distillation. This extracted water is regarded as the male principle, and the earth, or body, as the female principle. The water of the husband must now be joined in conjugal union to that of the wife; the body must, at intervals, drink of its own prepared water, and become ever purer, the more it drinks, till it turns most wonderfully white. Then it is called "our calx," and you must pour the water of our calx upon the body, until it is coagulated, becoming tinged, and a most bright quality returns to it, and the body itself is saturated with its own moisture. If you wish to obtain the red tincture, you should dissolve and coagulate, and go through the whole process over again. Verily, this is God's own truth, an accurate, simple, and plain statement of the requirements of our Art.

Explanation of the Emerald Table of Hermes.

Hermes is right in saying that our Art is true, and has been rightly handed down by the Sages; all doubts concerning it have arisen through false interpretation of the mystic language of the philosophers. But, since they are loth to confess their own ignorance, their readers prefer to say that the words of the Sages are imposture and falsehood. The fault really lies with the ignorant reader, who does not understand the style of the Philosophers. If, in the interpretation of our books, they would suffer themselves to be guided by the teaching of Nature, rather than by their own foolish notions, they would not miss the mark so hopelessly. By the words which follow: "That which is above is also that which is below," he describes the Matter of our Art, which, though one, is divided into two things, the volatile water which rises upward, and the earth which lies at the bottom, and becomes fixed. But when the reunion takes place, the body becomes spirit, and the spirit becomes body, the earth is changed into water and becomes volatile, the water is transmuted into body, and becomes fixed. When bodies become spirits, and spirits bodies, your work is finished; for then that which rises upward and that which descends downward become *one* body. Therefore the Sage says that that which is above is that which is below, meaning that, after having been separated into two substances (from being one substance), they are again joined together into one substance, *i.e.*, an union which can never be dissolved, and possesses such virtue and efficacy that it can do in one moment what the Sun cannot accomplish in a thousand years. And this miracle is wrought by a thing which is despised and rejected by the multitude. Again, the Sage tells us that all things were created, and are still generated, from one first substance, and consist of the same elementary material; and in this first substance God has appointed the four elements, which represent a common material into which it might perhaps be possible to resolve all things. Its development is brought about by the distillation of the Sun and Moon. For it is operated upon by the natural heat of the Sun-and Moon, which stirs up its internal action, and multiplies each thing after its kind, imparting to the substance a specific form. The soul, or nutritive principle, is the earth which receives the rays of the Sun and Moon, and therewith feeds her children as with mother's milk. Thus the Sun is the father, the Moon is the mother, the earth the nurse—and in this substance is that which we require. He who can take it and prepare it is truly to be envied. It is separated by the Sun and Moon in the form of a vapour, and collected in the place where it is found. When Hermes adds that "the air bears it in its womb, the earth is its nurse, the whole world its Father," he means that when the substance of our Stone is dissolved, then the wind bears it in its womb, *i.e.*, the air bears up the substance in the form of water, in which is hid fire, the soul of the Stone; and fire is the Father of the whole world. Thus, the volatile substance rises upward, while that which remains at the bottom, is the "whole world" (seeing that our Art is compared to a "small world"). Hence Hermes calls fire the father of the whole world, because it is the Sun of our Art, and air, Moon, and water ascend from it; the earth is the nurse of the Stone, *i.e.*, when the earth receives the rays of the Sun and Moon, a new body is born, like a new foetus in the mother's womb. The earth receives and digests the light of Sun and Moon, and imparts food to its fœtus day by day, till it becomes great and strong, and puts off its blackness and defilement, and is changed to a different colour. This, "child," which is called "our daughter," represents our Stone, which is born anew of the Sun and Moon, as you may easily see, when the spirit, or the water that ascended, is gradually transmuted into the body, and the body is born anew, and grows and increases in size like the fœtus in the mother's womb. Thus the Stone is generated from the first substance, which contains the four elements; it is brought forth by two things, the body and the spirit; the wind bears it in its womb, for it carries the Stone upward from earth to heaven, and down again from heaven to earth. Thus the Stone receives increase from above and from below, and is born a second time, just as every other fœtus is generated in the maternal womb; as all created things bring forth their young, even so does the air, or wind, bring forth our Stone. When Hermes adds, "Its power, or virtue, is entire, when it is transmuted into earth," he means that when the spirit is transmuted into the body, it receives its full strength and virtue. For as yet the spirit is volatile, and not fixed, or permanent. If it is to be fixed, we must proceed as the baker does in baking bread. We must impart only a little of the spirit to the body at a time, just as the baker only puts a little leaven to his meal, and with it leavens the whole lump. The spirit, which is *our* leaven, in like fashion transmutes the whole body into its own substance. Therefore the body must be leavened again and again, until the whole lump is thoroughly pervaded with the power of the leaven. In our Art the body leavens the spirit, and transmutes it into one body, and the spirit leavens the body, and transmutes it into one spirit. And the two, when they have become one, receive power to leaven all things, into which they are injected, with their own virtue.

The Sage continues: "If you gently separate the earth from the water, the subtle from the hard, the Stone ascends from earth to heaven, and again descends from heaven to earth, and receives its virtue from above and from below. By this process you obtain the glory and brightness of the whole world. With it you can put to flight poverty, disease, and weariness; for it overcomes the subtle mercury, and penetrates all hard and firm bodies." He means that all who would accomplish this task must separate the moist from the dry, the water from the earth. The water, or fire, being subtle, ascends, while the body is hard, and remains where it is. The separation must be accomplished by gentle heat, *i.e.*, in the temperate bath of the Sages, which acts slowly, and is neither too hot nor too cold. Then the Stone ascends to heaven, and again descends from heaven to earth. The spirit and body are first separated, then again joined together by gentle coction, of a temperature resembling that with which a hen hatches her eggs. Such is the preparation of the substance, which is worth the whole world, whence it is also called a "little world." The possession of the Stone will yield you the greatest delight, and unspeakably precious comfort. It will also set forth to you in a typical form the creation of the world. It will enable you to cast out all disease from the human body, to drive away poverty, and to have a good understanding of the secrets of Nature. The Stone has virtue to transmute mercury into gold and silver, and to penetrate all hard and firm bodies, such as precious stones and metals. You cannot ask a better gift of God than this gift, which is greater than all other gifts. Hence Hermes may justly call himself by the proud title of "Hermes Trismegistus, who holds the three parts of the whole world of wisdom."

==============

ANOTHER TRACT,

CORRESPONDING TO THE FIRST, WHICH MAY BE
READ WITH GREAT PROFIT.

PREFACE.

We may justly wonder that the Sages who have written about this most precious and secret Art, have thought it necessary to invent so many occult and allegorical expressions, by means of which our Art is concealed not only from the unworthy, but from earnest and diligent students of the truth. Foolish persons, indeed, who read their books, and hear of the riches and all the other good things which this Art affords, experience a pleasant tickling sensation in their ears, and straightway behold visions of themselves sitting on golden thrones, and commanding all the treasures of the universe; they fancy that the Art can be learned in the twinkling of an eye, soon come to regard themselves as great

Doctors, and are unable to conceive the possibility of their making a mistake, or being led astray by the Sages. Much less are they aware that it has always been the custom of the philosophers to conceal the fundamental facts of this Art, and to reveal them to their own sons and disciples only in sententious allegorical sayings. It is impossible to read through all that the Sages have ever written on this subject; but it is a still more hopeless undertaking to gather from their books a full and sufficient knowledge of our Art, unless, indeed, God opens your understanding, and gives you a real insight into the natural properties of things, and thereby into the sayings of those who speak of them. For it is Nature alone that accomplishes the various processes of our Art, and a right understanding of Nature will furnish you with eyes wherewith to perceive the secrets thereof. Thus Bason says: "Take care not to add anything else; for it is the property of our substance to overcome all other things." And Bondinus tells us that the whole process is accomplished by means of the water which issues from the Stone. Alphidius declares that the Philosopher's Stone contains four different natures, and thereby possesses a virtue and efficacy such as are found in no other stone. Therefore, the question of the Royal Sage Haly, whether there is another stone upon earth which may be compared with our Stone, and possesses the same wonderful properties, is answered by Morienus in the following words: "I am aware of no other stone of equal excellence, potency, and virtue; for it contains the four elements in a visible form, and is singular of its kind among all the created things of the world. If, therefore, any person should take any [other] Stone but the one demanded by this Magistery, his labours must result in failure." Moreover, the ancient Sage Arros says: "Our Stone is useless for our purpose, until it be purged of its gross earth." In like manner we are informed by Morienus that "unless the body be purged of its grossness, it cannot be united to its spirit; but when it has put off its gross nature, the spirit joins itself to it, and delights in it, because both have been freed from all impurity." The truth of his words is attested by Ascanius in "The Crowd," who says: "Spirits cannot join themselves to impure bodies; but when the body has been well purged, and digested by coction, the spirit becomes united to it, amidst a phenomenal exhibition of all the colours in the world, and the imperfect body is tinged with the indestructible colour of the ferment; this ferment is the soul, in and through which the spirit is joined to the body, and transmuted with the body into the colour of the ferment, whereupon all three become one thing." Hence it is well, though somewhat enigmatically said by the Sages, that there takes place a conjugal union of husband and wife, and that of the two a child is born after their likeness, just as men generate men, metals metals, and all other things that which is like them.

Hence all that would exercise this Art must know the properties of the most noble substance thereof, and follow the guidance of Nature. But many enquirers conduct their operations at haphazard, they grope in the dark, and do not know whether their art be an imitation of Nature, or not. Yet they undertake to correct, and intensify, the operation of Nature. Of such persons Arnold says that they approach our Art as the ass goes up to the crib, not knowing for what it opens its mouth. For they do not know what they would do, nor are they aware that they must listen to the teaching of Nature. They seek to do the works of Nature, but they will not watch the hand of her whom they pretend to imitate. Yet our Art has a true foundation in natural fact. For Nature prepares the metals in the earth, some perfect, like gold and silver; others imperfect, like Venus, Mars, Saturn, and Jupiter, according to the labour and influence of the planets. He, then, who would accomplish our Magistery, and desires to participate in this most noble Art, must know the seed from which the metals are naturally generated in the earth, which seed we remove by Nature, and purify and prepare it by Art, making it so glorious, and full of wonderful potency, that with it we can impart instant purity and perfection to the imperfect bodies of men and metals. This seed we must extract from perfect, pure, and mature bodies, if we would attain the desired end. Now, in order that you may the more readily attain this knowledge, I have composed the following Tract concerning the first principle of Nature, and the creation and generation of man — which the student of our Magistery should diligently peruse, consider, and digest. Then he will not so easily miss the right path.

The Fear of the Lord is the Beginning of Wisdom.

All true Sages and philosophers have earnestly sought to obtain a knowledge of Almighty God as He is revealed in His marvellous works; this knowledge they attained, in so far as it can be attained by the human mind, by diligently considering the origin and first principles of all things. For they were enabled to realize the omnipotence of the Creator by the contemplation of the secret powers, and miraculous virtues, which He has infused into natural things. They were led to consider how they might employ their knowledge for the good of the human race, and how they might reveal it to others, and they received wisdom to expound the first principles of natural things, but more especially the birth and death of man, in something like the following way: In the beginning God created all things out of a subtle liquid, or impalpable vapour which was neither moist, nor dry, nor cold, nor hot, nor light, nor dark, but a confused chaos. This subtle vapour God first changed into water, which He then separated into a hard and a liquid part, or into earth and water. Out or elementary water He further evolved air, and out of elementary earth He brought forth fire, that is, elementary fire. And it may still be seen that the two first elements contain the two last; for daily experience teaches us that in water there is air, and that in earth there is fire. Out of these God created the firmament, the Sun, the Moon, and the Stars, and all other natural objects. At last He created a being in His own image, which He formed out of moist earth—i.e., for the most part out of earth (which encloses fire) moistened with water (containing air). Hence it is said that man was created out of the four elements, and he is called a "small world." But man lay like one dead upon the ground, until God breathed into his nostrils the spirit of life, and Adam became a living soul. In like manner God created all other animals, and all plants and minerals, out of the four elements. Then God set Adam in the Garden of Eden, in Paradise, which He had planted with His own hands, and in which flourished all manner of flowers, fruit, roots, herbs, leaves, and grass. Then Adam's heart was filled with joy, and he understood the great power of his Creator, and praised and magnified Him with his lips; at that time he suffered no lack of any thing, having all that his heart desired, and he was appointed lord of all other creatures. Therefore, the eternal Creator bade the holy angels bring every other living being to Adam, that all might acknowledge him as their lord, and that Adam might give to each one its own name, and distinguish one from the other.

Now when God beheld the animals walking about in Paradise, each with its own mate (except Adam, for whom no mate was found); when God saw them approaching him, and yet eager to flee from him, because of the reverence and awe with which he inspired them –God said: "It is not good for man to be alone"; therefore He caused a deep sleep to fall upon Adam, and taking one of his ribs, not far from his heart, He formed it into a beautiful woman. This woman God brought unto the man, calling her Eve, and gave her to him for a wife, that he might protect her, that she might obey him, and that they might be fruitful and multiply.

The Glory and Excellence of Adam.

God had appointed that Adam and Eve should spend a thousand years in Paradise, and then be translated, body and soul, to the Eternal Life of Heaven; the same glorious destiny was in reserve for their posterity. For as yet man was pure, good, and sinless, and not subject or liable to any kind of distemper, or sickness. He was acceptable and perfect in the sight of His Creator, who had made him in His own image, and given him all the produce of Paradise to eat, except the fruit of the Tree of Knowledge, from which he was to abstain on pain of eternal punishment, both bodily and spiritual. But when he gave ear to the seducing words of the Evil One, and ate the forbidden fruit, he straightway became poor and wretched, perceived his own nakedness, and concealed himself amongst the trees of the garden. He had deserved eternal death, and it would have fallen upon him, if the Son of God, our Lord and Saviour Jesus Christ, had not promised to give satisfaction for him. Yet in this world God punished Adam with a heavy yoke of wretchedness, tribulation, poverty, and disease, followed by the bitter agony of death. He also drove him forth from Paradise, and laid a heavy curse upon the ground, that thenceforward it should not bring forth fruit of its own accord, but that it should bear thorns and thistles. Now, when Adam found himself in the midst of a wild and uncultivated earth, compelled to gain his bread by tilling the field in the sweat of his brow, and to endure much suffering, care, and anxiety, he began to think seriously of what he had done to provoke the wrath of God, to experience deep sorrow for his grievous sin, and to implore God's gracious mercy and forgiveness. His prayers appeased the paternal heart ofGod, and induced Him to ease the grievous yoke laid upon Adam. The central fact of his punishment, however, remained, and death, though deferred, at length overtook him.

But, as I say, God mitigated the punishment of Adam, and took away from his neck the grievous yoke of suffering, by shewing him the means of warding off the strokes of impending calamity. For this purpose the natural properties of things were revealed to Adam by the inspiration of the Holy Spirit; and he was taught to prepare medicines out of herbs, stones, and metals, wherewith he might alleviate his hard lot, ward off disease, and keep his body in good health until the end of his days, which, however, was known to God alone. For, although from the very beginning Adam had a clear insight into the working of the natural world, the greatest of all secrets was still hidden from him, till God one day called him into Paradise, and set forth to him this marvellous mystery — the mystery of our Stone — in the following words:

"Behold, Adam, here are two things, the one fixed and immutable, the other volatile and inconstant. The great virtue and potency that slumber in them you must not reveal to all your sons. For I created them for a special purpose, which I will now no longer conceal from you." Now, when Adam had learned the mystery out of God's own mouth, he kept it a strict secret from all his sons, until at length, towards the close of his life, he obtained leave from God to make the preparation of the Stone known to his son Seth. Unless Adam had possessed the knowledge of this great mystery he would not have been able to prolong his life to the age of 300 (let alone 900) years. For he was never for a <u>moment</u> free from an agonizing sense of his guilt, and of the terrible evils which he had, by his disobedience, brought upon himself and his posterity, who, through his fault, were one and all involved in the condemnation of eternal death. If we consider this, it must appear amazing that Adam could keep alive even so long as a single year after his fall; and we thereby clearly perceive (from the fact that he attained to so great a length of days) that the goodness of God must have furnished him with some life-preserving remedy. If Adam had not possessed our Medicine, or Tincture, he could not have borne up under so much tribulation, anxiety, wretchedness,grief, sorrow, and disease. But against all these ills he used our Medicine, which preserved his limbs and his strength from decay, braced his faculties, comforted his heart, refreshed his spirit, relieved his anxiety, fortified his mortal body against all manner of disease, and, in short, guarded him from all evil until the last hour of his life.

At length, however, Adam found that the Remedy had no longer any power to strengthen him, or to prolong his life. So he began to consider his end, refrained from applying the Medicine any more, threw himself upon the mercy of God, and sent his son Seth (to whom he had confided the secret), to the gate of Paradise, to demand some of the fruit of the Tree of Life. His request was denied him, whereupon he returned, and carried back to his father the answer of the Angel. It was heavy news for Adam, who now felt that his end was approaching, and therefore sent Seth a second time to fetch the oil of mercy. Before he could return, Adam died; but, at the bidding of God, Seth obtained from the Angel some olive-stones from the Tree of the Oil of Mercy, and planted them on his father's grave, where they grew into the tree from which the Cross of our Blessed Redeemer was made. Thus, though in a carnal sense the Oil was denied to Adam, and brought him no surcease from temporal death; yet, in a spiritual sense, it was freely given to him and obtained for him and all his offspring eternal life, and free, gracious, and merciful forgiveness of all their sins, concerning which God promised that He would remember them no more.

Thus, through the Heavenly Tree of Life, God fulfilled the prayer of our first parent Adam, and granted his request in a way which he had not looked for; and he now tastes the joy which is at the right hand of God, and is for ever removed from the hostile power of hunger, thirst, heat, cold, death, and all the other evils which flesh is heir to. Let us then diligently strive to realize that the Mystery of the Redemption is the most precious, the most excellent, and the most awful of the mysteries revealed by God to man, a mystery which no human thought can sound, and which no human lips can ever fully utter. But of this Awful Mystery, or Medicine of the Soul, God has also bestowed upon us an earthly antitype, or Medicine of the Body, by means of which wretched man may, even in this world, secure himself against all bodily distempers, put to. flight anxiety and care, and refresh and comfort his heart in the hour of trouble — namely, the Mystery of the Sages, or the Medicine of the Philosophers. If, therefore, a man would be perfectly happy in this world, and in the world to come, he should earnestly and devoutly strive to become possessed of these two Remedies; and for this purpose, he should turn to God with his whole heart, and ask for His gracious help, without which neither can be obtained; and, above all, he should be most eager to receive that Remedy by which the soul is healed of the mortal disease of sin.

This is the true fountain of the Sages; and there is nothing like it upon earth, but one eternal thing, by which the mortal body may, in this vale of tears, be fortified against all accidental disease, shielded from the pangs of poverty, and rendered sound, healthy, and strong, being protected against all mischances to the very end; and by which also metallic bodies may be changed into gold through a quickening of the process which Nature uses in the heart of the earth. The preparation and effects of this Stone are not unjustly considered to bear a close analogy to the creation of the world; therefore, I thought well to give an account of it from the very beginning.

I will now proceed briefly to expound my view of this Art, which, as all Sages testify, corresponds most closely to the creation and generation of man. I will attempt to make my meaning as plain as I dare, for the glory of the Holy Trinity, and the good of all Christian believers. When God had created the world, and adorned it with all manner of green things, herbs, roots, leaves, flowers, grass, and also with animals and minerals, he blessed them, and appointed that everything should bring forth fruit and seed after its kind. Only Adam (who is our Matter) was not yet in a position to produce any fruit out of himself. Before he could propagate his species, it was necessary that a part of him should be taken away, and again joined to him, *i.e.*, his wife Eve. Hereunto we must understand that so long as our substance is still gross and undivided, it can produce no fruit. It must first be divided, the subtle from the gross, or the water from the earth. The water is Eve, or the spirit; the earth Adam, or the body. And as the male is useless for purposes of generation until it be united to the female, so our earth is dead till it is quickened by the union with water. This is what that ancient Sage, Hermes, means when he says that the dead must be raised to life, and the feeble made strong.

It is necessary, then, to unite body and soul, and to change that which is below into that which is above, *i.e.*, body into spirit, and spirit into body. By this expression you are to understand not that the spirit by itself is changed into a body, or that the body by itself is changed into a spirit, but that both are united, and that the spirit, or water, dissolves, or resuscitates the body, or earth, while the body attracts the spirit, or water; and that they are thus joined into one substance, the earth being softened by the water, and the water hardened by the earth — as the boys in the street pour water on dry dust, and knead the whole into one mass. For this reason the Sages call our process child's play, in which the death of one is the life of the other, *i.e.*, in which the hardness of the one is softened by the other, and *vice versa*, seeing that the two are nothing but body and spirit originally belonging together. When contemplating this union, the Sage, Hermes, bursts forth into the following exclamation: "Oh, how strong, victorious, and precious is this nature that so unspeakably comforts its supplementary nature!" This nature is water, which stirs up and quickens the nature of the body. Hence it is said that Adam, or the body, would be dead without Eve, the spirit; for when the water has been distilled from our substance, the body lies dead and barren at the bottom of the alembic, and is described by the Sages as being, after the loss of its spirit, black, poisonous, and deadly. If the body is to be resuscitated, it must be rendered fit for generation by being purged of its blackness and fetid smell, and then its sweat or spirit must be restored to it; the spirit cannot conceive unless the body be allowed to embrace its Eve, or spirit. Senior says that the higher vapour must be brought back to the lower vapour; the Divine water is the King that descends from heaven, and leads the soul back to its body which is thereby quickened from the dead. Observe that in the body there is hidden fixed *salt*, which slumbers there just as the male seed slumbered in Adam. This the spirit, or Eve, attracts, and thus becomes pregnant; that is to say: The seed of the body, which we call fixed salt, is extracted from the body by its own water (which has before been separated from it), and is rendered so subtle and volatile that it ascends with the spirit to heaven. Then we say that the fixed has become volatile, that the dead has been revived, and that the body has received life from its spirit. On this account the water is called by some Sages the living water of the man, since it is extracted from the body, or man; and Lucas enjoins us to take it, and heat it after the fashion of Nature. Other Sages call the body the "black soil," because in it the fixed salt is concealed from view, like the seed in the ground. Others, again, call it the "black raven," which has in its maw the "white dove"; and the water which is distilled from the body they call the "virgin's milk," by which the white dove must be brought forth from the black raven. In short, these things are described by the Sages under a great variety of names; but the meaning of those names is the same. In this fashion the water is embraced by the body, and the seed of the body, or the fixed salt, makes the water pregnant. For the water dissolves the body, and bears upward with it some particles of the fixed salt; and the oftener this process is repeated, the thicker does the water become. Hence the repetition of the process is a most important point. Hermes says that when he saw the water gradually grow thicker and harder, he rejoiced, for thereby he knew that he should find what he sought. The water, then, must be poured upon the body, and heated with it, till the body is dissolved, and then again extracted till the body is coagulated. Thus the body must be well broken up, and purified by washing. This process of affusion and extraction must be repeated until all the salt, or potency and efficacy, has been extracted from the body. This is the case when the water becomes white and thick, and, in the cold, hard and solid like ice, while in the heat it melts like butter. Now, when nothing more can be extracted from the body, the residuum must be removed; for it is the superfluous part of the substance. This is what the Sages mean when they say: In the preparation we remove that which is superfluous; but otherwise our whole Magistery is accomplished with one single substance, nothing being added, and nothing taken away, except that which is really superfluous; for it possesses in abundance all that is needed, namely, the water, or "white, flaky earth," which must be injected into "living

p. 241

mercury," that so the transmutation into good and fixed silver may take place. But something much more noble and precious is concealed in this water (fixed salt), which grows and grows like the infant in the mother's womb. For as the embryo in the matrix, which is first a mere seed, grows, and is gradually transmuted into flesh and blood, *i.e.*, into a thicker substance, till at length the limbs are formed; so this water grows from the white colour which distinguishes it at first, till it is changed to another colour. (For the embryo, too, is transmuted from the natural colour of the embryo into flesh and blood.) The substance at length assuming a red colour, may be compared to the forming of the infant's limbs; it is then that we first see what is to become of it. When you perceive this final transmutation—the germ of which lay in the substance all along—you may well rejoice; for you have attained the object of your desire.

Thus I have described the union of the man and woman, that is to say, of the body and spirit, by means of which the child is conceived in the water, and the whiteness extracted from the black body. Nor do we need anything else, except, as Morienus says, time and patience. This coagulated water is the "white, flaky earth," in which the Sage bids us sow our gold and silver that they may bear fruit a hundred-thousand-fold. This is the "clear spring" of the Count of Trevisa, in which the King bathes, though not assisted by any of his ministers, who only watch his clothes until he has dried up the whole spring, when he makes all his ministers lords and kings such as he was at the time of his entering the bath. But now the King's dignity is three times as great as it was before; he wears a three-fold diadem on his head, and is arrayed in garments that shine like carbuncles and amethysts, and beneath them he wears the tunic of purity, and is bound with the girdle of righteousness. He is the most glorious King of life, whose power transcends all human thought. At his side is seated his pure and chaste queen, sprung of his own seed; and of these two are born many royal children. The redness is concealed and preserved in the whiteness, which must not be extracted, but subjected to gentle coction until its full crimson glory flames forth. This whiteness is thus referred to in "The Crowd": "If you see that after the blackness there follows a whiteness, be sure that after the whiteness will come a redness: for the redness slumbers in the whiteness, and should not be extracted, but gently heated, until the whole turns red." Let what I have now said suffice you.

HERMES [says]:

You must have a good knowledge of the True Principle of both Natural and Artificial Substances. For he who knows not the true First Principle will never attain to the end.

THE LOVE OF GOD AND

OF YOUR NEIGHBOUR

IS THE PERFECTION OF ALL WISDOM.

———

TO LOVE GOD IS THE HIGHEST WISDOM,

AND

TIME IS OUR POSSESSION.

———

UNTO HIM BE ALL HONOUR, PRAISE, AND

GLORY"

The Hermetic Museum, Vol. I, by Arthur Edward Waite, [1893]

CHAPTER SIX
Alchemical Catechism

"Alchemical Catechism

"A SHORT CATECHISM OF ALCHEMY

Q. What is the chief study of a Philosopher?
A. It is the investigation of the operations of Nature.

Q. What is the end of Nature?
A. God, Who is also its beginning.

Q. Whence are all things derived?
A. From one and indivisible Nature.

Q. Into how many regions is Nature separated?
A. Into four palmary regions.

Q. Which are they?
A. The dry, the moist, the warm, and the cold, which are the four elementary qualities, whence all things originate.

Q. How is Nature differentiated?
A. Into male and female.

Q. To what may we compare Nature?
A. To Mercury.

Q. Give a concise definition of Nature.
A. It is not visible, though it operates visibly; for it is

simply a volatile spirit, fulfilling its office in bodies, and animated by the universal spirit-the divine breath, the central and universal fire, which vivifies all things that exist.

Q. What should be the qualities possessed by the examiners of Nature?
A. They should be like unto Nature herself. That is to say, they should be truthful, simple, patient, and persevering.

Q. What matters should subsequently engross their attention?
A. The philosophers should most carefully ascertain whether their designs are in harmony with Nature, and of a possible and attainable kind; if they would accomplish by their own power anything that is usually performed by the power of Nature, they must imitate her in every detail.

Q. What method must be followed in order to produce something which shall be developed to a superior degree than Nature herself develops it.
A. The manner of its improvement must be studied, and this is invariably operated by means of a like nature. For example, if it be desired to develop the intrinsic virtue of a given metal beyond its natural condition, the chemist must avail himself of the metallic nature itself, and must be able to discriminate between its male and female differentiations.

Q. Where does the metallic nature store her seeds?
A. In the four elements.

Q. With what materials can the philosopher alone accomplish anything?
A. With the germ of the given matter; this is its elixir or quintessence, more precious by far, and more useful, to the artist, than is Nature herself. Before the philosopher has extracted the seed, or germ, Nature, in his behalf, will be ready to perform her duty.

Q. What is the germ, or seed, of any substance?
A. It is the most subtle and perfect decoction and digestion of the substance itself; or, rather, it is the Balm of Sulphur, which is identical with the Radical Moisture of Metals.

Q. By what is this seed, or germ, engendered?
A. By the four elements, subject to the will of the Supreme Being, and through the direct intervention of the imagination of Nature.

Q. After what manner do the four elements operate?
A. By means of an incessant and uniform motion, each one, according to its quality, depositing its seed in the centre of the earth, where it is subjected to action and digested, and is subsequently expelled in an outward direction by the laws of movement.

Q. What do the philosophers understand by the centre of the earth?
A. A certain void place where nothing may repose, and the existence of which is assumed.

Q. Where, then, do the four elements expel and deposit their seeds?
A. In the ex-centre, or in the margin and

circumference of the centre, which, after it has appropriated a portion, casts out the surplus into the region of excrement, scoriae, fire, and formless chaos.

Q. Illustrate this teaching by an example.
A. Take any level table, and set in its centre a vase filled with water; surround the vase with several things of various colours, especially salt, taking care that a proper distance intervenes between them all. Then pour out the water from the vase, and it will flow in streams here and there; one will encounter a substance of a red colour, and will assume a tinge of red; another will pass over the salt, and will contract a saline flavour; for it is certain that water does not modify the places which it traverses, but the diverse characteristics of places change the nature of water. In the same way the seed which is deposited by the four elements at the centre of the earth is subject to a variety of modifications in the places through which it passes, so that every existing substance is produced in the likeness of its channel, and when a seed on its arrival at a certain point encounters pure earth and pure water, a pure substance results, but the contrary in an opposite case.

Q. After what manner do the elements procreate this seed?
A. In order to the complete elucidation of this point, it must be observed that there are two gross and heavy elements and two that are volatile in character. Two, in like manner, are dry and two humid, one out of the four being actually excessively dry, and the other excessively moist. They are also masculine and

feminine. Now, each of them has a marked tendency to reproduce its own species within its own sphere. Moreover, they are never in repose, but are perpetually interacting, and each of them separates, of and by itself, the most subtle portion thereof. Their general place of meeting is in the centre, even the centre of the Archeus, that servant of Nature, where coming to mix their several seeds, they agitate and finally expel them to the exterior.

Q. What is the true and the first matter of all metals?
A. The first matter, properly so called, is dual in its essence, or is in itself of a twofold nature; one, nevertheless, cannot create a metal without the concurrence of the other. The first and the palmary essence is an aerial humidity, blended with a warm air, in the form of a fatty water, which adheres to all substances indiscriminately, whether they are pure or impure.

Q. How has this humidity been named by Philosophers?
A. Mercury.

Q. By what is it governed?
A. By the rays of the Sun and Moon.

Q. What is the second matter?
A. The warmth of the earth -otherwise, that dry heat which is termed Sulphur by the Philosophers.

Q. Can the entire material body be converted into seed?
A. Its eight-hundredth part only-that, namely, which

is secreted in the centre of the body in question, and may, for example, be seen in a grain of wheat.

Q. Of what use is the bulk of the matter as regards its seed?
A. It is useful as a safeguard against excessive heat, cold, moisture, or aridity, and, in general, all hurtful inclemency, against which it acts as an envelope.

Q. Would those artists who pretend to reduce the whole matter of any body into seed derive any advantage from the process, supposing it were possible to perform it?
A. None; on the contrary, their labour would be wholly unproductive, because nothing that is good can be accomplished by a deviation from natural methods.

Q. What, therefore, should be done?
A. The matter must be effectively separated from its impurities, for there is no metal, how pure soever, which is entirely free from imperfections, though their extent varies. Now all superfluities, cortices, and scoriae must be peeled off and purged out from the matter in order to discover its seed.

Q. What should receive the most careful attention of the Philosopher?
A. Assuredly, the end of Nature, and this is by no means to be looked for in the vulgar metals, because, these having issued already from the hands of the fashioner, it is no longer to be found therein.

Q. For what precise reason?
A. Because the vulgar metals, and chiefly gold, are absolutely dead, while ours, on the contrary, are absolutely living, and possess a soul.

Q. What is the life of metals?
A. It is no other substance than fire, when they are as yet imbedded in the mines.

Q. What is their death?
A. Their life and death are in reality one principle, for they die, as they live, by fire, but their death is from a fire of fusion.

Q. After what manner are metals conceived in the womb of the earth?
A. When the four elements have developed their power or virtue in the centre of the earth, and have deposited their seed, the Archeus of Nature, in the course of a distillatory process, sublimes them superficially by the warmth and energy of the perpetual movement.

Q. Into what does the wind resolve itself when it is distilled through the pores of the earth?
A. It resolves itself into water, whence all things spring; in this state it is merely a humid vapour, out of which there is subsequently evolved the principiated principle of all substances, which also serves as the first matter of the Philosophers.

Q. What then is this principiated principle, which is made use of as the first matter by the Children of Knowledge in the philosophic achievement?

A. It is this identical matter, which, the moment it is conceived, receives a permanent and unchangeable form.

Q. Are Saturn, Jupiter, Mars, Venus, the Sun, the Moon, etc., separately endowed with individual seed?
A. One is common to them all; their differences are to be accounted for by the: locality from which they are derived, not to speak of the fact that Nature completes her work with far greater rapidity in the procreation of silver than in that of gold, and so of the other metals, each in its own proportion.

Q. How is gold formed in the bowels of the earth?
A. When this vapour, of which we have spoken, is sublimed in the centre of the earth, and when it has passed through warm and pure places, where a certain sulphureous grease adheres to the channels, then this vapour, which the Philosophers have denominated their Mercury, becomes adapted and joined to this grease, which it sublimes with itself; from such amalgamation there is produced a certain unctuousness, which, abandoning the vaporous form, assumes that of grease, and is sublimised in other places, which have been cleansed by this preceding vapour, and the earth whereof has consequently been rendered more subtle, pure, and humid; it fills the pores of this earth, is joined thereto, and gold is produced as a result.

Q. How is Saturn engendered?
A. It occurs when the said unctuosity, or grease,

passes through places which are totally impure and cold.

Q. How is Venus brought forth?
A. She is produced in localities where the earth itself is pure, but is mingled with impure sulphur.

Q. What power does the vapour, which we have recently mentioned, possess in the centre of the earth?
A. By its continual progress it has the power of perpetually rarefying whatsoever is crude and impure, and of successively attracting to itself all that is pure around it.

Q. What is the seed of the first matter of all things?
A. The first matter of things, that is to say, the matter of principiating principles is begotten by Nature, without the assistance of any other seed; in other words, Nature receives the matter from the elements, whence it subsequently brings forth the seed.

Q. What, absolutely speaking, is therefore the seed of things?
A. The seed in a body is no other thing than a congealed air, or a humid vapour, which is useless except it be dissolved by a warm vapour.

Q. How is the generation of seed comprised in the metallic kingdom?
A. By the artifice of Archeus the four elements, in the first generation of Nature, distil a ponderous vapour of water into the centre of the earth ; this is the seed of metals, and it is called Mercury, not on account of its

essence, but because of its fluidity, and the facility with which it will adhere to each and every thing.

Q. Why is this vapour compared to sulphur?
A. Because of its internal heat.

Q. From what species of Mercury are we to conclude that the metals are composed?
A. The reference is exclusively to the Mercury of the Philosophers, and in no sense to the common or vulgar substance, which cannot become a seed, seeing that, like other metals, it already contains its own seed.

Q. What, therefore, must actually be accepted as the subject of our matter?
A. The seed alone, otherwise the fixed grain, and not the whole body, which is differentiated into Sulphur, or living male, and into Mercury, or living female.

Q. What operation must be afterwards performed
A. They must be joined together, so that they may form a germ, after which they will proceed to the procreation of a fruit which is conformed to their nature.

Q. What is the part of the artist in this operation?
A. The artist must do nothing but separate that which is subtle from that which is gross.

Q. To what, therefore, is the whole philosophic combination reduced?
A. The development of one into two, and the reduction of two into one, and nothing further.

Q. Whither must we turn for the seed and life of meals and minerals?
A. The seed of minerals is properly the water which exists in the centre
And the heart of the minerals.

Q. How does Nature operate by the help of Art?
A. Every seed, whatsoever its kind, is useless, unless by Nature or Art it is placed in a suitable matrix, where it receives its life by the coction of the germ! and by the congelation of the pure particle, or fixed grain.

Q. How is the seed subsequently nourished and preserved?
A. By the warmth of its body.

Q. What is therefore performed by the artist in the mineral kingdom?
A. He finishes what cannot be finished by Nature on account of the crudity of the air, which has permeated the pores of all bodies by its violence, but on the surface and not in the bowels of the earth.

Q. What correspondence have the metals among themselves?
A. It is necessary for a proper comprehension of the nature of this correspondence to consider the position of the planets, and to pay attention to Saturn, which is the highest of all, and then is succeeded by Jupiter, next by Mars, the Sun, Venus, Mercury, and, lastly, by the Moon. It must be observed that the influential virtues of the planets do not ascend but descend, and experience teaches us that Mars can be easily

converted into Venus, not Venus into Mars, which is of a lower sphere. So, also, Jupiter can be easily transmuted into Mercury, because Jupiter is superior to Mercury, the one being second after the firmament, the other second above the earth, and Saturn is highest of all, while the Moon is lowest. The Sun enters into all, but it is never ameliorated by its inferiors. It is clear that there is a large correspondence between Saturn and the Moon, in the middle of which is the Sun; but to all these changes the Philosopher should strive to administer the Sun.

Q. When the Philosophers speak of gold and silver, from which they extract their matter, are we to suppose that they refer to the vulgar gold and silver?
A. By no means; vulgar silver and gold are dead, while those of the Philosophers are full of life.

Q. What is the object of research among the Philosophers?
A. Proficiency in the art of perfecting what Nature has left imperfect in the mineral kingdom, and the attainment of the treasure of the Philosophical Stone.

Q. What is this Stone?
A. The Stone is nothing else than the radical humidity of the elements, perfectly purified and educed into a sovereign fixation, which causes it to perform such great things for health, life being resident exclusively in the humid radical.

Q. In what does the secret of accomplishing this admirable work consist?
A. It consists in knowing how to educe from

potentiality into activity the innate warmth, or the fire
of Nature, which is enclosed in the centre of the
radical humidity.

Q. What are the precautions which must be made use
of to guard against failure in the work?
A. Great pains must be taken to eliminate excrements
from the matter, and to conserve nothing but the
kernel, which contains all the virtue of the compound.

Q. Why does this medicine heal every species of
disease?
A. It is not on account of tile variety of its qualities,
but simply because it powerfully fortifies the natural
warmth, which it gently stimulates, while other
physics irritate it by too violent an action.

Q How can you demonstrate to me the truth of the art
in the matter of the tincture?
A. Firstly, its truth is founded on the fact that the
physical powder, being composed of the same
substance as the metals, namely, quicksilver, has the
faculty of combining with these in fusion, one nature
easily embracing another which is like itself.
Secondly, seeing that the imperfection of the base
metals is owing to the crudeness of their quicksilver,
and to that alone, the physical powder, which is a ripe
and decocted quicksilver, and, in itself a pure fire, can
easily communicate to them its own maturity, and
can transmute them into its nature, after it has
attracted their crude humidity, that is to say, their
quicksilver, which is the sole substance that

transmutes them, the rest being nothing but scoriae and excrements, which are rejected in projection.

Q. What road should the Philosopher follow that he may attain to the knowledge and execution of the physical work?
A. That precisely which was followed by the Great Architect of the Universe in the creation of the world, by observing how the chaos was evolved.

Q. What was the matter of the chaos?
A. It could be nothing else than a humid vapour, because water alone enters into all created substances, which all finish in a strange term, this term being a proper subject for the impression of all forms.

Q. Give me an example to illustrate what you have just stated.
A. An example may be found in the special productions of composite substances, the seeds of which invariably begin by resolving themselves into a certain humour, which is the chaos of the particular matter, whence issues, by a kind of irradiation, the complete form of the plant. Moreover, it should be observed that Holy Scripture makes no mention of anything except water as the material subject whereupon the Spirit of God brooded, nor of anything except light as the universal form of things.

Q. What profit may the Philosopher derive from these considerations, and what should he especially remark in the method of creation which was pursued by the Supreme Being?
A. In the first place he should observe the matter out

of which the world was made; he will see that out of this confused mass, the Sovereign Artist began by extracting light, that this light in the same moment dissolved the darkness which covered the face of the earth, and that it served as the universal form of the matter. He will then easily perceive that in the generation of all composite substances, a species of irradiation takes place, and a separation of light and darkness, wherein Nature is an undeviating copyist of her Creator. The Philosopher will equally understand after what manner, by the action of this light, the empyrean, or firmament which divides the superior and inferior waters, was subsequently produced; how the sky was studded with luminous bodies; and how the necessity for the moon arose, which was owing to the space intervening between the things above and the things below; for the moon is an intermediate torch between the superior and the inferior worlds, receiving the celestial influences and communicating them to the earth. Finally he will understand how the Creator, in the gathering of the waters, produced dry land.

Q. How many heavens can you enumerate?
A. Properly there is one only, which is the firmament that divides the waters from the waters. Nevertheless, three are admitted, of which the first is the space that is above the clouds. In this heaven the waters are rarefied, and fall upon the fixed stars, and it is also in this space that the planets and wandering stars perform their revolutions. The second heaven is the firmament of the fixed stars, while the third is the abode of the supercelestial waters.

Q. Why is the rarefaction of the waters confined to the first heaven?
A. Because it is in the nature of rarefied substances to ascend, and because God, in His eternal laws, has assigned its proper sphere to everything.

Q. Why does each celestial body invariably revolve about an axis?
A. It is by reason of the primeval impetus which it received, and by virtue of the same law which will cause any heavy substance suspended from a thread to turn with the same velocity, if the power which impels its motion be always equal.

Q. Why do the superior waters never descend?
A. Because of their extreme rarefaction. It is for this reason that a skilled chemist can derive more profit from the study of rarefaction than from any other science whatsoever.

Q. What is the matter of the firmament?
A. It is properly air, which is more suitable than water as a medium of light.

Q. After the separation of the waters from the dry earth, what was performed by the Creator to originate generation?
A. He created a certain light which was destined for this office; He placed it in the central fire, and moderated this fire by the humidity of water and by the coldness of earth, so as to keep a check upon its energy and adapt it to His design.

Q. What is the action of this central fire?

A. It continually operates upon the nearest humid matter, which it exalts into vapour; now this vapour is the mercury of Nature and the first matter of the three kingdoms.

Q. How is the sulphur of Nature subsequently formed?

A. By the interaction of the central fire and the mercurial vapour.

Q. How is the salt of the sea produced?

A. By the action of the same fire upon aqueous humidity, when the aerial humidity, which is contained therein, has been exhaled.

Q. What should be done by a truly wise Philosopher when he has once mastered the foundation and the order in the procedure of the Great Architect of the Universe in the construction of all that exists in Nature?

A. He should, as far as may be possible, become a faithful copyist of his Creator. In the physical chaos he should make his chaos such as the original actually was; he should separate the light from the darkness : he should form his firmament for the separation of the waters which are above from the waters which are below, and should successively accomplish, point by point, the entire sequence of the creative act.

Q. With what is this grand and sublime operation performed?

A. With one single corpuscle, or minute body, which, so to speak, contains nothing but faeces, filth, and abominations, but whence a certain tenebrous and mercurial humidity is extracted, which contains in itself all that is required by the Philosopher, because, as a fact, he is in search of nothing hut the true Mercury.

Q. What kind of mercury, therefore, must he make use of in performing the work? A. Of a mercury which, as such, is not found on the earth, but is extracted from bodies, yet not from vulgar mercury, as it has been falsely said.

Q. Why is the latter unfitted to the needs of our work? A. Because the wise artist must take notice that vulgar mercury has an insufficient quantity of sulphur, and he should consequently operate upon a body created by Nature, in which Nature herself has united the sulphur and mercury that it is the work of the artist to separate.

Q. What must he subsequently do?
A. He must purify them and join them anew together.

Q. How do you denominate the body of which we have been speaking?
A. The RUDE STONE, Or Chaos, or Iliaste, or Hyle-- that confused mass which is known but universally despised.

Q. As you have told me that Mercury is the one thing which the Philosopher must absolutely understand, will you give me a circumstantial description of it, so as to avoid misconception?
A. In respect of its nature, our Mercury is dual--fixed

and volatile; in regard to its motion, it is also dual, for it has a motion of ascent and of descent; by that of descent, it is the influence of plants, by which it stimulates the drooping fire of Nature, and this is its first office previous to congelation. By its ascensional movement, it rises, seeking to be purified, and as this is after congelation, it is considered to be the radical moisture of substances, which, beneath its vile scoriae, still preserves the nobility of its first origin.

Q. How many species of moisture do you suppose to be in each composite thing?
A. There are three--the Elementary, which is properly the vase of the other elements; the Radical, which, accurately speaking, is the oil, or balm, in which the entire virtue of the subject is resident--lastly, the Alimentary, the true natural dissolvent, which draws up the drooping internal fire, causing corruption and blackness by its humidity, and fostering and sustaining the subject.

Q. How many species of Mercury are there known to the Philosophers?
A. The Mercury of the Philosophers may be regarded under four aspects; the first is entitled the Mercury of bodies, which is actually their concealed seed; the second is the Mercury of Nature, which is the Bath or Vase of the Philosophers, otherwise the humid radical; to the third has been applied the designation, Mercury of the Philosophers, because it is found in their laboratory and in their minera. It is the sphere of Saturn; it is the Diana of the Wise; it is the true salt of metals, after the acquisition of which the true

philosophic work may be truly said to have begun. In its fourth aspect, it is called Common Mercury, which yet is not that of the Vulgar, but rather is properly the true air of the Philosophers, the true middle substance of water, the true secret and concealed fire, called also common fire, because it is common to all minerae, for it is the substance of metals, and thence do they derive their quantity and quality.

Q. How many operations art comprised in our work?
A. There is one only, which may be resolved into sublimation, and sublimation, according to Geber, is nothing other than the elevation of the dry matter by the mediation of fire, with adherence to its own vase.

Q. What precaution should be taken in reading the Hermetic Philosophers ?
A. Great care, above all, must be observed upon this point, lest what they say upon the subject should be interpreted literally and in accordance with the mere sound of the words: For the letter killeth, but the spirit giveth life.

Q. What books should be read in order to have an acquaintance with our science?
A. Among the ancients, all the works of Hermes should especially be studied; in the next place, a certain book, entitled The Passage of the Red Sea, and another, The Entrance into the Promised Land. Paracelsus also should be read before all among elder writers, and, among other treatises, his Chemical Pathway, or the Manual of Paracelsus, which contains all the mysteries of demonstrative physics and the

most arcane Kabbalah. This rare and unique manuscript work exists only in the Vatican Library, but Sendivogius had the good fortune to take a copy of it, which has helped in the illumination of the sages of our order. Secondly, Raymond Lully must be read, and his Vade Mecum above all, his dialogue called the Tree of Life, his testament, and his codicil. There must, however, be a certain precaution exercised in respect to the two last, because, like those of Geber, and also of Arnold de Villanova, they abound in false recipes and futile fictions, which seem to have been inserted with the object of more effectually disguising the truth from the ignorant. In the third place, the Turba Philosophorum which is a collection of ancient authors, contains much that is materially good, though there is much also which is valueless. Among mediaeval writers Zachary, Trevisan, Roger Bacon, and a certain anonymous author, whose book is entitled The Philosophers, should be held especially high in the estimation of the student. Among moderns the most worthy to be prized are John Fabricius, Francois de Nation, and Jean D'Espagnet, who wrote Physics Restored, though, to say the truth, he has imported some false precepts and fallacious opinions into his treatise.

Q. When may the Philosopher venture to undertake the work?
A. When he is, theoretically, able to extract, by means of a crude spirit, a digested spirit out of a body in dissolution, which digested spirit he must again rejoin to the vital oil.

Q. Explain me this theory in a clearer manner.

A. It may be demonstrated more completely in the actual process; the great experiment may be undertaken when the Philosopher, by the medium of a vegetable menstruurn, united to a mineral menstruum, is qualified to dissolve a third essential menstruum, with which menstruums united he must wash the earth, and then exalt it into a celestial quintessence, to compose the sulphureous thunderbolt, which instantaneously penetrates substances and destroys their excrements.

Q. Have those persons a proper acquaintance with Nature who pretend to make use of vulgar gold for seed, and of vulgar mercury for the dissolvent, or the earth in which it should be sown?

A. Assuredly not, because neither the one nor the other possesses the external agent--gold, because it has been deprived of it by decoction, and mercury because it has never had it.

Q. In seeking this auriferous seed elsewhere than in gold itself, is there no danger of producing a species of monster, since one appears to be departing from Nature?

A. It is undoubtedly true that in gold is contained the auriferous seed, and that in a more perfect condition than it is found in any other body; but this does not force us to make use of vulgar gold, for such a seed is equally found in each of the other metals, and is nothing else but that fixed grain which Nature has infused in the first congelation of mercury, all metals having one origin and a common substance, as will be ultimately unveiled to those who become worthy of receiving it by application and assiduous study.

Q. What follows from this doctrine?
A. It follows that, although the seed is more perfect in gold, it may be extracted much more easily from another body than from gold itself, other bodies being more open, that is to say, less digested, and less restricted in their humidity.

Q. Give me an example taken from Nature.
A. Vulgar gold may be likened to a fruit which, having come to a perfect maturity, has been cut off from its tree, and though it contains a most perfect and well-digested seed, notwithstanding, should anyone set it in the ground, with a view to its multiplication, much time, trouble, and attention will be consumed in the development of its vegetative capabilities. On the other hand, if a cutting, or a root, be taken from the same tree, and similarly planted, in a short time, and with no trouble, it will spring up and produce much fruit.

Q. Is it necessary that an amateur of this science should understand the formation of metals in the bowels of the earth if he wishes to complete his work ?
A. So indispensable is such a knowledge that should anyone fail, before all other studies, to apply himself to its attainment, and to imitate Nature point by point therein, he will never succeed in accomplishing anything but what is worthless.

Q. How, then, does Nature deposit metals in the bowels of the earth, and of what does she compose them ?

A. Nature manufactures them all out of sulphur and mercury, and forms them by their double vapour.

Q. What do you mean by this double vapour, and how can metals be formed thereby?

A. In order to a complete understanding of this question, it must first be stated that mercurial vapour is united to sulphureous vapour in a cavernous place which contains a saline water, which serves as their matrix. Thus is formed, firstly, the Vitriol of Nature; secondly, by the commotion of the elements, there is developed out of this Vitriol of Nature a new vapour, which is neither mercurial nor sulphureous, yet is allied to both these natures, and this, passing through places to which the grease of sulphur adheres, is joined therewith, and out of their union a glutinous substance is produced, otherwise, a formless mass, which is permeated by the vapour that fills these cavernous places. By this vapour, acting through the sulphur it contains, are produced the perfect metals, provided that the vapour and the locality are pure. If the locality and the vapour are impure, imperfect metals result. The terms perfection and imperfection have reference to various degrees of concoction.

Q. What is contained in this vapour?

A. A spirit of light and a spirit of fire, of the nature of the celestial bodies, which properly should be considered as the form of the universe.

Q. What does this vapour represent?
A. This vapour, thus impregnated by the universal
spirit, represents, in a fairly complete way, the
original Chaos, which contained all that was required
for the original creation, that is, universal matter and
universal form.

Q. And one cannot, notwithstanding, make use of
vulgar mercury in the process?
A. No, because vulgar mercury, as already made
plain, is devoid of external agent.

Q. Whence comes it that common mercury is without
its external agent?
A. Because in the exaltation of the double vapour, the
commotion has been so great and searching, that the
spirit, or agent, has evaporated, as occurs, with very
close similarity, in the fusion of metals. The result is
that the unique mercurial part is deprived of its
masculine or sulphureous agent, and consequently
can never be transmuted into gold by Nature.

Q. How many species of gold are distinguished by the
Philosophers?
A. Three sorts :--Astral Gold, Elementary Gold, and
Vulgar Gold.

Q. What is astral gold?
A. Astral Gold has its centre in the sun, which
communicates it by its rays to all inferior beings. It is
an igneous substance, which receives a continual
emanation of solar corpuscles that penetrate all things
sentient, vegetable, and mineral.

Q. What do you refer to under the term Elementary Gold ?

A. This is the most pure and fixed portion of the elements, and of all that is composed of them. All sublunary beings included in the three kingdoms contain in their inmost centre a precious grain of this elementary gold.

Q. Give me some description of Vulgar Gold ?

A. It is the most beautiful metal of our acquaintance, the best that Nature can produce, as perfect as it is unalterable in itself.

Q. Of what species of gold is the Stone of the Philosophers ?

A. It is of the second species, as being the most pure portion of all the metallic elements after its purification, when it is termed living philosophical gold. A perfect equilibrium and equality of the four elements enter into the Physical Stone, and four things are indispensable for the accomplishment of the work, namely, composition, allocation, mixture, and union, which, once performed according to the rules of art, will beget the lawful Son of the Sun, and the Phoenix which eternally rises out of its own ashes.

Q. What is actually the living gold of the Philosophers?

A. It is exclusively the fire of Mercury, or that igneous virtue, contained in the radical moisture, to which it has already communicated the fixity and the nature of the sulphur, whence it has emanated, the mercurial character of the whole substance of philosophical sulphur permitting it to be alternatively termed mercury.

Q. What other name is also given by the Philosophers to their living gold ?
A. They also term it their living sulphur, and their true fire; they recognize its existence in all bodies, and there is nothing that can subsist without it.

Q. Where must we look for our living gold, our living sulphur, and our true fire ?
A. In the house of Mercury.

Q. By what is this fire nourished?
A. By the air.

Q. Give me a comparative illustration of the power of this fire ?
A. To exemplify the attraction of this interior fire, there is no better comparison than that which is derived from the thunderbolt, which originally is simply a dry, terrestrial exhalation, united to a humid vapour. By exaltation, and by assuming the igneous nature, it acts on the humidity which is inherent to it; this it attracts to itself, transmutes it into its own nature, and then rapidly precipitates itself to the earth, where it is attracted by a fixed nature which is like unto its own.

Q. What should be done by the Philosopher after he has extracted his Mercury ?
A. He should develop it from potentiality into activity.

Q. Cannot Nature perform this of herself?

A. No; because she stops short after the first sublimation, and out of the matter which is thus disposed do the metals engender.

Q. What do the Philosophers understand by their gold and silver?

A. The Philosophers apply to their Sulphur the name of Gold, and to their Mercury the name of Silver.

Q. Whence are they derived?

A. I have already stated that they are derived from a homogeneous body wherein they are found in great abundance, whence also Philosophers know how to extract both by an admirable, and entirely philosophical, process.

Q. When this operation has been duly performed, to what other point of the practice must they next apply themselves?

A. To the confection of the philosophical amalgam, which must be done with great care, but can only be accomplished after the preparation and sublimation of the Mercury.

Q. When should your matter be combined with the living gold?

A. During the period of amalgamation only, that is to say, Sulphur is introduced into it by means of the amalgamation, and thenceforth there is one substance; the process is shortened by the addition of Sulphur, while the tincture at the same time is augmented.

Q. What is contained in the centre of the radical moisture ?
A. It contains and conceals Sulphur, which is covered with a hard rind.

Q. What must be done to apply it to the Great Work?
A. It must be drawn, out of its bonds with consummate skill, and by the method of putrefaction.

Q. Does Nature, in her work in the mines, possess a menstruum which is adapted to the dissolution and liberation of this sulphur?
A. No; because there is no local movement. Could Nature, unassisted, dissolve, putrefy, and purify the metallic body, she would herself provide us with !he Physical Stone, which is Sulphur exalted and increased in virtue.

Q. Can you elucidate this doctrine by an example?
A. By an enlargement of the previous comparison of a fruit, or a seed, which, in the first place, is put into the earth for its solution, and afterwards for its multiplication. Now, the Philosopher, who is in a position to discern what is good seed, extracts it from its centre, consigns it to its proper earth, when it has been well cured and prepared, and therein he rarefies it in such a manner that its prolific virtue is increased and indefinitely multiplied.

Q. In what does the whole secret of the seed consist ?
A. In the true knowledge of its proper earth.

Q. What do you understand by the seed in the work Of the Philosophers ?

A. I understand the interior heat, or the specific spirit, which is enclosed in the humid radical, which, in other words, is the middle substance of living silver, the proper sperm of metals, which contains its own seed.

Q. How do you set free the sulphur from its bonds?
A. By putrefaction.

Q. What is the earth of minerals ?
A. It is their proper menstruum.

Q. What pains must be taken by the Philosopher to extract that part which he requires?
A. He must take great pains to eliminate the fetid vapours and impure sulphurs, after which the seed must be injected.

Q. By what indication may the Artist be assured that he is in the right road at the beginning of his work?
A. When he finds that the dissolvent and the thing dissolved are converted into one form and one matter at the period of dissolution.

Q. How many solutions do you count in the Philosophic Work?
A. There are three. The first solution is that which reduces the crude and metallic body into its elements of sulphur and of living silver; the second is that of the physical body, and the third is the solution of the mineral earth.

Q. How is the metallic body reduced by the first solution into mercury, and then into sulphur?

A. By the secret artificial fire, which is the Burning Star.

Q. How is this operation performed?
A. By extracting from the subject, in the first place, the mercury or vapour of the elements, and, after purification, by using it to liberate the sulphur from its bonds, by corruption, of which blackness is the indication.

Q. How is the second solution performed ?
A. When the physical body is resolved into the two substances previously mentioned, and has acquired the celestial nature.

Q. What is the name which is applied by Philosophers to the Matter during this period?
A, It is called their Physical Chaos, and it is, in fact, the true First Matter, a name which can hardly be applied before the conjunction of the male--which is sulphur--with the female--which is silver.

Q. To what does the third solution refer?
A. It is the humectation of the mineral earth and it is closely bound up with multiplication.

Q. What fire must be made use of in our work ?
A. That fire which is used by Nature.

Q. What is the potency of this fire?
A. It dissolves everything that is in the world, because it is the principle of all dissolution and corruption.

Q. Why is it also termed Mercury ?
A. Because it is in its nature aerial, and a most subtle vapour, which partakes at the same time of sulphur, whence it has contracted some contamination.

Q. Where is this fire concealed ?
A. It is concealed in the subject of art.

Q. Who is it that is familiar with, and can produce, this fire?
A. It is known to the wise, who can both produce it and purify it.

Q. What is the essential potency and characteristic of this fire ?
A. It is excessively dry, and is continually in motion; it seeks only to disintegrate and to educe things from potentiality into actuality; it is that, in a word, which coming upon solid places in mines, circulates in a vaporous form upon the matter, and dissolves it.

Q. How may this fire be most easily distinguished?
A. By the sulphureous excrements in which it is enveloped, and by the saline environment with which it is clothed.

Q. What must be added to this fire so as to accentuate its capacity for incineration in the feminine species?
A. On account of its extreme dryness it requires to be moistened.

Q. How many philosophical fires do you enumerate ?
A. There are in all three--the natural, the unnatural, and the contra-natural.

Q. Explain to me these three species of fires.

A. The natural fire is the masculine fire, or the chief agent; the unnatural is the feminine, which is the dissolvent of Nature, nourishing a white smoke, and assuming that form. This smoke is quickly dissipated, unless much care be exercised, and it is almost incombustible, though by philosophical sublimation it becomes corporeal and resplendent. The contranatural fire is that which disintegrates compounds and has the power to unbind what has' been bound very closely by Nature.

Q. Where is our matter to be found?

A. It is to be found everywhere, but it must specially be sought in metallic nature, where it is more easily available than elsewhere.

Q. What kind must be preferred before all others ?

A. The most mature, the most appropriate, and the easiest; but care, before all things, must be taken that the metallic essence shall be present, not only potentially but in actuality, and that there is, moreover, a metallic splendour.

Q. Is everything contained in this subject?

A. Yes; but Nature, at the same time, must be assisted, so that the work may be perfected and hastened, and this by the means which are familiar to the higher grades of experiment.

Q. Is this subject exceedingly precious ?

A. It is vile, and originally is without native elegance; should anyone say that it is saleable, it is the species to which they refer, but, fundamentally, it is not saleable, because it is useful in our work alone.

Q. What does our Matter contain?
A. It contains Salt, Sulphur, and Mercury.

Q. What operation is it most important to be able to perform?
A. The successive extraction of the Salt, Sulphur, and Mercury.

Q. How is that done ?
A. By sole and perfect sublimation.

Q. What is in the first place extracted ?
A. Mercury in the form of a white smoke.

Q. What follows?
A. Igneous water, or Sulphur.

Q. What then?
A. Dissolution with purified salt, in the first place volatilising that which is fixed, and afterwards fixing that which is volatile into a precious earth, which is the Vase of the Philosophers, and is wholly perfect.

Q. When must the Philosopher begin his enterprise ?
A. At the moment of daybreak, for his energy must never be relaxed.

Q. When may he take his rest?
A. When the work has come to its perfection.

Q. At what hour is the end of the work ?
A. High noon, that is to say, the moment when the Sun is in its fullest power, and the Son of the Day-Star in its most brilliant splendour.

Q. What is the pass-word of Magnesia?
A. You know whether I can or should answer:--I reserve my speech.

Q. Give me the greeting of the Philosophers.
A. Begin ; I will reply to you.

Q. Are you an apprentice Philosopher?
A. My friends, and the wise, know me.

Q. What is the age of a Philosopher ?
A. From the moment of his researches to that of his discoveries, the Philosopher does not age."

The Alchemical Catechism

SOURCES

The Emerald Tablet of Hermes

A Letter from the Brothers of R. C. Concerning the Invisible, Magical Mountain, And the Treasure therein Contained

The Secret Works of Chiram One, From the Chaldean, Dr. Sigismund Bacstrom's Collection of Manuscripts on the Emerald Tablet, The Emerald Table, the Most Ancient Monument of the Chaldeans concerning the Lapis Philosophorum (the stone of the philosophers)

The Emerald Tablets of Thoth the Atlantean, Dr. Doreal, Great White Lodge, 1930

The Divine Pymander of Hermes, Hermes Trismegistus, Translated by John Everard, 1650

The Secret Teachings of all Ages, Manly P. Hall, 1928

Basil Valentine, His Triumphant Chariot of Antimony, with Annotations of Theodore Kirkringus (1678)

The Hermetic Museum, Vol. I, by Arthur Edward Waite, [1893]

The Alchemical Catechism

The Divine Pymander and the Emerald Tablets of Thoth Hermes Trismegistus

Including the Glory of the World, the Table of Paradise. the Science of the Philosophers Stone and the Alchemical Catechism

By Hermes Trismegistus, Translated by John Everard, Compiled by Marilynn Hughes

THE DIVINE PYMANDER AND THE EMERALD TABLET OF HERMES TRISMEGISTUS: Including the Glory of the World, the Table of Paradise. the Science of the Philosophers Stone and the Alchemical Catechism

For more info – http://outofbodytravel.org)

Printed by Amazon Italia Logistica S.r.l.
Torrazza Piemonte (TO), Italy

18704433R00263